Vulnerabilities, Challenges and Risks in Applied Linguistics

Full details of all our publications can be found on http://www.multilingual-matters.com, or by writing to Multilingual Matters, St Nicholas House, 31–34 High Street, Bristol BS1 2AW, UK.

Vulnerabilities, Challenges and Risks in Applied Linguistics

Edited by
Clare Cunningham and Christopher J. Hall

MULTILINGUAL MATTERS
Bristol • Blue Ridge Summit

DOI https://doi.org/10.21832/CUNNIN8236
Library of Congress Cataloging in Publication Data
A catalog record for this book is available from the Library of Congress.
Names: Cunningham, Clare, editor. | Hall, Christopher J., editor. | British Association for Applied Linguistics. Meeting (51st: 2018 : York St. John University)
Title: Vulnerabilities, Challenges and Risks in Applied Linguistics Edited by Clare Cunningham and Christopher J. Hall.
Description: Bristol, UK; Blue Ridge Summit: Multilingual Matters, 2021. | Based on papers mostly presented at the 51st annual meeting of the British Association of Applied Linguistics, 2018, at York St. John University. | Includes bibliographical references and index. | Summary: "The chapters in this book call attention to vulnerabilities, challenges and risks for applied linguists and the communities they work with across a broad range of contexts from the Global North and South, and in both signed and spoken languages. Together they provide insights on both academic and professional practice across several areas"— Provided by publisher.
Identifiers: LCCN 2021022388 (print) | LCCN 2021022389 (ebook) | ISBN 9781788928229 (paperback) | ISBN 9781788928236 (hardback) | ISBN 9781788928243 (pdf) | ISBN 9781788928250 (epub)
Subjects: LCSH: Applied linguistics—Congresses. | Applied linguistics—Study and teaching—Congresses.
Classification: LCC P129 .V85 2021 (print) | LCC P129 (ebook) | DDC 418—dc23 LC record available at https://lccn.loc.gov/2021022388
LC ebook record available at https://lccn.loc.gov/2021022389

British Library Cataloguing in Publication Data
A catalogue entry for this book is available from the British Library.

ISBN-13: 978-1-78892-823-6 (hbk)
ISBN-13: 978-1-78892-822-9 (pbk)

Multilingual Matters
UK: St Nicholas House, 31–34 High Street, Bristol BS1 2AW, UK.
USA: NBN, Blue Ridge Summit, PA, USA.

Website: www.multilingual-matters.com
Twitter: Multi_Ling_Mat
Facebook: https://www.facebook.com/multilingualmatters
Blog: www.channelviewpublications.wordpress.com

Copyright © 2021 Clare Cunningham, Christopher J. Hall and the authors of individual chapters.

All rights reserved. No part of this work may be reproduced in any form or by any means without permission in writing from the publisher.

The policy of Multilingual Matters/Channel View Publications is to use papers that are natural, renewable and recyclable products, made from wood grown in sustainable forests. In the manufacturing process of our books, and to further support our policy, preference is given to printers that have FSC and PEFC Chain of Custody certification. The FSC and/or PEFC logos will appear on those books where full certification has been granted to the printer concerned.

Typeset by Nova Techset Private Limited, Bengaluru and Chennai, India.
Printed and bound in the UK by the CPI Books Group Ltd.

Contents

	Contributors	vii
1	Introduction *Clare Cunningham and Christopher J. Hall*	1

Part 1: Communities

2	Can Southern Epistemological and Indigenous Ontological Orientations to Applied Linguistics Challenge its Ethnocentrism? *Cristine Gorski Severo and Sinfree B. Makoni*	15
3	Late Capitalism and New Challenges: Indigenous Communities Taking Risks in Defense of Vulnerable Languages and Territories in Guatemala and Colombia *Luz A. Murillo*	31
4	The Bumpy Journey Towards the Irish Sign Language Act: Critical Considerations and Personal Reflections of a Deaf Activist–Scholar *John Bosco Conama*	48
5	'Befriending' Risks, Vulnerabilities and Challenges: Researching Sexuality and Language in Educational Sites *Helen Sauntson*	63

Part 2: Policy

6	Challenging Constitutional Bilingualism with 'What if …': Counterfactual Histories and At-risk Minorities in Finland *Johanna Ennser-Kananen and Taina Saarinen*	81
7	UK Language Policy Quo vadis? Language Learning in the UK post Brexit *Ursula Lanvers*	97
8	Vulnerabilities, Challenges and Risks in Sign Language Recognition in Canada *Kristin Snoddon and Erin Wilkinson*	111

Part 3: Research

9 From the Outside Looking in: The Risks and Challenges of Analysing Extremist Discourses on Far-right and Manosphere Websites — 131
   Kate Barber

10 Critical Incidents in a Teacher–Researcher and Student–Participant Relationship: What Risks Can We Take? — 147
   Sal Consoli

11 Taking Risks in Literacy Research – Using an Interpreter in Multilingual Research Interviews — 162
   Annika Norlund Shaswar

Part 4: Education

12 A Challenge for Applied Linguistics: Developing a Novel Curriculum in the Field of Language and Integration — 183
   Liana Konstantinidou and Ursula Stadler

13 Teaching Controversial Issues in the Language Education of Adult Migrants to the UK: A Risk Worth Taking — 197
   Michael Hepworth

14 Access to English in Pakistan: Differences in Instruction as a Risk to Social Integration — 214
   Sham Haidar

15 Afterword — 231
   Christopher J. Hall and Clare Cunningham

Index — 236

Contributors

Kate Barber is in the final year of her PhD at the Centre for Language and Communication Research at Cardiff University, Wales. She has an LLB (Hons) Law degree and an MA in Forensic Linguistics. Her PhD examines the intersection of far-right extremism and misogyny through a corpus-assisted critical discourse analysis of extremists' blog posts discussing rape and sexual assault. Her wider research interests centre around narratives and counter-narratives, representations of identity, rape culture and online hate speech.

John Bosco Conama is the Director of the Centre for Deaf Studies in Trinity College Dublin. He is the Board Director of the Irish Deaf Society and he has been involved in many committees within the Civil Service and other government bodies to monitor the progress of Deaf and disabled people in society. His recent publications have focused on Deaf people in society, especially focusing on language rights and equality. He was awarded a European Label Language Ambassadorship for 2015. He currently sits on the Disability Advisory Committee under the aegis of the Irish Human Rights and Equality Commission.

Sal Consoli is Assistant Professor in the Department of English at the Hong Kong Polytechnic University. His research focuses on the psychology of language learning and teaching as well as research ethics and reflexivity in applied linguistics. His work has been largely influenced by the epistemological and methodological traditions of narrative inquiry and practitioner research. Sal is co-founder of the Forum on Language Learning Motivation and serves on the Executive Committee of the British Association of Applied Linguistics.

Clare Cunningham is a Senior Lecturer in English language and linguistics at York St John University in the UK. Her research has principally been focused on the attitudes, beliefs and knowledge of teachers with regards to multilingualism and she has published on this topic in *Language and Education*, *Language, Culture and Curriculum*, *Power and Education* and *Linguistics and Education*. She is currently engaged in a large-scale pan-European project furthering this research through a comparative study within the AILA Research Network *Affective and Social Factors in Home Language Maintenance*. Another research interest is in the area of eco-linguistics and she is currently involved in two research projects in this area, one focused on students' discourses about ecojustice in the higher education curriculum and another exploring childrens' written eco-narratives.

Johanna Ennser-Kananen is a university lecturer of English at the University of Jyväskylä and Docent of multilingual and multicultural education at the Centre for Applied Language Studies. Her current work focuses on linguistically and culturally sustaining (teacher) education and epistemological justice in educational contexts. She is the co-editor of the *Routledge Handbook of Educational Linguistics* and has published in *The Modern Language Journal, The International Review of Education, The Encyclopedia of Applied Linguistics* and *The International Journal of Language Studies*, among others.

Sham Haidar was born in Buner Khyber Pakhtunkhwa, Pakistan. He completed doctoral studies from Warner School of Education, University of Rochester, USA. He is currently serving as an assistant professor in the Department of English, Air University Islamabad, Pakistan. His research interests lie in sociolinguistics, equity in education, language and power, language ideology, English and globalisation, language instruction and technology, Teaching English to Speakers of Other Languages and critical discourse analysis. He has published articles in journals including *International Journal of Bilingual Education and Bilingualism, English Today, Asia Pacific Journal Education* and *Journal of Education and Educational Development*.

Christopher J. Hall is Professor of Applied Linguistics at York St John University in the UK. His current research focuses on conceptualisations of English from the perspective of Global Englishes. He has authored several books, book chapters and journal articles, including *Mapping Applied Linguistics: A Guide for Students and Practitioners* (co-author) and *Ontologies of English: Conceptualising the Language for Learning, Teaching, and Assessment* (co-editor). He also co-created the online course for teachers, *Changing Englishes* (www.changingenglishes.online), now in its second edition.

Michael Hepworth is a senior lecturer in TESOL and Education at the University of Sunderland and also works as a lecturer at the University of Leeds and the Open University. Before this, he worked as a Teaching Fellow at the University of Leeds, completing his PhD on Spoken Argumentation in the Adult ESOL classroom. His research interests lie in argumentation and in critical pedagogies and he has published a book chapter on Argumentation and Citizenship in the Adult ESOL classroom (2019). He is an experienced ESOL teacher and teacher educator and has worked as an English teacher in state comprehensive schools.

Liana Konstantinidou is Professor of German as a Foreign and Second Language at the Zurich University of Applied Sciences and Co-Head of the Institute of Language Competence. Her research focuses on the teaching of writing in vocational education and training and on writing assessment. In her projects, she also deals with the topic of language and integration as well as with language skills promotion for specific purposes. She has several years of experience in the management and implementation of international and national research projects and a broad network in the field of literacy promotion.

Ursula Lanvers is Associate Professor of Language Education at the University of York, UK. She joined the Department of Education in York in 2016. Before this, she worked at the Open University and University of Exeter as a lecturer in modern languages. She has published widely on language learner motivation especially for students with English as a first language (e.g. 'Contradictory others and the habitus of languages: Surveying the L2 motivation landscape in the United Kingdom', *The Modern Language Journal*, 2017), and on language education policy. A further strong interest of hers is Englishisation in education; she recently edited a Special Edition on Englishisation in European education systems in the *European Journal of Language Policy*.

Sinfree Makoni teaches in the Department of Applied Linguistics and Program in African Studies at Pennsylvania State University, USA, and is an extraordinary professor at the University of the North West, South Africa. His main research interests are language and politics and Southern Theories. His most recent books are: *Innovations and Challenges to Applied Linguistics from the Global South* (co-authored with Alastair Pennycook, Routledge) and *Language Planning and Policy: Ideologies, Ethnicities, and Semiotic Spaces of Power* (co-edited with Ashraf Abdelhay and Cristine Severo, Cambridge Scholars Publishing).

Luz Murillo is an educational anthropologist who studies the biliteracy development of Indigenous, immigrant and Latinx children, families and teachers. A native of Colombia, she earned her doctoral degree in Language, Reading and Culture at the University of Arizona, USA. Dr Murillo has taught courses in reading/writing/literacy, language and culture, and ethnography for bilingual educators at universities in the US, Mexico and Colombia. Her research has been published in English, Spanish and TexMex in journals like *Anthropology & Education Quarterly*, *Language Arts* and *Lectura y Vida*. Currently, she runs the

Biliteracy Enrichment after-school programme at the Centro Cultural Hispano de San Marcos, where Texas State students gain hands-on experience in Spanish and English literacy by tutoring dual language students from San Marcos CISD.

Annika Norlund Shaswar is a senior lecturer in Language Teaching and Learning at the Department of Language Studies at Umeå University in Sweden. Her research centres on multilingual literacy, basic literacy education for adult second language learners, digital literacy practices and genre pedagogy. She has researched the literacy practices of adult second language learners of Swedish and is particularly interested in the connections between literacy practices in everyday life and those in educational contexts. She has also studied how literacy practices of adult second language learners can be used a resource for the development of pedagogical practices in second language education.

Taina Saarinen is a Research Professor of higher education at the University of Jyväskylä, with a previous position in language education policy. She has published widely on higher education, language education policy and contemporary and historical language policies, and her latest research interests focus on new nationalism in higher education. She has recently published in journals such as *Higher Education*, *Rethinking History* and *Language Policy*, and is currently editing a volume on a new material turn in language education with Johanna Ennser-Kananen. She particularly enjoys multidisciplinary and comparative contexts, which often make unobserved gaps in the existing research visible.

Helen Sauntson is Professor of English Language and Linguistics at York St John University, UK. Her research areas are language in education and language, gender and sexuality. She has published a range of book chapters and journal articles in these areas and has authored and edited nine books. She is co-editor of the Palgrave Studies in Language, Gender and Sexuality book series.

Cristine Gorski Severo is Associate Professor at the Department of Portuguese and at the Post-Graduate Program of Linguistics, Federal University of Santa Catarina, Brazil. She has received two PhDs from the Federal University of Santa Catarina, one in Language Planning and Policy and the other in Interdisciplinary Studies. She has conducted research on colonial linguistics, language policy, African languages and resistance. Her research experience includes comparative research of primary sources in Portuguese and Spanish language related to colonisation and forms of resistance through language. Her publications include *Language Planning and Policy: Ideologies, Ethnicities and Semiotic Spaces of Power* (2020), edited with Sinfree Makoni and Ashraf Abdalhay.

Kristin Snoddon is an Associate Professor with the School of Early Childhood Studies, Ryerson University, Toronto, Canada. Her research and professional experience include collaborative work with deaf communities in developing sign language and early literacy programming for young deaf children and their parents. Additionally, she analyses policy issues related to inclusive education, sign language rights and acquisition planning for American Sign Language. She has served as Co-ordinator for the World Federation of the Deaf's Expert Group on Deaf Education.

Ursula Stadler Gamsa is Co-Head of the Institute of Language Competence. After a first degree in primary education she taught for many years German as a second language in Swiss schools and institutions and worked in educational projects and institutions in China, Pakistan and the UK. Her second degree is in German, Chinese and General Linguistics. At the Zurich University of Applied Sciences she teaches classes in professional communication and intercultural management as well as in the linguistics of writing. Her projects cover topics of professional writing, especially writing in social work.

Erin Wilkinson is Associate Professor in the Department of Linguistics at the University of New Mexico. Her research interests include bilingualism in signing populations, language change and variation in signed languages, and signed language typology. Her current studies in collaboration with other researchers examine bilingualism in highly diverse communities with respect to language socialisation and language planning and policy. She also collaboratively explores what linguistic structures are re-structured over time in signed languages and what are possible factors that contribute to language change and variation in signed languages in the lens of usage-based theory.

1 Introduction

Clare Cunningham and Christopher J. Hall

The global community is currently experiencing deeply unsettling times, with language use at the heart of many of the challenges that confront us. The risks we face operate in new and renewed contexts of social, political and economic instability. They are often associated with new technologies and sociopolitical movements which place in jeopardy the rights and wellbeing of marginalised or vulnerable groups. At the same time, new currents in applied linguistics over the past couple of decades (manifested notably in the so-called 'critical turn', 'social turn' and 'multilingual turn') have inevitably focused attention on new sources of data with their own risks, e.g. in ethnographic, ecological, narrative and critical late modern approaches. They have also presented new challenges for teaching and demanded a reconsideration of appropriate research methodologies and attendant risks (to data, researchers and participants). Clearly, it is time for applied linguists to think through the vulnerabilities, challenges and risks implicated in our discipline and to learn from our shared experiences.

This book was originally conceived during the annual meeting of the British Association for Applied Linguistics, held in 2018 at York St John University under the theme of *Taking Risks in Applied Linguistics*. The theme was chosen in recognition of the need for focused discussion of risk in applied linguistics, given rapid change and consequent uncertainty both in world affairs and in the discipline itself. (As it happens, this uncertainty has increased considerably since the time of the conference, given the global pandemic which paralysed the planet in 2020 and is still causing immense suffering as we go to press.) Most chapter contributions are developed from papers presented at the event in York, but as we considered work for inclusion in this volume and received initial feedback from reviewers, we quickly realised two things: first, that in many papers the theme of 'risk' spilled over into the neighbouring conceptual fields of 'vulnerabilities' and 'challenges'; and second, that to do fuller justice to the theme, we needed to commission additional chapters covering contexts and regions that were under-represented at the 2018 conference. At the forefront of our minds also was the understanding that Applied Linguistics is centrally concerned with action: that it is informed by theory, but only inasmuch as the theory underpins practice designed to solve or mitigate social problems or helps us understand such problems so that solutions or mitigations may be sought (Hall et al., 2017). This focus on action motivated the dual consideration here of: (a) risk arising from the contexts in which applied linguistic problems are embedded; and (b) risk in the way these applied linguistic problems are researched and addressed.

The result is the present volume, which is intended as a contribution to both research and practice in Applied Linguistics, showcasing recent work which addresses the inter-related issues of risk, challenges and vulnerability in a range of contexts. In this introductory chapter, we briefly discuss and define these inter-related concepts, and then introduce the chapters to follow.

Risk, Vulnerabilities and Challenges

For the purposes of this book, we understand risk as: (a) the perceived or real probability of actions having unwanted or unintended outcomes or consequences; and (b) the perceived or real potential causes of these outcomes or consequences. Vulnerabilities and challenges are closely aligned with these two senses of risk: we can define vulnerability as susceptibility to harm (i.e. exposure to the probability of unwanted or unintended outcomes or consequences); and challenges can be viewed as those factors which constitute obstacles to the achievement of desired/intended outcomes (i.e. cause them not to be met or to lead to unwanted or unintended consequences). Figure 1.1 provides a schematic representation of this relationship.

With this relationship in mind, we now make some brief comments about how the three concepts have been viewed within the broader human sciences and make some initial points of contact with themes and practices in applied linguistics, in order to contextualise the perspectives provided in the chapters that follow.

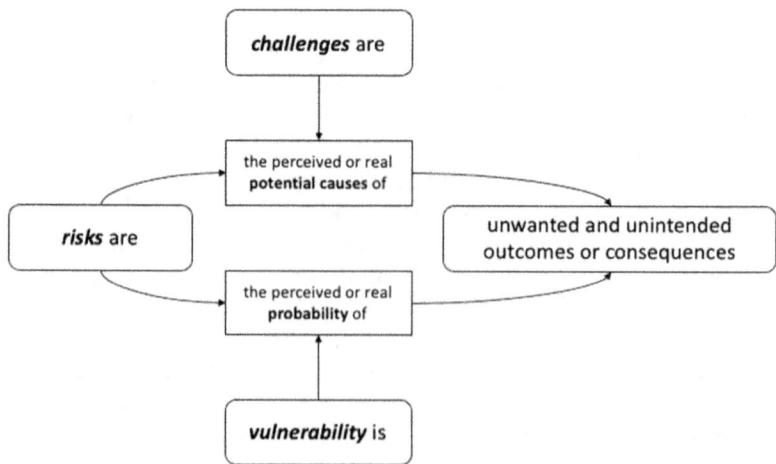

Figure 1.1 A sketch of the relationship between risk, vulnerability and challenges

Risk

The word *risk* was originally associated with the activity of 'sailing in unchartered waters' and later with the purely negative concept of 'danger' (Denney, 2005: 3). Although contemporary technical definitions focus on statistical probability, in everyday use the term most frequently reflects qualitative senses involving the cause and likelihood of unwanted events (Boholm *et al.*, 2016). In his hugely influential book *Risk Society* (published in English in 1992), Beck observed that, in the modern age, many of these undesirable outcomes are unintended, such as antibiotic resistance. This resonated with many beyond his own discipline of sociology, as did his argument that globalised society constructs and prescribes risk in part through its own reflexive processes, which are themselves inherently limited. He noted that the factors that have contributed to exacerbating the risks of our age stem, in fact, from the well-meaning actions of some of the groups who were most involved in risk management. He went on to point out that the most problematic aspect of many of these 'manufactured risks' is their global nature, which means that humanity cannot escape from their effects.

While more recent socially-oriented risk researchers, for the most part, consider risk to be a socially constructed concept (Burgess *et al.*, 2018), relating as much in some circumstances to the perception of risk as the likelihood of real harm, there has been much debate also about the boundaries between objective and manufactured risk. Climate change is, of course, one of the most deleterious examples of an objective risk (Beck, 1986/1992), to which the entire planet is vulnerable, and one to which applied linguists are increasingly attending (see below). And of course the Covid-19 pandemic has confronted humanity with risk, both objective and manufactured, of an unprecedented magnitude. The world today is very different from the one in which over 300 applied linguists from over 40 countries travelled to York for the British Association for Applied Linguists (BAAL) conference three years ago. The Covid-19 pandemic has heightened our awareness of the global and multifaceted nature of risk, especially for the most vulnerable members of our communities.

Vulnerabilities

Kasperson and Kasperson (2005) discuss the unequal distribution of risk rendering some communities more vulnerable to harm in the modern world. Vulnerability is therefore intimately connected with risk, as Power (2007) makes clear in his work on how risk management has, in many cases, increased *organisational uncertainty* and *individual insecurity*. Based on this literature, we take vulnerability to refer to the state or quality which renders communities, leaders, participants and researchers (as individuals or as part of organisations), as well as their policies and research projects, more susceptible or exposed to actions and situations that can result in undesirable outcomes.

However, there is also value in reframing vulnerability in a more positive light, as an important tool in resistance and activism work, as Butler (2004) and Butler *et al.* (2016) discuss at length. The vulnerability of the interdependence we have as humans can be seen as a way into reimagining how our relationships could be, with Hirsch (2016: 80) noting that vulnerability can be re-construed as 'a radical openness towards surprising possibilities'. Samata (2019) offers a thorough exploration of the importance of Butler's approach to vulnerability and resistance for applied linguistics. In her paper she argues that adopting a Butlerian framing of a 'linguistic precariat', instead of the more typical deficit construction of a limited linguistic capital, would perhaps establish a basis from which to resist. Samata (2019) notes that this construction may be useful for a number of populations: in migrant communities, amongst sign language users and in groups where first languages are suppressed, many of which are under discussion in this volume.

Vulnerability can also be seen as a property of applied linguistics itself, because of the discipline's inherent concern with social practice beyond academia. Kramsch (2015), for example, posits that the discipline is vulnerable to being manipulated, both intellectually (because of the drive to have measurable results and accountability) and professionally (in terms of the potential for budget cuts). Power (2007) argues that the demands and intensification of an audit culture as a demonstration of good governance have increased an organisation's risks of reputational damage, and it could well be argued that this is particularly true in academia.

Applied linguistics also continues to be vulnerable to 'culturist reduction' caused by a 'large culture' paradigm (Holliday, 1999). This is problematised, along with multiple other challenges for applied linguistics in and beyond the Global South, by Pennycook and Makoni (2020). As applied linguists we need to challenge ourselves to be individually and collectively vulnerable, to be open to learning about and critiquing the highly problematic history of applied linguistics, for example, and to take appropriate actions in our teaching, research and activism as a result of this work. The discipline needs to take risks to meet the challenge of working for social and linguistic justice, wherever we see that it may be lacking.

Challenges

Beck (1986/1992) highlighted that a key societal challenge is the public distrust in expert systems for dealing with the risks that present themselves. In recent times, we have seen this become increasingly prevalent, even encouraged by politicians, and then further amplified and distorted by the media (Kasperson & Kasperson, 2005). This was seen explicitly in reports of Michael Gove's infamous statement ('I think the people of this country have had enough of experts') in the lead-up to the UK's referendum on whether to remain in the European Union. The public distrust engendered through these means has also been seen in the conspiracy theories and misinformation spread globally during the Covid-19 pandemic. This is, of course, important for applied linguists to reflect on in terms of the discipline's positioning and claimed expertise. It perhaps reinforces the need to amplify voices from the communities we work with.

Returning to climate change as perhaps the most significant risk to humanity, and one from which many others stem and will continue to grow, we see that the challenges abound, including those around how the discourse is framed. One of the challenges set by Stibbe (2021) in the burgeoning field of eco-linguistics is to find new stories to replace those *stories-we-live-by* that are destructive, such as those stemming from the 'dark side of modernization' (Burgess *et al.*, 2018: 3). He suggests that humanity may actually find some of those 'new' stories-to-live-by in some of communities seen to be the most vulnerable, for example in Indigenous groups globally, some of which we read about in the following chapters. Hickman (2019) finds new ways of talking about climate change in discussing feelings about it with children, another group particularly vulnerable to its effects. The reframing of such vulnerability as fertile ground for resistance and activism (Butler, 2016; Hirsch, 2016) is useful here too, with the time right to 'galvanise a sense of urgency about the need for change' (Hirsch, 2016: 80).

Key to the discussions in this book, therefore, is the question: what is the role of the applied linguist in playing a more active role and pushing for social justice in everyday society? In our view it is to challenge and seek to redress societal problems that have language-related causes and/or solutions, especially with more vulnerable communities and individuals. Cowal and Leung (2020) characterise the role of the Activist Applied Linguist as being to address or solve 'wicked problems', a term they borrow from social policy studies, and Beck celebrates the double-edged sword of individualism by noting that the uncertainty that can be caused by the norms of the past can be offset by the opportunities to play a more active role in challenging unhelpful systems and averting potential future disasters (Burgess *et al.*, 2018). The recent arrival of chapters on applied linguistic activism in introductory handbooks for the discipline should be applauded; we hope that the chapters in this volume will complement such initiatives by inviting deeper reflection on and understanding of the risks, challenges and vulnerabilities associated with such activism.

Structure of the Book

This book is divided into four sections which allow us to explore thematically the nature of some of the risks, challenges and vulnerabilities faced by applied linguists and the people their work is focused around.

The opening part, *Communities*, presents a series of studies on the risks and challenges experienced by applied linguists working to ameliorate the position of the communities of the Global South and those representing and working with members of the deaf community and the LGBTQ+ community. These and other marginalised communities are perhaps well-positioned to utilise the vulnerability often societally ascribed to them to bring about change. Part 2, *Policy*, brings together chapters which consider the role of policy in challenging linguistic inequalities, including a flight of the imagination with regards to Finnish language policy, a critique of Anglophone countries' language policy and an exploration of the challenges of getting a language recognised as such in the first place. The third part, *Research*, considers the role of the applied linguistics researcher, and includes chapters on the vulnerability of researchers when dealing with extremist discourses online, risks to the notion of 'good data' and challenges in relationship-building in research and in working with interpreters in research interviews. The final part, *Education*, takes us into the classroom, and offers three chapters covering the potential for an increased role for Applied Linguistics in designing socially just curricula, the challenge of introducing controversial topics in ESOL classes and the risks to social integration that the continued hegemonic status of English poses in one particular nation in the Global South.

Part 1: Communities

In the first chapter, **Severo** and **Makoni** ask applied linguists to consider the vulnerability of their discipline when construed uniquely according to the dominant epistemologies and ontologies of the Global North. They also point out the risks to alternative Southern epistemologies and Indigenous ontologies posed by unchallenged Northern legacies of colonialism and white male heteronormativity. As an illustration of the ideas that can be mobilised to challenge the 'epistemic racism' of the Eurocentric model of language, they present the African-Brazilian Quilombist movement and metaphors of land and mangrove. They suggest that these ideas can afford powerful analytical perspectives which highlight alternative conceptions of territoriality, reconfigure the regimes of visibility and discourse and recognise equally the aesthetic, ecological and political dimensions of language.

Murillo's chapter complements the previous one by exploring how social inequalities in Latin America are discursively constructed and may be challenged and disrupted through language and by embracing alternative epistemologies. Murillo recounts the challenges arising from late capitalism which confront vulnerable Indigenous communities in Guatemala and Colombia and the risks taken by activists and applied linguists who work to protect their languages and territories. Using her own fieldwork in the schools and communities of Q'anjob'al and Arhuaco speakers,

Murillo vividly describes the risks – often physical – experienced by activists, educators and researchers. She concludes by advocating 'epistemic disobedience' to engender 'radical hope' for the future. Her work here directly answers Butler's (2004) challenge to see potential vulnerability as a tool for resistance and activism.

Conama focuses on another vulnerable community of language users, this time in Ireland, and like Murillo adopts a personal perspective, describing his own role as an activist–scholar working to achieve official recognition of Irish Sign Language. Against the familiar backdrop of neoliberal inequalities, Conama depicts the challenges he and fellow activists have faced along the 'bumpy road' to the 2017 Irish Sign Language Act, including the 'audist' indifference of policymakers, their undermining of Deaf leadership, the unfair distribution of state resources for signed vs spoken languages, and official failure to understand that languages are more than means for accessing information. Conama also highlights the mental and emotional toll of challenging the linguistic inequalities which remain endemic in contemporary society.

In her chapter, **Sauntson** explores the vulnerabilities of researchers working on language and sexuality, and the real and perceived risks they face in doing so, especially in the many contexts where the issue is still treated as 'taboo'. Like the previous two chapters, Sauntson reports on her own personal experience, calling attention to the professional pressures that researchers in the area can be subjected to, especially in the light of largely unchallenged neoliberal conceptions of successful higher education careers. Focusing on the continuing ubiquity of heteronormative discrimination in schools, Sauntson points out that structural forms of homophobia have been overlooked. Informed by Pakuła's theorisation of risk in this area, she presents a series of case studies which lead to the proposal of strategies that educators, institutions, and publishers can take to embrace the challenges and 'befriend' the risks.

Part 2: Policy

Taking a novel approach to our theme, **Ensser-Kananen** and **Saarinen** use the alternative epistemology of 'counterfactual histories' to explore the risks posed by Finnish language policy to speakers of minority languages. They argue that the future orientation of risk, the sense of uncertainty it involves and its potential to be manipulated by powerful groups make it a useful lens through which to analyse the potential inequalities associated with official language policy. Asking what might have happened if Swedish had been named a minority language of Finland, rather than given national status, allows them to problematise the idealisation of Finland as a model of bilingualism, and to identify the non-linguistic factors that might lead language policies to perpetuate privilege rather than protect the disenfranchised.

Lanvers uncovers the vulnerabilities inherent in the UK's language learning policies in the contexts of longstanding Anglophone linguaphobia and the withdrawal of the UK from the European Union. She reviews the current state of language learning and public discourse around it in the constituent nations of the UK, points out the heightened politicisation of the issue since Brexit and explores the consequences of Brexit for English in Europe and language learning in the UK. Lanvers concludes that the privileged position of (British) English in the EU is unlikely to be challenged as a result of Brexit, and that the risks of continued complacency regarding the language needs of the UK show no immediate signs of dissipating. She also argues that, as well as a significant challenge, Brexit may represent an opportunity to tackle monolingual mindsets.

In their chapter, **Snoddon** and **Wilkinson** explore the vulnerabilities, challenges and risks associated with sign language policy in Canada, contrasting two legislative treatments in which sign languages are conceptualised either as disability accommodations or as the linguistic resources of Indigenous communities. Noting that deaf Indigenous people are 'doubly vulnerable', Snoddon and Wilkinson track the risks and challenges of the two sets of legislation and the problems, both conceptual and structural, which will complicate fulfilment of their policy objectives. They conclude that mainstream deaf community advocates, as well as policymakers, must consider language in the broader context of identity and culture, but that the 'happy accident' of Indigenous sign language protection may inadvertently result in more attention being paid to the vulnerabilities of non-Indigenous sign language users.

Part 3: Research

In **Barber's** chapter on analysing online discourses, the particular focus is on the work she has conducted in extremist discourses. She offers an insight into the ethical dimensions, reflecting on the role of the researcher in handling the risks to victims and in preventing an uncritical dissemination of 'hateful rhetoric', as well as how to protect the researcher from harm as a result of being exposed to such views for an extended period. Barber questions whether it is possible or even desirable to adopt an emic stance in working with extremist online discourses, and usefully discusses the value of framing one's research carefully to ensure that researcher positionality is clear. Connecting with Kasperson and Kasperson's (2005) writings about the challenges posed by inflammatory and distorted media coverage, the chapter concludes with a reflection on the rise of far-right rhetoric in mainstream media, an issue which is becoming increasingly urgent following the murder by a police officer of George Floyd and the subsequent Black Lives Matter protests of 2020.

In his chapter, **Consoli** shares some personal research stories which allow us to reflect on the roles, relationships and ethical responsibilities inherent in 'messy' applied linguistics research. He discusses the extent to which research roles can change during the course of a study, and the challenges to relationships that this can trigger. The tensions he focuses on highlight the power of making oneself as a researcher vulnerable to scrutiny and allow him to raise the question of what risks are worth taking in obtaining strong (or 'good enough') research data. Consoli's research focus was concerned with student motivations for undertaking pre-sessional modules, but his reflections take us well beyond the research topic into areas that will be of interest to many readers around the challenges of fostering rapport, and the risks in using humour, with participants. His discussions of critical incidents allow him to explore the balance between being constantly aware of the ethical considerations needed towards participants and the potential for obtaining 'superb data'.

Norlund Shaswar explores the challenges and risks in conducting research interviews alongside an interpreter. She discusses relevant literature in terms of the impact of a researcher's particular paradigm: positivists view the interpreter as a neutral figure, where the main risk is that the interpretation could be 'wrong'; constructivists are more concerned about the risks to contextual factors and the privileging of certain perspectives. Norlund Shaswar examines the increased complexity of interpreted interaction and threats to co-construction in an interview for a project on digital literacies practices. The chapter offers an insight into the practical aspects of working with an interpreter in research interviews (e.g. optimal seating plans and how much information to provide in advance), but the focus is on data, showing the importance of the researcher and interpreter working together and the risks to the project if they are misaligned in their stance.

Part 4: Education

Konstantinidou and **Stadler's** chapter takes us to the heart of the role of applied linguistics in tackling some of the greatest social challenges that face our societies. They explore the process of launching a new undergraduate programme on Language and Integration in Switzerland, setting this decision against the background of political discussions on language skills for migrants. The careful procedure undertaken to ensure that this novel curriculum would meet the needs of students and stakeholders is meticulously presented, offering a valuable model for applied linguists interested in providing this challenge to their own students. Konstantinidou and Stadler raise some important questions for applied linguists around the value of our discipline and its limitations in tackling societal issues, challenging the reader to acknowledge the key role of transdisciplinary research in which applied linguistics can perform a leading role.

Hepworth's chapter takes us right into the language classroom, considering the challenge of using controversy as a pedagogical tool. While not a novel area for discussion, he points out that despite research on the opportunities that discussing controversial issues affords, it remains a risk that many teachers avoid. The settings he describes are adult ESOL (English to Speakers of Other Languages) classes in the UK, in a post-Brexit environment in which evidence of an increase in nationalism and discrimination based on xenophobia is growing. By presenting excerpts which allow the reader access into these teaching spaces, Hepworth offsets the issues of the risk of offence and reluctance to participate in discussing controversial topics to reveal an environment in which students can develop as 'critical agents' as well as gain significant language and social skills.

In the final chapter, **Haidar** takes us full circle back to the Global South in focusing on the divisive role of English in the Pakistani school system. He explores the processes that lead to differing levels of English proficiency in the population and asks how access to English can be construed as a risk to the social integration of students from different school systems. His research shows the reader only too clearly the risks posed by the hegemonic status of English that was discussed in the first chapter of this volume. On the basis of interview data with teachers and students in both 'elite' and 'general' schools, he graphically documents their understanding of their language learning and usage experiences and of the social ramifications and expectations of life beyond the school that are perpetuated through the differentiated systems.

Concluding Remarks

By calling attention to vulnerabilities, challenges and risks in applied linguistics – in the communities we work with, the policies we critique and propose, the research we conduct, and the educational contexts we engage with – we intend the papers collected here to provide insights and benefits for academic and professional practice in several ways: first, by raising awareness of aspects of our current research and teaching that we engage with on a daily basis but perhaps should scrutinise more explicitly, such as our own vulnerabilities as researchers; second, by identifying potential limitations in our epistemologies and suggesting new approaches to understanding; third, by exposing challenges inherent in the repertoire of research methods and pedagogies we employ and thereby helping us anticipate them; and finally, by providing some insight into which aspects of our practical responses to language-related problems are more or less effective, so that we can better manage the risks and overcome the challenges involved. We return to our view for the future in the Afterword.

References

Beck, U. (1986/1992) *Risk Society: Towards a New Modernity*. London: Sage.
Boholm, M., Möller, N. and Hansson, S.O. (2016) The concepts of risk, safety, and security: Applications in everyday language. *Risk Analysis* 36 (2), 320–338.

Burgess, A., Wardman, J. and Mythen, G. (2018) Considering risk: Placing the work of Ulrich Beck in context. *Journal of Risk Research* 21 (1), 1–5.

Butler, J. (2004) *Precarious Life: The Powers of Mourning and Violence*. London: Verso.

Butler, J. (2016) Rethinking vulnerability and resistance. In J. Butler, Z. Gambetti and L. Sabsay (eds) *Vulnerability in Resistance* (pp. 12–27). Durham, NC: Duke University Press.

Butler, J., Gambetti, Z. and Sabsay, L. (2016) Introduction. In J. Butler, Z. Gambetti and L. Sabsay (eds) *Vulnerability in Resistance* (pp. 1–11). Durham, NC: Duke University Press.

Cowal, J. and Leung, G. (2020) Activist applied linguistics. In S. Conrad, A. Hartig and L. Santelmann (eds) *The Cambridge Introduction to Applied Linguistics* (pp. 308–324). Cambridge: Cambridge University Press.

Denney, D. (2005) *Risk and Society*. London: Sage.

Hall, C.J., Smith, P.H. and Wicaksono, R. (2017) *Mapping Applied Linguistics. A Guide for Students and Practitioners* (2nd edn). London: Routledge.

Hickman, C. (2019) Children and climate change: Exploring children's feelings about climate change using Free Association Narrative Interview methodology. In P. Hoggett (ed.) *Climate Psychology: On Indifference to Disaster* (pp. 41–60). Cham: Palgrave Macmillan.

Hirsch, M. (2016) Vulnerable times. In J. Butler, Z. Gambetti and L. Sabsay (eds) *Vulnerability in Resistance* (pp. 76–98). Durham, NC: Duke University Press.

Holliday, A. (1999) Small cultures. *Applied Linguistics* 20 (2), 237–264.

Kasperson, J.X. and Kasperson, R.E. (2005) *Social Contours of Risk. Volume I: Publics, Risk Communication and the Social*. Abingdon: Routledge.

Kramsch, C. (2015) Applied linguistics: A theory of the practice. *Applied Linguistics* 36 (4), 454–465.

Pennycook, A. and Makoni, S. (2019) *Innovations and Challenges in Applied Linguistics from the Global South*. London: Routledge.

Power, M. (2007) *Organized Uncertainty: Designing a World of Risk Management*. Oxford: Oxford University Press.

Samata, S. (2019) Linguistic precariat: Judith Butler's 'rethinking vulnerability and resistance' as a useful perspective for applied linguistics. *Applied Linguistics Review* 10 (2), 163–177.

Stibbe, A. (2021) *Ecolinguistics: Language, Ecology and the Stories We Live By* (2nd edn). London: Routledge.

Part 1
Communities

2 Can Southern Epistemological and Indigenous Ontological Orientations to Applied Linguistics Challenge its Ethnocentrism?

Cristine Gorski Severo and Sinfree B. Makoni

Introduction

In this chapter, we argue that applied linguistics has come a long way from when definitions and debates revolved around the distinctions between applied linguistics and 'linguistics applied' (Davies & Elder, 2006) or when it was taken as axiomatic that applied linguistics, unlike linguistics, addressed issues in the 'real world' (Brumfit, 1995). However, in this chapter, we seek to demonstrate how applied linguistics can take on the challenge of developing further than how it was characterized by Davies and Elder and, subsequently, by Brumfit if it is viewed through Southern epistemologies and Indigenous ontologies (Makoni, 1998, 2003; Pennycook, 2018; Pennycook & Makoni, 2019). In the chapter, we also seek to illustrate that Southern epistemologies and Indigenous ontologies render it feasible to move beyond the impasse that critical applied linguistics (CAL) faces because CAL continues to subscribe to universalism characteristics of Eurocentric scholarship. Southern epistemologies and Indigenous ontologies are not the same as CAL; if anything, they seek to address some of the limitations that have become apparent in CAL in the Global South, as the latter has 'run out of steam' (Pennycook & Makoni, 2019) and because its hegemonic universalism entrenches differences between the Global North and Global South.

We conclude by showing how the benefits of using Southern epistemologies and Indigenous ontologies outweigh the risks of not using such approaches in applied linguistics in the Global South. The Southern epistemologies and Indigenous ontologies that we are developing involve a mobilization of and a construction of an 'assemblage' (Kroskrity, 2018; Pennycook, 2018) of Indigenous and non-Western ontologies of language and multilingualism, and wherever possible, we capitalize on perspectives of marginalized communities in either the Global North or Global South (Hauck & Heurich, 2018). The epistemological and Indigenous ontological 'assemblages' include Indigenous multilingual typologies that include spiritual aspects of language (Di Carlo, 2016). In the epistemological and ontological 'assemblages', language is not separated from the other aspects of one's being that are central to an individual's life, such as their spirituality, because language is life, and life is language, which provides spiritual sustenance (Ferguson, 2013). Language in this framework is not an abstraction; it has animacy (Ferguson, 2019).

In this chapter, we aim to contribute to a development of Southern epistemologies and Indigenous ontologies toward applied linguistics by using lay perspectives as analytical heuristics that originate in integrationism (Pablé & Hutton, 2015). Southern epistemologies and Indigenous ontologies render it feasible to decolonialize applied linguistics. We are developing Southern epistemologies and Indigenous ontologies in applied linguistics, drawing on the work of Connell (2007). Southern epistemologies and Indigenous ontologies in applied linguistics are 'multicentered' and 'represent diverse social experiences' and conflicting forms of knowledge that may accommodate the needs of social movements, all of which are relevant to a democratizing applied linguistics. In terms of Southern epistemologies and Indigenous ontologies, we consider colonialism and post-colonialism – in both a broad and narrow sense – as important frameworks from which to discuss the meanings of language, language learning, and applied linguistics.

Southern epistemologies and Indigenous ontologies do not constitute a fixed body of knowledge but, rather, an emergent set of possibilities. They constitute an orientation toward language and applied linguistics that is at the intersection of decoloniality and Indigenous perspectives of language. Interest in the Global South and Southern epistemologies and Indigenous ontologies is occurring at the same time that there is a 'decolonial turn' marked by a massive shift in knowledge production comparable with the 'linguistic' and 'pragmatic turns' that we have previously witnessed. The 'decolonial turn' is occurring across many disciplines in the social sciences and humanities and within applied linguistics. Although the concept of decolonization is controversial, we construe it in this chapter to be a 'political and epistemic project that surfaces from local histories elsewhere and otherwise, which seeks to speak back to this world system that affects all aspects of society' (García & Baca, 2019: 2). Moreover, we echo García and Baca's contention that decoloniality emerges from hope and vision such that it is possible to explore 'border thinking' as the site of knowledge and epistemic alternatives that move us beyond Western categories of epistemology and ontologies. This further leads us to mobilize Indigenous and non-Western categories about language and multilingualism in applied linguistics, which are both based on 'land', as we illustrate in this chapter, and in other 'waves of knowing' (Ingersoll, 2016, drawing on the sea, which Ingersoll refers to as 'seascape epistemology').

This chapter is a continuation of discussions of the possible and desirable contribution of Southern epistemologies and Indigenous ontologies to applied linguistics, as proposed recently by Pennycook and Makoni (2019: 34), in which 'our goal here is to seek ways of expanding the analytical repertoires of applied linguistics by drawing on southern thought'. We are arguing for an applied linguistics whose goal is to 'disrupt' Global Northern hegemony over applied linguistics in the Global South, thereby creating conditions in which applied linguistics in the Global South can enter into a dialogue with applied linguistics that originate in the Global North or other regions in the Global South. It will be easier for the Global South to enter into a dialogue with the Global North when the hegemony of Global North applied linguistics in the Global South is 'disrupted'. The dialogue between Global North and Global South applied linguistics is not equivalent to a 'delinking' of Global North applied linguistics from the Global South or vice versa. A 'delinking' of the Global South applied linguistics from the Global North is politically desirable, as we strive to move toward a more egalitarian politics of knowledge, but is not feasible owing to the 'entanglement' in applied linguistics between the Global North and Global South. Neither decolonial thinking nor epistemologies of the South and Indigenous ontologies claim to replace a previous incorrect paradigm with a correct one but, rather, offer paradigms of complexity that, rather than seeking authenticity, seek justice and horizontality.

We approach issues about risks and vulnerabilities in two different senses. We explore the nature of the risks and vulnerabilities to applied linguistics if it does not address issues raised by alternative approaches to applied linguistics emerging from the Global South. The second sense of risks we address is the risks which alternative approaches are faced with themselves if they constitute alternative frameworks to applied linguistics in the Global North. We understand that 'Epistemological or civilizational racism is deeply embedded in academic knowledge systems in the Global North and by extension can be found in applied linguistics. It privileges "White" epistemological assumptions about knowledge, regarding them as norms against other forms of knowledge have to be measured' (Pennycook & Makoni, 2020: 104). Disciplines such as applied linguistics and anthropology are 'historically viscerally' (Rajagopalan, 2020) tied to colonialism and racism.

In this chapter, we illustrate the analytical value of Southern epistemologies and Indigenous ontologies in Global South applied linguistics of

Quilombism, the land and mangrove metaphors. Language is a product of individual and community perspectives and is grounded not only in socio-historical contexts but on 'land' as well. We situate the ontology of language on land and on the mangrove. We believe that this is important because 'land' – with all of the multiple metaphorical meanings associated with it – in some colonial and post-colonial contexts, has been a site of protracted conflict both in Africa and in the Diaspora, such as is seen in Brazil. By interpreting such examples in terms of Southern epistemologies and Indigenous ontologies, we may identify a lay-oriented conception to language that includes politics, aesthetics and ethics, with the objective to denaturalize and de-Westernize universal 'linguistic-cognitive rules' about language, second language learning and applied linguistics.

We address the following questions: in what ways can Southern epistemologies and Indigenous ontologies be used as instruments to challenge and undercut the recalcitrant colonial legacy in applied linguistics? In what ways can Southern epistemologies and Indigenous ontologies be used to challenge Global Northern hegemony in applied linguistics, as we seriously address issues about the politics of knowledge production, distribution and dissemination? Is it feasible to establish a dialogue between Global North and Global South applied linguistics in an applied linguistics animated by Southern epistemologies and Indigenous ontologies? All of these questions have a direct bearing on the politics of knowledge production, dissemination and circulation, which is an important component in a development of applied linguistics of the Global South.

The chapter is organized as follows. First, we present an overview of Southern epistemologies and ontologies in applied linguistics, followed by a discussion of two interconnected epistemological and ontological frameworks – Quilombism and the metaphors of land and the mangrove, thereby establishing areas of contact between such approaches and Southern epistemologies and ontologies.

Southern Epistemologies and Indigenous Ontologies in Applied Linguistics in the Global South

We argue that, if applied linguistics aims at integrating Southern epistemologies and Indigenous ontologies in the social sciences and humanities (Cusicanqui, 2012; Lander, 2000; Quijano, 2000; Santos & Meneses, 2010), it has to face some epistemic, ethical and political challenges and risks. We must problematize core concepts in applied linguistics, such as language, learning and applied linguistics. 'What is language?' should be a central question, instead of engagement in foreclosing debates about the 'natures' of language (Hauck & Hank, 2018) by adopting universal methodological and theoretical frameworks that assume that the nature of language is a settled matter. We therefore advocate a contextualized applied linguistics that is the product of a continuous and ongoing reflection of individual experimentation and creativity with the local in a decolonizing applied linguistics.

Both Southern epistemologies and Indigenous ontologies are political and ethical projects related to power relations, race, gender and ethnicity, all of which have a bearing on the nature of applied linguistics. Southern epistemologies and Indigenous ontologies demand of us that we pay attention to colonial and post-colonial experiences and call upon us to challenge the White male heteronormative basis upon which contemporary applied linguistics is grounded. We ask, 'Why is my applied linguistics White and male?' Southern epistemologies and Indigenous ontologies help us to understand what counts as language from multiple perspectives, which means that we should be able to use new metaphors and narratives to describe languages, all of which are relevant in our conceptualization and ways of 'doing' Southern epistemology and Indigenous ontology in applied linguistics.

'Doing' southern epistemology and Indigenous ontology includes considering experiences of resistance and histories of struggle by local people in both colonial and post-colonial contexts. We should be able to consider the way resistance plays a major role in framing what counts as applied linguistics from the perspective of those who were created as the 'other' in applied linguistics. In Southern perspectives, the 'coloniality of power' (Quijano, 2000) has to do with the way colonial practices have continued to exist even after many previously colonized countries became nominally independent. Colonial culture and structures have been reinforced by capitalism and neoliberalism, which include the ratified use of hierarchical and racial categories to describe the 'other', who are euphemistically described as language users, second language learners, speakers of New Englishes or Global Englishes, language learners and so forth, categorizations that reinforce a mythical status of some Western-educated, native speaker of English. Coloniality concerns several interconnected issues, such as economy, authority, natural resources, gender, sexuality, identity and knowledge production (Cusicanqui, 2012; Lander, 2000; Quijano, 2000; Santos & Meneses, 2010). Local knowledge production also concerns wondering about what language – communicative practices – should be used to narrate how colonial power can be subverted or contested.

We argue that a critical Southern perspective must consider how applied linguistics helped to shape what we understand as language – as language practices – in colonized contexts. Coloniality and post-coloniality cannot be reduced to geographical or temporal aspects (Pennycook & Makoni, 2019), but rather, must consider evolving power relations that submit some to the systematic control of others. This means that history cannot be reduced to a linear and chronological perspective that has been used to shape the ideas of 'pre' and 'post': 'There is no post or pre in this vision of history that is not linear or teleological but rather moves in cycles and spirals and sets out on a course without neglecting to return to the same point' (Cusicanqui, 2012: 96). We should be able to understand the underlying epistemological and ontological mechanisms of such control, which means considering language as a political and constructed category that, together with race and gender, helped to shape and hierarchize people's lives, depending on which languages they are native speakers of or whether or not they are native speakers.

In terms of applied linguistics, we postulate, 'Racism impacts not only the people, texts, or semiosis that we investigate in our research, but also us – teachers, researchers, and students in applied linguistics – in many ways' (Kubota, 2019: 1). This means that Southern perspectives illuminate the historical process by which we have created the use of language as a category of differentiation, control and hierarchization. We are aware that some concepts in applied linguistics, such as mother tongue, foreign language, proficiency, language extinction, language revitalization, language families and language diversity, are grounded in colonial templates (Heller & McElhinny, 2017; Irvine, 2009; Kubota, 2019; Leonard, 2017; Pennycook & Makoni, 2019; Severo, 2019; Smith, 1999)

In the following section, we explore the conceptual value of two Southern political metaphors: the Quilombo and the land and mangrove metaphors. We understand such epistemological and ontological frames in terms of ethnic and gender resistance. Although the Quilombo is a political, juridical, ethical and historical movement connected to the colonial era and slavery in Brazil, the mangrove can be seen as a cultural, political and musical movement that is connected to the way it captures the rhythms of the mangrove, understood as a metaphor of the periphery, juxtaposition, transition and ambiguity (instead of opposition, similarity, discreteness or differentiation). The mangrove is also related to the role played by women who harvest crabs in Brazil. We argue that the metaphor of the mangrove can help us to understand and narrate gender and language issues.

Integrating Perspectives of Southern Epistemologies and Indigenous Ontological Frameworks

In this section, we explore the underlying epistemologies of two political and sociocultural movements: Quilombism and its connection to the evolving concept of Quilombo and African-Brazilian struggles for rights as well as the cultural movement of *Manguebit/MangueBeat* (rhythm of the mangrove). Although other local concepts and practices also could be considered, we opted for these worldviews because they link peripheral experiences historically connected to modes of political, cultural and moral living. We argue that these movements and metaphors enable us to articulate language and applied linguistics in terms of land, belonging, sharing, being, singing, dancing, claiming and constructing a complex interconnected vision of language. By focusing on such metaphors and movements, we seek to connect local issues and demands with a cross-border perspective that underlines diasporic movements of resistance.

Language is not static, and its status is not a pre-given reality. Each subdomain in applied linguistics creates its vision of language anew in its theorization and practice. For example, second language acquisition with a strong emphasis on the cognitive and images of language influenced by cognition and computers frames language differently from sociolinguistics or language teaching. Analytical frameworks of language in language teaching are undergirded by different understandings of language. We advocate a radically contextualized concept of language, which means that laypeople's opinions and practices (Pablé, 2019) matter in terms of defining not only what counts as language but also the way that language can be approached only from an integrated understanding of local experiences. Although we understand that a radically contextualized concept of language may run the risk of reinforcing what counts as authenticity, we argue that universal and ahistorical theories should be consistently understood in terms of local experiences and submitted for interpretation.

We start by exploring the ideas of *Quilombo* and *Quilombismo* (Quilombism) and how they are connected to African-Brazilian struggles for rights, visibility and justice. The term *Quilombo* is related to the political, juridical and sociocultural struggle of African-Brazilians for recognition and citizenship, which is connected to the history of slavery that brought around 5 million African people to Brazil. The term *Quilombo* has had several meanings since the colonial era in Brazil. It is related to modes of living, places, resistance, popular movements and ethical issues (Leite, 1999). In the Brazilian Constitution of 1988, the use of the expression *Remanescentes de Quilombo* (Remainders of the Quilombos communities) designated a group that has a right to land. Since then, such an expression has been broadly used by African Brazilians, scholars and jurists. The concepts of *Quilombo* and *Quilombismo* also are connected to the term *Black*, which includes two perspectives: the historical experience of Africans who, under slavery, have been treated as being ahistorical and non-human; and the political and cultural experience of Africans and their descendants toward the creation of a sense of solidarity and community (Leite, 1999).

Quilombism was a term used by Abdias do Nascimento (1980), an African-Brazilian writer, activist and scholar, who founded the *Teatro Experimental do Negro* (The Black Experimental Theater) in 1944 in Brazil and wrote, among other treatises, the *Manifesto da Convenção Nacional do Negro à Nação Brasileira* (Manifesto of the Black National Convention to the Brazilian Nation), in 1945. For Nascimento, Quilombism is related to an 'idea-force, a source of energy inspiring models of dynamic organization, since the fifteenth century' (1980: 153), which still has to be realized. The underlying epistemology of Quilombism challenges the Eurocentric theories that helped historically to shape the stereotypical concepts of race, identity and language used to define and describe Africans' experience: 'For centuries we have carried the burden of the crimes and falsities of "scientific" Eurocentrism, its dogmas imposed upon our being as the brands of a definitive, "universal" truth' (Nascimento, 1980: 159). Nascimento's ideas have historically helped to shape the Brazilian Black Movement, which can be noticed by how his concept of Quilombism has been revisited by important Black scholars and cultural leaders, for example, Nei Lopes who in his Brazilian Encyclopedia of African Diaspora (2011) described in a lengthy treatise Abdias Nascimento's political, epistemological and cultural contribution to Afro-Brazilian movements.

Considering Quilombism as a critical perspective to Eurocentric visions means:

(1) To question historical authoritarianism in its several modalities, which includes the use of a Greco-Latin and Christian concept of language that has helped to shape universal frameworks that have been used in regard to Indigenous African languages as 'European scripts' (Makoni & Meinhof, 2004; Severo & Makoni, 2015). We understand that applied linguistics has been caught up in a Eurocentric model of language that underlies the contemporary and modern approaches to language.
(2) To problematize the racialized epistemologies that have been used to frame 'Bantu' languages as a language family that was constructed under the 19th century comparative linguistics (Abdelhay *et al.*, forthcoming). Such problematization includes the descriptive, structuralist and ethnolinguistic framework that has been used to describe what counts as 'African languages' in diaspora, such as the idea of Afro-Brazilian Portuguese.
(3) To be careful about the politics to be adopted (Nascimento, 1980), avoiding the acritical reproduction of colonizing power relations that work by silencing and erasing histories, narratives and peoples' vision. This means that we should be able to avoid commonplace, dualistic and simplistic interpretations of power relations.
(4) To avoid the reproduction of language harmonization ideologies (Makoni, 2016), such as the idea that Brazilian Portuguese has been the product of a harmonious contact between African Bantu Languages and European Portuguese. This ideology perpetuates the idea that an alleged linguistic democracy in Brazil would follow the myth of Brazil's being a racial democracy fictitiously favored by 'miscegenation'.
(5) To understand that language is the product of an open-ended and indeterminate process: 'What orthodox linguistics cannot take on board is the notion that in verbal communication both form and meaning function as indeterminate variables' (Harris & Haas, 2011: 501).

(6) To expand the meanings of 'land' by considering not only the right to acquire geographical land but also symbolic forms of territorialization, such as the idea of language as a dwelling place. Land has to do with different forms of spacialization, which means, on the one hand, control, use of space and new forms of socialization, and on the other hand, issues of forced eviction and negative stereotypes (Leite, 1999).

(7) To expand the conception of language in an educational context in which oral tradition and other language practices may be seriously considered. This means that systematization and standardization should not be a condition for teaching languages (Deumert, 2010).

Another example of Southern epistemologies and ontologies is the Brazilian cultural movement of *Manguebit/MangueBeat*. The hybrid word *Manguebit*, whose symbol is a crab, mixes the ideas of mangrove, rhythm (beat) and technology (bit). Just as 'land' has been a powerful means of defining the several meanings related to territorialization, belonging and resistance in Quilombism, the word 'mangue' (mangrove) also carries political and critical meanings related to cultural and economic movements of historically subalternized and excluded people in Brazil. The mangrove can be seen as an 'in between' metaphor – it is located between the land and the sea – and as an integrated and antibinary process – the mangrove includes the sea and the land. The mangrove is a 'form of artistic thinking' that reminds us of 'collapsing land-bound notions of being-in-the-world and reminding us not to forget the ocean' (Deumert, 2019: para. 9). On the other hand, the mangrove is also a metaphor that problematizes poverty and hunger from the perspective of the so-called 'amphibious individuals' who live between the margins of the capitalist world and the agrarian society: 'Amphibian beings: inhabitants of land and water, half men and half animals. Fed in childhood with crab broth: this mud milk' (Castro, 1967: 12).

The manguebit is a cultural and political movement that started in the outskirts of Recife, a city in northern Brazil, in the 1990s. Such an artistic movement subverts the ideas of marginality and periphery by promoting new forms of collectivism, participation, construction of visibility and social voices. Just as Nascimento wrote a manifesto to elucidate his perspective on *Quilombismo*, the manguebit movement produced the *Manifesto Caranguejos com Cérebro* (Crabs with Brain Manifesto). The leaders of the movement were Chico Science and Nação Zumbi (Zumbi Nation), who mixed in local aesthetic elements, such as the African Brazilian rhythm Maracatu, with modern ones, such as hip hop and the punk subculture (Guimarães & Carvalho, 2016). Such cultural movements also used alternative modes of diffusion, such as social networking, flyers, libraries, street theater groups and communitarian modes of communication, such as local radio programs. The multiplicity and complexity of the manguebit movement reflects the integrated and yet indeterminate ecosystem of mangroves, which 'are constituted by fluid borders separating and linking diverse elements such as water, roots, mud, crabs, reptiles, mollusks, fish, insects, birds, plants, flowers, and lichen among other things' (Walter, 2005: 128).

Recife is considered, culturally and economically, a peripheral place in Brazil, in contrast to São Paulo and Rio de Janeiro, which reinforce the political agenda of the movement in relation to the cultural national scenario. The city of Recife was built over a big mangrove, and the mangrove is the place where poor people live. By using modern elements, the mangue movement helped to resignify the meanings of regional, popular, traditional and authentic. This meant a deconstruction of cultural and social binaries, such as periphery and urbanity, regional and central, and popular and erudite. The mangue movement is about new modes of occupying the public space by creating new forms of visibility that are strongly related to social and economic resistance. It is also about the (conflictual and dialogical) relation with otherness that underlies the concept of politics: 'I want to regard the mangrove as a concrete utopian symbol and space of identity formation based on inclusive otherness through antagonistic complementarity' (Walter, 2005: 129).

Inspired by Deleuze and Guattari's (1980) ideas, Deumert (2019: para. 2) proposes a rhizomatic interpretation of the mangrove: 'Thinking-with the rhizome allows us to capture the multiplicities, assemblages and interconnections that shape the social world, and give it meaning'. Such dialogicity implied in the mangrove metaphor has a deep connection with the way communication, arts and culture work by approximating, aggregating, resisting and creating an evolving sense of political belonging and social struggles. One example of the several initiatives that integrate the mangue movement is the Solidarity Resistance Network (SRN), a network of more than 60 urban communitarian groups committed to new modes of organization (Martins, 2009). The SRN has a connection to the right, to the city (Lefebvre, 1996) and to urban social movements. In addition, the SRN is about renewed forms of distribution of spaces, times, communication and forms of activities, turning visible and audible what has been historically invisibilized. In terms of strategies of communication, the SRN includes visual arts, audiovisual techniques, songs and graffiti (Martins, 2009).

A multimodal language used with political and aesthetic issues characterizes such practices as graffiti, which carries several meanings, relates to youth identity, urbanity and creativity: 'By creating signs, symbols and motifs that convey meanings and messages, urban space is transformed by its adornment and co-option as a canvas for the expression of identity, status, style and culture' (Zieleniec, 2016: 13). In this context, communication, arts and culture play an integrated role in the SRN. This means that politics and aesthetics play a joint role, in which aesthetics is seen as 'a delimitation of spaces and times, of the visible and the invisible, of speech and noise, that simultaneously determines the place and the stakes of politics as a form of experience' (Rancière, 2004: 13).

By reconfiguring the regime of visibility and the regime of discourses, which define what can be said and seen by whom, the mangue movement politically acts by using language as an important element of emancipation. The mangue movement is an example of how the regime of (language) politics is also aesthetically configured. Southern perspectives to applied linguistics may help us to recognize language aesthetics and communication by connecting language to its modes of distribution in space and time, helping to create new regimes of visibility, as in the example of graffiti and street theater in urban and peripheral spaces illustrates. It is not a coincidence that both Nascimento and the manguebit have used the arts, which include the public use of language, as a political instrument of self-emancipation. In addition, both have used the manifesto as a discursive genre, which signals its political and visual roles. Curiously, the root verb 'manifest' comes from the old French *manifester*, which means 'to make evident to the eye'. The manifesto also can be taken as an example of truth telling, a way of denouncing regimes of oppression and exclusion and a search for new political or artistic orientations and movements (Amidon, 2003). Manguebit provides opportunities to forge a utopian vision of social life.

In terms of its economic and social aspects, the mangrove is also strongly related to the collective harvest of crabs by women in several areas of Brazil, as the region of Maragogipe in the state of Bahia, located in the northeast of Brazil. The mangroves are considered complex coastal areas, places of intense biological recycling, a mixture of sea and river, of trees and water (fluvial trees), and of air and land (Oliveira, 1993). It is a kind of biological 'third space' and, metaphorically, we argue that it works as a cultural 'third space' (Bhabha, 1994), an ambivalent and indeterminate space in-between, where historical meanings are open to negotiation and interpretation. By proposing this metaphorical interpretation, we highlight the role that women play in the post-colonial process of meaning negotiation.

It is not a coincidence that, in the African-Brazilian religious symbolism of *Candomblé*, there is the image of an old wise woman, *Nanã*, who, in some parts of Brazil, is associated with the mangrove, fertility, agriculture and the transition between land and sea; *Nanã* is known as 'a Véia do mangue' (the old lady of the mangrove; Oliveira, 1993). Another hybrid religious symbol related to the mangrove is the *Oxumaré*, for half of the year a man who lives in the sea, and for the other half a woman who lives in the river. In the Brazilian religious sincretism, *Oxumaré* is considered the Catholic Saint Bartolomeu. There also is a deep connection between women's social practice of crab harvesting and environmental issues: the rhythms of the tide and of the harvesting are directly influenced by the moon. Pollution affects the social and economic exploration of the mangrove, which is why women also play an important role in environmental protection practices. By worshipping the local mythical symbolism of *Nanã*, these women follow a harvesting ritual that balances environmental and economic exploration (Oliveira, 1993).

Some language practices related to the harvest of crabs in the mangrove are songs. Women sing as a strategy to attract crabs (*aratu*) to the surface. Such songs are generally a solitary performance, a relationship between the woman and the crab. One example is the following song (Dantas, 2010: 45–46):

> Chega aratuzinho, vem pra minha isquinha. Quando for de noite você está na panelinha
>
> [Come little aratu, come to my little bait. When night comes you will be in my little pan]
>
> Ururu, urru já vem o aratu/Ururu, urru, ururu aratu
>
> [Ururu, urru, there it comes the aratu/Ururu, urru, ururu aratu]

We understand that songs play an important role in shaping both social relations and language. We argue that songs should be taken as frameworks to understand what counts as language, which may vary according to the local and cultural contexts involved. Songs thus ontologically constitute a form of interaction between humans and animals, thereby creating a type of applied linguistics that does not revolve around the human, but rather takes into serious consideration human/animal interaction as part of an important aspect of applied linguistics practice. For example, for the Yaminawá shamans in Brazil, 'Learning to be a shaman is learning to sing, to intone the powerful chant rhythms' (Townsley, 1993: 457), which occurs in ritualistic religious practices. We argue that the local meaning and practice of singing should be considered an important framework to define what counts as language.

Conclusion

In this chapter, we sought to illustrate how an applied linguistics from the Global South can utilize its metaphors to enhance our understanding of the nature of applied linguistics and not be dependent on analytical metaphors from the Global North. We selected Quilombism and the metaphors of the land and mangrove to describe these analytical metaphors of language, language learning and applied linguistics. The analytical metaphors create alternative models of applied linguistics that are potentially relevant to applied linguistics in the Global North.

We return to issues about risks and vulnerabilities which are the key touchstone concepts in this volume. Epistemic racism constitutes the cornerstone of knowledge structures of Westernized universities and the way most applied linguistics is practised intellectually within them. It therefore logically means that applied linguistics as a displine cannot escape the 'epistemological racism' characteristic of Westernized universities in which it is practised. Applied linguistics in the Global North and, indeed to some extent, even in the geographical South, runs the risks of being permeated by the 'epistemic racism' of Western cultural ethnocentricism unless it opens and renders itself susceptible and vulnerable to other ways of doing applied linguistics which come from diverse Indigenous cosmovisions. We argue that if we are to 'recuperate an applied linguistics with a heart, we will need to put our minds to retrieving the discipline's spirit of compassion by standing with Indigenous peoples and other marginalized communities, and not on the sidelines, in their struggles against structural violence' (Gomes, 2013: 14).

There are, however, risks in incoporating orientations from the Global South, particularly its Indigenous cosmovisions. The following are the risks which we have to bear in mind as enumerated by Grosfoguel (2013):

(1) Can we produce a radical anti-systemic politics beyond identity politics?
(2) Is it possible to articulate a critical cosmopolitianism beyond nationalism and colonialism?
(3) Can we produce knowledge beyond Third World and Eurocentric fundamentalisms?
(4) Can we overcome the traditional dichotomy between political economy and cultural studies?
(5) How can we overcome Eurocentric modernity, without throwing away the best of modernity as many Third World fundamentalists do?

There are also risks in including alternative epistemologies in applied linguistics, since including them in applied linguistics may alter the character of the epistemologies. For example, alternative Indigenous epistemologies are 'inherently heterogeneous, incohoate, pluri-and multi-epistemic, and potentially emergent' (Pennycook & Makoni, 2020: 117). Incorporating them into applied linguistics demands that they be normative, thus consequently changing their character from variable to normative.

Our conclusion in this chapter is that an applied linguistics that draws on Southern epistemologies and Indigenous ontologies is, indeed, possible and desirable, can be mobilized for use in the Global South and may serve as a powerful corrective in some areas in the applied linguistics of the Global North.

References

Abdelhay, A., Makoni, S.B. and Severo, C.G. (forthcoming) Colonial heteronormative ideologies and the racializing discourse of 'language families'. In E. Hurst, L. Marten, N. Kula and J. Zeller (eds) *Oxford Guide to the Bantu Languages*. Oxford: Oxford University Press.

Amidon, S.R. (2003) Manifestoes: A study in genre. Open Access Dissertations (paper 682). http://digitalcommons.uri.edu/oa_diss/682.

Bhabha, H.K. (1994) *The Location of Culture*. New York: Routledge.

Brumfit, C. (1995) Teacher professionalism and research. In G. Cook and B. Seidholfer (eds) *Principles and Practices in Applied Linguistics* (pp. 27–41). Oxford: Oxford University Press.

Castro, Josué de (1967) *Homens e Caranguejos* [Men and Crabs]. São Paulo: Brasiliense.

Connell, R. (2007) *Southern Theory: The Global Dynamics of Knowledge in the Social Sciences*. Cambridge: Polity Press.

Cusicanqui, S.R. (2012) Ch'ixinakax Utxiwa: A reflection on the practices and discourses of decolonization. *The South Atlantic Quarterly* 111 (1), 95–109. doi:10.1215/0038 2876-1472612

Dantas, V.M.C.S. (2010) Nas Marés da Vida: Histórias e Saberes das Mulheres Marisqueiras [In the tides of life: Stories and knowledge of women who work in the mangrove] (Unpublished doctoral dissertation). Federal University of Rio Grande do Norte, Brazil.

Davies, A. and Elder, C. (eds) (2006) *The Handbook of Applied Linguistics*. Oxford: Wiley Blackwell.

Deleuze, G. and Guattari, F. (1980) *A Thousand Plateaus*. Minneapolis, MN: University of Minnesota Press.

Deumert, A. (2010) Imbodela Aamakhumsha: Reflections on standardization and destandardization. *Multilingua* 29, 243–264. doi:10.1515/mult.2010.012.

Deumert, A. (2019) *The Mangrove or Moving With and Beyond the Rhizome*. See https://www.diggitmagazine.com/column/mangrove-or-moving-and-beyond-rhizome?fbcli d=IwAR3NX7WZZ3WjBJzEo7pkDAlqCxpMbQQFabOsejXmmeAcY-35aFB0ph mRKyg

Di Carlo, P. (2016) Multilingualism, affiliation and spiritual insecurity. From phenomena to processes in language documentation. In M. Seyfeddinipur (ed.) *African Language Documentation: New Data, Methods And Approaches* (pp. 71–104). Honolulu, HI: University of Howai'i Press.

Ferguson, J. (2013) Khanna Bardyng? Where are you going? Rural–urban connections and the fluidity of Sakha-Russian speakers (Unpublished doctoral dissertation). University of Aberdeen, Aberdeen.

Ferguson, J. (2019) *Words Like Birds: Sakha Language Discourse and Practices in the City*. Lincoln, NE: University of Nebraska Press.

García, R. and Baca, D. (2019) *Rhetorics Elsewhere and Otherwise: Contested Modernities, Decolonial Visions*. Champaign, IL: National Council of Teachers of English.

Gomes, A. (2013) Anthropology and the politics of indigeneity. *Anthropological Forum* 23 (1), 5–15.

Grosfoguel, R. (2013) The structure of knowledge in westernized universities: Epistemic racism/sexism and the four genocides in the long 16th century. *Human Architecture: Journal of the Sociology of Knowledge* 11 (1), 73–80.

Guimarães, R.G. and Carvalho, C. (2016) O Movimento Manguebeat na Mudança da Realidade Sociopolítica de Pernambuco. *Political and Cultural Review, Salvador* 9 (1), 110–133.

Harris, R. and Haas, M. (2011) The question is not whether integrationism can survive outside linguistics, but whether linguistics can survive outside integrationism: An interview with Roy Harris. *Language Sciences* 33, 498–501.

Hauck, G. and Heurich, J.D. (2018) Language in the Amerindian imagination: An inquiry into linguistic natures. *Language and Communication* 63, 1–8.

Heller, M. and McElhinny, B. (2017) *Language, Capitalism, Colonialism: Toward a Critical History*. Toronto: University of Toronto Press.

Ingersoll, K.A. (2016) *Waves of Knowing: A Seascape Epistemology*. Durham, NC: Duke University Press.

Irvine, J. (2009) Subjected words: African linguistics and the colonial encounter. *Language and Communication* 28, 323–324.

Kroskrity, P. (2018) On recognizing persistence in the indigenous language ideologies of multilingualism in two Native American communities. *Language and Communication* 62, 133–144.

Kubota, R. (2019) Confronting epistemological racism, decolonizing scholarly knowledge: Race and gender in applied linguistics. *Applied Linguistics* 33, 1–22. doi:10.1093/applin/amz033

Lander, E. (ed.) (2000) *La Colonialidad del Saber: Eurocentrismo y Ciencias Sociales, Perspectivas Latino-Americana*s. Buenos Aires: Clacso.

Lefebvre, H. (1996) *Writings on Cities*. Edited and translated by E. Kofman and E. Lebas. Cambridge, MA: Wiley-Blackwell.

Leite, I.B. (1999) Quilombos e quilombolas. *Horizontes Antropológicos*, Porto Alegre 5 (10), 123–149. doi:10.1590/S0104-71831999000100006

Leonard, W. (2017) Producing language reclamation by decolonising 'language'. In W. Leonard and H. De Kome (eds) *Language Documentation and Description* (pp. 15–36). London: El Publishing.

Lopes, Nei (2011) *Enciclopédia brasileira da diáspora africana* [Brazilian Encyclopedia of African Diaspora]. São Paulo: Selo Negro.

Makoni, S.B. (1998) In the beginning was the missionaries' word: The European invention of African languages: The case of Shona in Zimbabwe. In K. Prah (ed.) *Between Extinction and Distinction: The Harmonization and Standardization of African Languages* (pp. 157–165). Johannesburg: Wits University Press.

Makoni, S.B. (2003) From misinvention to disinvention of language: An approach to multilingualism and the South African constitution. In S.B. Makoni, G. Smitherman, A. Spears, and A. Ball (eds) *Black Linguistics, Language, Society and Politics in Africa and the Americas* (pp. 132–151). London: Routledge.

Makoni, S.B. (2016) Romanticizing differences and managing diversities: A perspective on harmonization, language policy, and planning. *Language Policy* 15 (3), 223–234. doi:10.1007/s10993-015-9375-x

Makoni, S.B. and Meinhof, U. (2004) Western perspectives in applied linguistics in Africa. *AILA Review* 17, 77–104. doi:10.1075/aila.17.09mak

Martins, A. de M. (2009) Rede de Resistência Solidária: Resistência e Cotidiano Na Luta Pelo Direito à Cidade em Recife-PE. Unpublished Master's Dissertation, Universidade de Brasília, Brasília, 2009.

Nascimento, A. (1980) Quilombismo: An Afro-Brazilian Political Alternative. *Journal of Black Studies* 11 (2), 141–178.

Oliveira, N.M. de (1993) Rainha Das Águas, Dona do Mangue: Um Estudo do Trabalho Feminino No Meio Ambiente Marinho [Queen of the Sea, Lady of the Mangroves: A Study of Women's Survival in the Marine Environment]. *Revista Brasileira de Estudos de População* 10 (1/2), 71–88.

Pablé, A. (2019) In what sense is integrational theory lay-oriented? *Language Sciences* 72 (1), 150–159.

Pablé, A. and Hutton, C. (2015) *Signs, Meaning and Experience: Intergrational Approaches to Linguistics and Semiotics*. Berlin: Mouton de Gruyter.

Pennycook, A. (2018) *Posthumanism Applied Linguistics*. London: Routledge.

Pennycook, A. and Makoni, S.B. (2019) *Innovations and Challenges in Applied Linguists from the Global South*. New York: Routledge.

Quijano, A. (2000) Colonialidad del poder y clasificación social. *Journal of World-Systems Research* 11 (2), 342–386.

Rajagopalan, K. (2020) Linguistics, colonialism and the urgent need to enact appropriate language policies to counteract the latter's baleful fallout on former colonies. In A.

Abdelhay, S. Makoni and C. Severo (eds) *Language Planning and Policy: Ideologies, Ethnicities and Semiotic Spaces of Power.* Newcastle upon Tyne: Cambridge Scholars.

Rancière, J. (2004) *The Politics of Aesthetics: The Distribution of the Sensible.* New York: Continuum.

Santos, B.S. and Meneses, M.P. (eds) (2010) *Epistemologias do Sul* [Epistemologies of the South]. São Paulo: Cortez.

Severo, C.G. (2019) *Os Jesuítas e as Línguas: Brasil a África* [The Jesuits and the Languages in Colonial Brazil and Africa]. Campinas, Brazil: Pontes.

Severo, C. and Makoni, S.B. (2015) *Políticas Linguísticas Brasil-África* [Language Policy Brazil-Africa] Florianópolis, Brazil: Insular.

Smith, L. (1999) *Decolonizing Methodologies: Research and Indigenous People.* London: Zed Books.

Townsley, G. (1993) Song paths: The ways and means of Yaminahua Shamanic knowledge. *L'Homme* XXIII, 449–468.

Walter, R. (2005) The poetics and politics of identity at the crossroads of cultural difference and diversity. *Ilha do Desterro* 48, 115–134.

Zieleniec, A. (2016) The right to write the city: Lefebvre and graffiti. *Environnement Urbain/Urban Environment* 10, 1–20. See http://journals.openedition.org/eue/1421

3 Late Capitalism and New Challenges: Indigenous Communities Taking Risks in Defense of Vulnerable Languages and Territories in Guatemala and Colombia

Luz A. Murillo

Introduction

In his classic work *Imagined Communities*, Benedict Anderson (2006) helped researchers understand the role of linguistic imperialism in the conformation of nation states, where the erasure of Indigenous languages and dispossession of their territories constituted a central aspect of the process of European modernity. Five centuries after the 'Enlightenment' spread Eurocentric views of modernity through Christianization and schooling in Spanish (Mignolo, 2012), contemporary Indigenous communities in Latin America are facing new forms of social inequality and economic instability through the spread of 'new' corporations in their territories. To be Indigenous and to speak an Indigenous language in Latin America, as in much of the world, has historically meant facing personal and communal risks from ideologies and institutions of the dominant society, including those involved in state-sponsored violence, often on behalf of global economic interests. Indigenous children have been exposed to particular kinds of risk in Latin American schools (Mignolo & Walsh, 2018).

In this chapter, I draw on decolonizing methodologies (Severo & Makoni, Chapter 2; Tuhiwai-Smith, 2013), to describe the ways applied linguists and speakers of Q'anjob'al in Guatemala take risks to comply with longstanding state mandates to educate children in their Mayan/Indigenous languages and Spanish, and navigate contradictory globalizing, market-based mandates that redefine bilingualism as Spanish/English and render the Indigenous languages 'irrelevant' once again. The chapter also describes the challenges experienced by Indigenous communities and researchers in Colombia seeking to defend their languages and cultural practices in semi-autonomous territories of the Sierra Nevada de Santa Marta. Taking risks in the maintenance and study of Indigenous language practices in late capitalism helps us understand how inequalities in Latin America are constructed, challenged and sometimes disrupted through language (Heller & McElhinny, 2017). This chapter demonstrates how taking risks and fostering radical hope (Diaz, 2016) as epistemic disobedience (Mignolo, 2009) supports efforts by linguistically minoritized communities to survive aggressive and sophisticated forms of global capitalism.

Colonialism and Indigenous Communities in Latin America

In his classic work *Imagined Communities*, Benedict Anderson (2006) describes the role of linguistic imposition and cultural homogenization in the conformation of nation states, where the erasure of Indigenous languages and dispossession of their territories constituted an organizing principle in the process of European modernization and the 'discovery' of the Americas. As Walter Mignolo makes clear in his analysis of the economic reformulation of the Americas through colonization, European powers approached the new (to them) world with the goal of incorporating it into the world economic system, and 'The image of a new continent discovered one happy day in October of 1492 is, indeed, an ideological construction presupposing that America was an already existing entity awaiting discovery' (Mignolo, 1992: 301–302). Thus, Latin American countries are the result of European thinking about nationalism and an ideology of national independence in which a creole mentality of European ideas and values, including beliefs about Indigenous peoples and their languages, was dominant (Anderson, 2006). What is important for applied linguists to understand is that the territory we know as Latin America was invaded and forcibly assimilated into a European-dominated world economic and political system with a long history of subjugating local populations and eliminating Indigenous ways of knowing the world, including languages and child socialization (Severo & Makoni, Chapter 2).

The period of colonization of Amerindians was successful for European economic powers and colonial elites, not only at the level of materiality, but also through the colonization of language. Through missionaries the colonial powers Spain and Portugal sought to reorganize 'Amerindian speech by writing grammars, Amerindian writing systems by introducing the Latin Alphabet, and Amerindian memories by implanting Renaissance discursive genres conceived in the experience of alphabetic writing' (Mignolo, 1992: 304). In this way, the histories and memories of

Indigenous groups in Latin America were told by missionaries and 'men of letters' who assumed that only through alphabetic writing could these histories be shared. This was the most effective way to silence Indigenous stories, intersecting with and arguably even more lasting than the spread of smallpox and other devastating European diseases, enslaved labor and genocide (Bell & Delacroix, 2019).

As a result of colonization, Amerindian writings all but disappeared, as books (codices), murals and other forms of writing were burned and otherwise destroyed, banned and driven underground (Chacón, 2018). Despite the loss of these autochthonous forms of literacy, millions of people in Latin America still speak Amerindian languages and try to live according to the worldviews of their pre-Columbian ancestors. As we will see, they include Indigenous peoples from Guatemala, where Mayan writing systems were among the most sophisticated forms of writing in the world at the time of the Conquest.

This chapter is grounded in the resilience of Indigenous communities and the radical hopes that sustain users and defenders of Indigenous languages. I document challenges that Indigenous groups, applied linguists and linguistic anthropologists face in the resurgence of Indigenous movements in communities in Guatemala and Colombia and in the context of military repression threatening to silence Indigenous and subaltern voices. One goal of the chapter is to link Indigenous movements, documented in las Americas since at least 1781 (Rivera-Cusicanqui, 2010), with contemporary cases of the risks faced by Indigenous groups and applied linguists working in Indigenous communities (Snoddon & Wilkinson, Chapter 8). The chapter is organized as follows: first, I present a brief analysis of the 'new' ways late capitalism is seeking to take over Indigenous territories and natural resources. I next describe the theoretical framework and research methods I used to understand how Indigenous peoples in two communities are responding to territorial and existential threats from globalized forms of capital. Findings point to the appropriation of Indigenous schools to heal colonial wounds, re-appropriate lands and defend natural resources. I offer implications for research and practice, as well as recommendations for applied linguists wishing to support Indigenous movements.

Theoretical Orientations

In this section I outline a historically grounded theoretical framework for our analysis of late capitalism and the new risks it creates for Indigenous communities and languages. Historically, Latin America has been a source of raw materials, first to feed Europe and later to supply markets in the US. According to Eduardo Galeano, 'the ultimate goal of the Latin American colonial economy from its inception … was to serve the development of capitalism somewhere else' (Galeano, 1997: 45). As noted above, the development of the industrialized West was accomplished through the displacement of Indigenous populations from their territories in an attempt to not only appropriate their labor and land, but also replace their cultural practices and languages with Spanish and other colonial languages. Central to this process of linguistic and cultural erasure (Chacón, 2018) was the colonial project of civilizing Indigenous 'barbarians' through religion, language homogenization and alphabetical literacy.

Five centuries after the 'Enlightenment' spread Eurocentric views of modernity through Christianization and schooling in Latin, Spanish and Portuguese, contemporary Indigenous communities in Latin America are facing new forms of social inequality and economic instability owing to the spread of new extracting corporations in their territories. In different forms and at different times, Indigenous peoples in Latin America have responded to the coloniality of power. Despite ongoing efforts to portray Indigenous and other non-dominant knowledges as inferior and deficient by placing 'hegemonic forms of knowledge into the perspective of the subaltern' (Mignolo, 2012: 12), Indigenous resistance movements have emerged in response to the reconfigurations of late capitalism and the ongoing coloniality of power 'enacting concrete processes, struggles, and practices of resurgent and insurgent action and thought, including in the spheres of knowledge, territory-land, state, and life itself' (Mignolo & Walsh, 2018: 9).

Throughout Latin America, Indigenous movements continue to organize around the maintenance and recovery of ancestral territories. In this endeavor, language, education and the natural world are central aspects of Indigenous peoples' struggle for self-determination. Furthermore, the importance of place in the *cosmovisiones* (worldviews) of Indigenous peoples is becoming more widely understood (Severo & Makoni, Chapter 2), as is the fact that Indigenous communities in Latin America have often rooted their political struggles in the sacredness of their lands (Murillo, 2009) and the understanding that important forms of wisdom about taking care of the Earth are encoded primarily in Indigenous languages (Gorenflo *et al.*, 2012). These emerging Indigenous movements in Latin America demonstrate that 'non-Western Knowledges and praxis of living-knowing were not killed in the Americas' (Mignolo & Walsh, 2018: 207). Around 700 Indigenous languages are still alive in Latin America (UNICEF, 2009), one of the world's most resilient regions in terms of linguistic diversity. Indigenous peoples in Latin America are engaging in processes of cultural and linguistic revitalization inspired by movements in Canada, Hawaii and New Zealand, and many individuals and groups are reclaiming their indigeneity, including some who no longer speak the Indigenous language (Murillo, 2009; Snoddon & Wilkinson, Chapter 8).

In the context of these historic and persistent inequalities, I am interested in the challenges faced by speakers of Indigenous languages and applied linguists whose work focuses on protecting Indigenous languages and territories. Epistemic disobedience, as a theoretical guide, is an intentional de-linking of knowledge from the 'magic' of Anderson's 'imagined communities' promised in Western ideas of modernity through coloniality. Epistemic disobedience means questioning and rethinking ways of knowing and ways of valuing knowledge to include Indigenous worldviews and epistemologies. To practice epistemic obedience in applied linguistics we need to research and use methods that reflect a belief that ways of knowing did not begin with European colonization of the Americas. Because Western imperial knowledge is hegemonic and epistemically non-democratic (Mignolo, 2012), the assertion of alternative worldviews and epistemologies that have been developed by Indigenous peoples can be unsettling to authority. To be perceived as rejecting or threatening dominant interests carries potential risks for Indigenous activists. Despite discourses of educational and linguistic justice by the Guatemalan and Colombian governments, these risks can extend to researchers and educators who participate in projects that challenge the primacy of epistemologies inherited from European traditions and which aim to 'decolonize' knowledges (Severo & Makoni, Chapter 2).

I also want to connect the notion of taking risks in defense of vulnerable Indigenous languages and cultures with Jonathan Lear's (2006) theory of radical hope, which can be summarized as envisioning and working toward a more just society, one that we have never experienced. Lear (2006: 104) writes

> What makes this hope radical is that it is directed toward a future goodness that transcends the current ability to understand what it is. Radical hope anticipates a good for which those who have the hope as yet lack the appropriate concepts with which to understand it. What would it be for such hope to be justified.

Lear suggests that radical hope is 'intimately bound to the question of how to live' (2006: 105) in times and situations that seem otherwise hopeless. I am proposing that those who work to promote and protect Indigenous cultures may approach their activities with something very much like radical hope. Given the abject history of schooling for Indigenous children in national education systems around the world, for example, those who envision a different type of treatment, one where Indigenous languages are honored and taught, are working towards a goal of which there are few examples and which may be, therefore, difficult to conceive (Ennser-Kananen & Saarinen, Chapter 6). To begin to imagine the outlines of a better future for speakers of Indigenous languages despite aggressive incursions of global capitalism expanding in the region, our starting point is a different understanding of Latin America's past.

Methods

This study of challenges faced by Indigenous communities and by applied linguists who work with them is based on my research with schools and families in Q'anjob'al communities in northwestern Guatemala and in an Arhuaco community in the Sierra Nevada de Santa Marta mountains in northern Colombia. The Colombian data come from my dissertation research and subsequent fieldwork in Simunurwa between 2008 and 2014; the Guatemalan data were gathered in 2016 as part of a professional development project for teachers working with Indigenous immigrant children and families in the US Midwest. Each study took place in Indigenous communities with long histories of experiencing state-sponsored violence, Western capitalist structures and laws that threaten their way of life and cultural existence.

I gathered the data presented in this chapter using a combination of ethnographic approaches and techniques with historical research methods. Because I mean to portray speakers of Q'anjob'al and Ika as agents engaged in shaping their own educational trajectories and not merely subjects of government policies and victims of global capitalism (Conama, Chapter 4), I have been interested in learning from Indigenous scholars and always working to avoid imposing my Eurocentric views on language practices in bilingual Indigenous communities. Both projects sought to practice what Linda Tuhiwai-Smith describes as 'decolonizing methodologies' aimed at dismantling the perpetuation of 'imperialism through the ways in which knowledge about Indigenous peoples was collected, classified and then represented in various ways to the West, and then through the eyes of the West, back to those who have been colonized' (Tuhiwai-Smith, 2013: 1–2).

In this sense, the research contexts were very different. In Guatemala, I was immersed in a transnational community, strongly influenced by residents' international migration experiences and the *remesas* (remittances) received from family members in the US. In the Sierra Nevada de Santa Marta, I was immersed in a highly spiritual and intensely political situation in which a consistent discourse of 'we, the Indigenous people' imbued every interaction I had with the Arhuacos. In both places, I was fortunate that permissions to spend time in schools were granted by local rather than national authorities. In Guatemala, authorization came from the local education coordinator. I was granted permission to live and study in Simunurwa by the *mamo*, a religious leader and the highest authority in the region.

As Tuhiwai-Smith (2013) notes, for many Indigenous groups oracy, including debate, formal speech making, structured silence and other conventions that shape oral tradition, remains an important means of developing trust and sharing information, strategies, advice, contacts and ideas. Speakers of Q'anjob'al and Ika traditionally have lived an oral culture (alphabetic writing and reading of their languages were first imposed by religious and national government authorities), and face-to-face conversations and interviews were my most powerful research tools. At both sites, I visited schools, engaged in non-participant observation, interviewed teachers and families, and spoke with children. Classroom observations focused on bilingual instruction in reading, writing and mathematics, in Q'anjob'al/Spanish in Guatemala and in Ika/Spanish in Colombia. Home visits led to audiotaped recorded interviews in which parents and elders spoke of their own language and literacy experiences in and out of school. Most conversations and formal interviews were conducted in Spanish and most people I had the opportunity to talk with were bilingual to some degree. Eulalia Gonzalez in Guatemala and Antolino Torres in Colombia translated during the conversations with dominant speakers of Q'anjobal and Ika. The risks associated with reliance on interpreters during multilingual research interviews (Norlund Shaswar, Chapter 11) were mitigated by the fact that both interpreters were local Indigenous educators and were familiar with the epistemological and theoretical bases of the study.

Peligros (dangers) and Taking Risks in Guatemala

I begin my account of taking risks in Indigenous communities in Guatemala by locating them geographically, politically and linguistically in Mesoamerica, the culturally distinct region encompassing central Mexico and Guatemala and extending into Honduras. At the arrival of the Spaniards, the Mesoamerican population was around 6 million Indigenous people (Rosenblat, 1967). The Indigenous population in Guatemala has been politically and economically marginalized since the Spanish conquest and over five centuries of colonial and post-colonial domination, a bloody civil war from 1960–1996 and ongoing state-sponsored genocide against Indigenous peoples. Across rural Guatemala, Mayan communities have struggled to remain on their lands. For much of the last century, the US government has intervened on the wrong side of those struggles, contributing to the violent displacement of Indigenous Guatemalans that continues to this day (Grandin & Oglesby, 2019).

The most commonly spoken Indigenous languages in Guatemala are the Mayan languages: Q'eqchi', Kiche', Mam and Kaqchikel, each with at least 500,000 speakers. The overall national poverty rate for the Indigenous population is 79%, far higher than for their mestizo/ladino counterparts. Longstanding economic disparities continue to exist for Indigenous groups in Guatemala (Flood *et al.*, 2019), which helps explain why many Indigenous Guatemalans seek refuge in the US and other nations.

At the beginning of the 1900s, the Q'eqchi'-Maya lived mainly in Guatemala's northern highlands but were pushed out as coffee planters, members of Guatemala's military elite and European and North American investors took their lands 'through legal chicanery and violence' (Grandin & Klein, 2011). The civil war in Guatemala was driven by the US government's desire to control raw materials and labor and to gain political control in the name of anti-communism and democracy. The San Francisco massacre on 17 June 1982 near the town of Yalambojoch in Santa Eulalia,

Huehuetenango was one of the most violent in Guatemala's history as government soldiers killed more than 350 people in a single day (Sepputat, 2000). Thousands of residents fled the region, many being captured and killed by the Guatemalan army. Others reached the Mexican border and settled in refugee camps or in Mexico's southern states, or risked the long, dangerous journey to the US, 'beginning the great movement of Indigenous Guatemalans to *El Norte*' (Grandin & Oglesby, 2019). Most Indigenous migrant Guatemalans living in the midwestern US are from this region.

Ironically, migration seems to be the only reparation Indigenous peoples in Guatemala have ever had. The primary destination for Guatemalan migrants is the US, where government officials characterize immigrants and their children as 'illegals', families with children seeking asylum are separated at the US border with Mexico, and state legislatures have passed overtly racist anti-immigration and ant-immigrant laws. Currently there are proposals to tax or prohibit the sending of remittances by Guatemalans to their families in Guatemala, and the US federal government has recently pressured the Guatemalan government to detain asylum seekers from El Salvador and Honduras in Guatemala (PBS Newshour, 2019).

In the context of territorial incursions and forced dislocation, speakers of Q'anjob'al and other Indigenous languages in Guatemala now face continuous encroachment by corporations in what Povinelli (2011: 18) calls 'accumulation by dispossession' (2011: 18) that is 'not a historical event but an ongoing process' (2011: 35). As Grandin and Oglesby state:

> Instead of pursuing a people-centered rural development, the Guatemalan government's postwar strategy, backed by international development loans, has been to open large swaths of the country for foreign investment in megaprojects like mining and hydroelectric dams …. There is not a single Maya name among the list of investors in these projects, where the profits go to international conglomerates in association with elite family networks in Guatemala. (Grandin & Oglesby, 2019: 20–21)

The immense sums of money involved in such projects, along with desire for the raw materials and natural resources held within Indigenous territories, make it risky for anyone be perceived as resisting 'progress' and 'development'.

Speakers of Mayan languages in Guatemala have taken risks to keep their languages at the center of their cultural practices, as have applied linguists working with Indigenous communities to maintain and revitalize their languages. For example, research by applied linguists at the Universidad Rafael Saldivar is used to produce materials for mother tongue literacy with support from the *Fondo de Desarrollo Indígena Guatemalteco* (FODIGUA). In addition, the work of Garzón *et al.* (1998) on linguistic revitalization, and the tireless Peruvian applied linguist, Luis Enrique López Hurtado, defending Indigenous languages in Guatemala and across Latin America, are examples of applied linguists taking physical and academic risks in order to support the maintenance and revitalization of Indigenous languages. These risks include being detained and questioned by government authorities. Scholars may also be denied the right to travel to certain regions or discouraged from pursuing research critical of national language and education policies.

To illustrate these risks, I share findings from fieldwork with Q'anjob'al speakers in and around Santa Eulalia, a small city close to the site of the San Francisco massacre. Q'anjob'al is a Mayan language spoken by approximately 150,000 people (Eberhard *et al.*, 2019), primarily in Huehuetenango, immigrant communities in southern Mexico and the midwestern US. I was introduced to these communities through my work with educators in a school district in central Illinois where the number of Indigenous Guatemalan families was growing rapidly. As a professor of biliteracy education at the local university, I was invited to help develop professional development workshops for teachers working with Indigenous students. The teachers felt that the district's Spanish/English transitional bilingual and dual language immersion programmes were not working because, in their view, the Indigenous children spoke little Spanish. When schools are unprepared to work with children who speak minoritized languages at home, a concern arises that teachers will come to regard children as 'uneducable'. The challenges are compounded by assumptions about the connection between language and race (Rosa, 2019), as users of different languages are racialized into stratified social categories. Generally, Indigenous Guatemalans in Illinois were looked down upon by White and African American speakers of English, as well as by Mexican immigrants who identified as white or mestizo (Farr, 2006).

To learn about the Q'anjob'al-speaking immigrant community in Illinois, I visited schools in sending communities around Santa Eulalia to talk with teachers and document the educational experiences of speakers of Q'anjob'al. My university supervisors initially opposed the trip because Guatemala was considered a dangerous country by the US State Department. Eventually, the project was sponsored by the university's Center for Latin American and Caribbean Studies and I spent a month in spring 2016 in Huehuetenango. I also visited the national offices of the Ministry of Education's *Dirección General de Educación Intercultural Bilingüe* in Guatemala City.

In the process of studying language, education and transnational migration in Santa Eulalia, I learned about the challenges and potential risks facing Indigenous people. These are bilingual communities where almost everyone speaks Q'anjob'al and Spanish. Except for early Sunday mass in the Catholic Church conducted only in Spanish, I heard Q'anjob'al and Spanish used together nearly everywhere I went. For example, on public transportation I heard Christian radio stations broadcast programmes in Q'anjob'al and commercials and public service announcements in Spanish. Despite widespread bilingualism, people, including teachers and education officials, did not present themselves as Indigenous, but rather as mestizos who speak a Mayan language and Spanish. This apparent separation of ethnicity and linguistic identity may reflect a desire to depoliticize language in response to state violence against Indigenous people. Rather than 'risks' (*amenazas*), the Guatemalans I met spoke of *peligros* (dangers), including political repression and the murders of Indigenous activists. This stance – presenting oneself as bilingual but not Indigenous – may reflect the high levels of risk associated with being Indian in Guatemala.

Another example of risk relates to the language(s) of classroom instruction. Although the Guatemalan national curriculum requires primary school teachers in the *Programa Intercultural Bilingüe* to teach in both the Indigenous language and Spanish, most materials I observed were aimed at the acquisition of Spanish. In the villages, for example, teachers used Q'anjob'al during informal interactions with children and colleagues, while instruction was delivered mostly in Spanish. In urban schools, Spanish appeared to be even more dominant, although I heard many students speaking Q'anjob'al amongst themselves. Additional research can help us better understand this particular diglossic situation. However, as is the case for some Indigenous languages (Romaine, 2007), it seems plausible that bilinguals in Huehuetenango regard Q'anjob'al as a language of orality and are not necessarily convinced of the relevance of writing it.

Q'anjob'al migration to the US is more complex than the Illinois teachers were aware of. Behind the obvious 'desire for a better life', a migration trope that many teachers can articulate, are the historic and current threats of violence experienced by Indigenous communities from the state and private interests acting in collaboration with or with approval from the state. At the same time they are pushed to leave Guatemala, Indigenous Guatemalans are also being recruited to work in the US Midwest by international corporations, because, as Mexican workers become more organized, Guatemalans are regarded as a more compliant source of labor. Guatemalan teachers with family members living in the US told me that when recruiters arrive seeking to hire workers for jobs in US agriculture and poultry plants young people often jump at the chance. As a result of these political and economic threats, residents of Sta. Eulalia have developed transnational social networks (Duff, 2015) spanning several generations and normalizing migration to the US and dependence on the remittances that migrants send home.

The Guatemalan Ministry of Education's use of Indigenous languages as languages of instruction, primarily through publishing and distributing textbooks and educational materials in Q'anjob'al, has not brought about a more justice-oriented education. Using the Indigenous language to convey the national curriculum or to sing the national anthem can reinforce the coloniality of power historically imposed on Indigenous education in Latin America (Walsh, 2017). To truly nurture and preserve linguistic diversity, simply inserting Indigenous languages into the present structures of the national curriculum is insufficient. Until the forms of structural racism that position Indigenous communities and their languages as obstacles to the ideals of nation state, modernity and progress are challenged and replaced, the school, by itself, holds limited power to change dominant perceptions of Indigenous learners.

Applied linguists and anthropologists working with Indigenous schools and communities seek to generate knowledge they hope will positively impact policy and practice. Back in Illinois, I shared my findings through professional development workshops for ESL and bilingual teachers. I wanted to humanize the idea of Q'anjob'al migrant children and families for teachers who felt unprepared and understandably anxious about teaching them. In addition to providing information about Q'anjob'al speakers' bilingualism and mestizo identity, the predominance of Spanish in instruction and the safety, economic, and political motivations behind decisions to migrate, I wanted teachers to gain a sense of what classrooms in Sta. Eulalia looked and sounded like. I hoped to challenge misconceptions teachers might hold about Indigenous people, about education in Latin America and, by extension, the educability of Indigenous children. I was struck by teachers' positive reactions to images and descriptions of Guatemalan classrooms, sparsely furnished but beautifully decorated with teacher-made posters and examples of student work in Q'anjob'al and Spanish. They were surprised to learn that becoming an elementary school teacher in Guatemala requires a pre-university year and then three years of full-time university study to learn to teach young children. Some teachers remarked that the formation of teachers in Guatemala is probably more rigorous than teacher preparation in the US, where preservice teachers often receive only two years of education courses.

Between la Guerilla, Narcotraficantes and Paramilitares: Taking Risks in Colombia

Because I am a native of Colombia and conducted dissertation research in the Sierra Nevada de Santa Marta, my history with the Arhuaco community is a long one. Indigenous peoples in Colombia comprise barely 3% of the country's total inhabitants (Ng'weno, 2007), compared with numerically and proportionally larger Indigenous populations in Mexico, Guatemala, Ecuador, Bolivia and Peru. Within Colombia, the Arhuaco, or Ika as they also call themselves, are a relatively small group of 18,000, approximately one-third of the populations of the Nasa and Wayu, the largest Indigenous groups in the country.

The Sierra Nevada de Santa Marta, home of the Arhuaco people and central element of their cosmology and political discourse, presents a remarkably diverse biolinguistic ecology. This snow-capped mountain range rises dramatically from the Caribbean coastal plain and supports unique species of flora and fauna. The region's natural resources have attracted non-Indigenous farmers, *guerrillas* (anti-government soldiers), *narcotraficantes* (drug dealers) and *paras* (paramilitary forces). In response to the presence of these last three groups, and to protect the radio and television towers that connect the coastal states of Cesar and Magdalena with the interior of the country, Colombian army troops have been a regular presence in the Sierra Nevada since the 1960s. Those entering the *resguardo*, the land reserve granted by the Colombian government located within the states of Cesar, Magdalena and Guajira (Frank, 1990), must pass a military check point. Anyone bringing in food supplies must justify the amount to satisfy the government's policy of controlling food and preventing access by the guerrillas.

Currently, four Indigenous peoples live in the Sierra Nevada: the Kogui, the Wiwa, the Kankuamo and the Arhuacos. With the introduction of Catholic mission schools in 1740, these groups moved away from Spanish settlements on the coast and the lowland plains to secluded higher elevations (Trillos, 1996). The relative isolation of the Sierra Nevada continues to be an important factor in the continued vitality of Arhuaco culture (Elsass, 1995), with most settlements on the southeastern flanks of the mountain, from the lower, temperate zones to the highest, coldest elevations.

According to Arhuaco tradition, the Indigenous groups in the Sierra Nevada were created to protect *Ka' gimmiri nivisaku ni* (the mountain; or Mother Earth). For them, the mountain is a sacred place, the center of the world, where nature is understood as the embodiment of a living force that maintains and sustains the universe, the Arhuaco people and the Ika language. Like the Maori, whose survival as a people 'has come from our knowledge of our contexts, our environment, not from some active beneficence of our Earth Mother' (Tuhiwai-Smith, 2013: 12–13), the Arhuaco regard their knowledge of and relationship with the Sierra Nevada as central to cultural and linguistic survival and the basis of political struggle. Antolino Torres, a teacher at the bilingual school in the village of Simunurwa, described this relationship:

> Our language and Arhuaco culture couldn't exist without the land. Our language is endangered as long as our ancestral lands are threatened. Otherwise, it's not in trouble. We have conversations with the land, of course we do; that's what the spiritual *trabajos* and the *pagamentos* (tasks and offerings) are for. Our language is strong because we live in the Sierra, that's why. [Personal communication, February 2000]

Interdependencies between biological and linguistic diversity and implications for political resistance have begun to receive attention from applied linguists and other scientists (Harmon, 1996). The Arhuacos understand these inter-connections very well. Torres's point that Ika remains vital 'because we live in the Sierra, that's why' emphasizes this view, reminding us that, in the case of the Arhuaco, language and culture cannot be understood separately from territory.

Ethnolinguistic maintenance among the Arhuaco is also rooted in strong feelings of pride in being Indian and in speaking Ika (Trillos, 1986). Spanish is the national language of Colombia and a language of power and prestige in the Sierra Nevada, but it has not replaced Ika, which continues to be the home and community language for most Arhuacos. Ika is also the language that keeps Simunurwa residents 'safe' from the risks of violence surrounding their territory. For example, when I asked Antolino Torres, my colleague and translator, about starting my language classes in Ika, his response was revealing: 'I am going to teach you just the basics because a language is learned in the *vivencia*, the lived experience, but the truth is that we don't want the *bunachis* (lit., the whites) to understand our language very well ... if they did, how would we keep our movement safe?' Before beginning my research at the school, I was encouraged to participate in a spiritual 'trabajo' [task], and followed the instruction of the *mamo* (spiritual leader) while Antolino patiently translated for me. Once the *limpieza* (spiritual cleansing) was finished, Antolino explained the reasons for that particular task and what we had accomplished, prefacing his explanation with the comment 'I will tell you only what as a *bunachi* (white person) you are allowed to know'. These examples suggest the power of Ika to protect forms of knowledge available only to the Arhuaco. In this view, language is a form of wealth closely guarded by the wise. When Ika's power is diminished, through generational language loss or through sharing too much of it with *bunachi*, the community becomes more vulnerable.

Despite previous research experience in non-Indigenous communities in the Caribbean region of Colombia, I found challenging the spiritual tasks I was required to perform to gain permission to live and conduct research in Simunurwa. Tuhiwai-Smith describes such tasks as 'part of a larger set of judgments on criteria that a researcher cannot prepare for, such as: Is her spirit clear? Does she have a good heart? What other baggage are they carrying? Are they useful to us? Can they actually do anything?' (Tuhiwai-Smith, 2013: 10). After meeting these conditions and agreeing to share my findings with community leaders before making them publicly available, I was permitted to undertake a study of schooling and the maintenance of Arhuaco culture and language (Murillo, 2009). I lived in Simunurwa for 14 months in 2000 and 2001 and visited yearly between 2002 and 2014.

The bilingual primary school was my point of entry to other domains. At the Arhuacos' request, I taught classes in Spanish and advised a youth group learning local traditions. I studied Ika at the school and learned to greet and share basic conversation with elders and young children. My work at the school led me to form close friendships with several Indigenous teachers who became cultural informants and valued critics of my interpretations of Arhuaco efforts to decolonize schooling.

An event I experienced in 2000, a paramilitary attack near to the Arhuaco *resguardo* suggests the risks facing Indigenous peoples in the Sierra Nevada de Santa Marta. In March, 2000 I was in Simunurwa when a paramilitary group attacked the nearby town of Pueblo Bello and assassinated several people as punishment for (allegedly) supporting the guerrillas. Later that day, the community nurse came to the house where I was staying to deliver a message from the health center: as the only *bunachis* in the village, the nurse and I must remain in hiding until the danger had passed. Because the paramilitary forces had taken over Pueblo Bello, the health center staff there feared that they would come to Simunurwa next in search of guerrilla collaborators.

On the night of the attack, Vicencio, a member of the youth group I was advising, shared the story of how he had been detained, interrogated and eventually released by the paramilitary. Pueblo Bello had suddenly become full of vehicles transporting strongly armed men and women, and Vicencio was detained with several other people. He described how two men and a woman pointed their guns at them and demanded that each person show identification. While everybody was showing their *cédula de ciudadanía* (citizenship card), one of the armed men was checking a list to see if any of their names matched. When it was Vicencio's turn to be questioned by the paramilitary officers, he said that, as an Arhuaco, he did not carry a citizenship card. The man requesting his identification told him he could go, but to leave his supply of coca leaves behind. After this, he made it back to Simunurwa without incident. Another community member, Efrain Ramos (personal communication) said that, owing to increased international attention being given to Indigenous peoples, armed groups must now 'think twice before they disappear an Arhuaco'. After reflecting on Vicencio and Efrain's descriptions of the attack, I understood that the Arhuaco also display their cultural resistance, including child language socialization and schooling in Ika, as a means of protecting their young people from attacks by external forces and from recruitment into the Colombian military, guerilla and paramilitary forces.

Armed violence has receded somewhat since 2014, but Indigenous groups in the Sierra Nevada de Santa Marta face new threats to their territories from extractive corporations mining for gold, gems and materials for construction. Despite accords signed between the Colombian government and the four Indigenous groups living in the region in 1973 and 1995 (Murillo, 2009), mining has become an imminent environmental threat. Currently, there are 132 projects approved by the Colombian Agencia Nacional Minera (National Mining Agency) and nearly twice that number of proposals by international agencies are pending approval (Cote, 2017).

Colombia's Commissioner for Human Rights of Indigenous Peoples, Leonor Zalabata described the environmental threats: 'The Sierra holds mineral wealth that dates back to the creation of the world, and these natural treasures, (…) now form a threat to us because environmental permits are being granted for mineral and hydrocarbon exploitation' (Center for World Indigenous Studies, 2018). Arhuaco leaders have led protests against legal and illegal gold mining that is poisoning rivers with mercury and blocking access to sacred sites where spiritual practices are observed. As the number of mining permits increases, Indigenous leaders insist that corporations do not obtain, or even seek, approval before beginning extraction activities. They accuse the Colombian government of siding with the corporations and presenting Indigenous people as 'anti-development' and anti-Colombian (Cote, 2017). In response, the Arhuaco are organizing to protect their territory from mining interests. In February 2019, hundreds of Arhuaco gathered around a big bonfire to play and dance to traditional music (Valerio Ramos, personal communication) in protest against renewed attacks on their livelihood. Currently, Arhuaco lawyers aided by non-Indigenous lawyers are petitioning courts to stop mining corporations from encroaching on Indigenous territory.

Discussion

What can we learn about taking risks from these two cases of Indigenous education? Broadly, studying the risks involved in defending Indigenous languages and territories helps us understand how inequalities in Latin America are constructed, challenged and potentially disrupted through language (Heller & McElhinny, 2017). In Santa Eulalia and Simunurwa we see clear evidence for claims that the ultimate purpose of the Latin American economy has been, during and post-colonialism, to sustain global capitalism (Galeano, 1997; Mignolo, 2012). Although it is difficult to compare risk and vulnerabilities across geographies and temporalities, Indigenous groups to may find it even more difficult to defend their languages and territories today because national elites in Guatemala and Colombia are increasingly sponsored by powerful foreign investors.

Such threats have not prevented Indigenous communities from confronting new and invasive forms of global capitalism. Expressions of Indigenous knowledge give voice to epistemic disobedience (Mignolo, 2009), enacting and symbolizing resistance to attempts to dispossess them of their lands and languages. Indigenous people live these risks and activists, including educators, respond to them with what I have characterized as radical hope for a more just, sustainable and as yet unknown future (Diaz, 2016). We have seen how Q'anjob'al speakers in Guatemala and Illinois have responded to decades of state violence through forced and induced migration, downplaying their Indigenous identity, emphasizing Spanish (in school) and mestizo origins, and developing transnational migration networks in the US. In Colombia, Arhuaco leaders use Ika to preserve and protect specialized forms of knowledge, and promote use of their language in school as emblem of the Indigenous cultural identity that affords some protection against the (para) militarization of the Sierra Nevada de Santa Marta.

The defense of territory, biodiversity and language in Indigenous communities in Guatemala, Colombia and elsewhere in Latin America is sometimes accompanied by applied linguists and anthropologists. To contribute to this work, researchers must embrace new research paradigms, from a posture of studying about Indigenous languages to one of understanding language use within broader struggles for territorial and economic autonomy. Moving toward adopting new research methodologies and approaches is one way that researchers can practice radical hope. Adopting new approaches can also expose researchers to unforeseen vulnerabilities and challenges. I hope that this chapter provides useful guidance in this endeavor.

References

Anderson, B. (2006) *Imagined Communities: Reflections on the Origin and Spread of Nationalism*. London: Verso Books.

Bell, M.K. and Delacroix, J. (2019) Ned Blackhawk Q&A: Understanding indigenous enslavement. *Teaching Tolerance, 63* https://www.learningforjustice.org/magazine/fall-2019/ned-blackhawk-qa-understanding-indigenous-enslavement.

Center for World Indigenous Studies (2018) Colombia in focus: The Arhuacos' last stand in the heights of the Sierra Nevada. *Intercontinental Cry*, October. See https://intercontinentalcry.org/the-arhuacos-last-stand-in-the-heights-of-the-sierra-nevada/ (accessed 16 September 2019).

Chacón, G.E. (2018) *Indigenous Cosmolectics: Kab'awil and the Making of Maya and Zapotec Literatures*. Chapel Hill, NC: University of North Carolina Press.

Cote, J. (2017) La preocupante radiografía de la Sierra Nevada por cuenta de la minería. *Semana Sostenible*, 3 September. See https://sostenibilidad.semana.com/medio-ambiente/articulo/mineria-en-la-sierra-nevada-de-santa-marta-indigenas-denuncian-afectaciones/38555

Diaz, J. (2016) Under President Trump, radical hope is our best weapon. *The New Yorker*, 21 November.

Duff, P.A. (2015) Transnationalism, multilingualism, and identity. *Annual Review of Applied Linguistics 35*, 57–80.

Eberhard, D.M., Simons, G.F. and Fennig, C.D. (eds) (2019) *Ethnologue: Languages of the World*. Twenty-second edition. Dallas, TX: SIL International. See http://www.ethnologue.com

Elsass, P. (1995) *Strategies for Survival. The Psychology of Cultural Resilience in Ethnic Minorities*. New York: New York University Press.

Farr, M. (2006) *Rancheros in Chicagoacán*. Austin, TX: University of Texas.

Flood, D., Chary, A., Rohloff, P. and Henderson, B. (2019) Language as health: Healing in indigenous communities in Guatemala through the revitalization of Mayan languages. In N. Avinery, L.R. Graham, E.J. Johnson, R.C. Riner and J. Rosa (eds) *Language and Social Justice in Practice* (pp. 136–144). London: Routledge.

Frank, P. (1990) *Ika Syntax: Studies in the Languages of Colombia*, vol. 1. Dallas, TX: Summer Institute of Linguistics.

Galeano, E. (1997) *Open Veins of Latin America: Five Centuries of the Pillage of a Continent*. New York: Monthly Review Press.

Garzón, S., McKenna, R., Wuqu', A. and Becker, J. (1998) *The Life of our Language: Kaqchikel Maya Maintenance, Shift, and Revitalization*. Austin, TX: University of Texas Press.

Gorenflo, L.J., Romaine, S., Mittermeier, R.A. and Walker-Painemilla, K. (2012) Co-occurrence of linguistic and biological diversity in biodiversity hotspots and high biodiversity wilderness areas. *Proceedings of the National Academy of Sciences of the United States of America* 109 (21), 8032–8037. See https://doi.org/10.1073/pnas.1117511109.

Grandin, G. and Klein, N. (2011) *The Last Colonial Massacre: Latin America in the Cold War*. Chicago, IL: University of Chicago Press.

Grandin, G. and Oglesby, E. (2019) Washington trained. *The Nation* 11 (18), 19–26.

Harmon, D. (1996) Losing species, losing languages. Connections between biological and linguistic diversity. *Southwest Journal of Linguistics* 15, 89–108.

Heller, M. and McElhinny, B. (2017). *Language, Capitalism, Colonialism*. Toronto: University of Toronto Press.

Lear, J. (2006) *Radical Hope*. Cambridge, MA: Harvard University Press.

Mignolo, W. (1992) On the colonization of Amerindian languages and memories: Renaissance theories of writing and the discontinuity of the classical tradition. *Comparative Studies in Society and History* 34 (4), 301–330.

Mignolo, W. (2009) Epistemic disobedience, independent thought, and decolonial freedom. *Theory, Culture and Society* 27 (7–8), 159–181.

Mignolo, W. (2012) *Local Histories/Global Designs: Coloniality, Subaltern Knowledges, and Border Thinking*. Princeton, NJ: Princeton University Press.

Mignolo, W. and Walsh, C. (2018) *On Decoloniality. Concepts, Analytics, Praxis*. London: Duke University Press.

Murillo, L.A. (2009) 'This great emptiness we are feeling': Toward a decolonization of schooling in Simunurwa, Colombia. *Anthropology and Education Quarterly* 40 (4), 421–437.

Ng'weno, B. (2007) Can ethnicity replace race? Afro-Colombians, indigeneity, and the Colombian multicultural state. *Journal of Latin American and Caribbean Anthropology* 12 (2), 414–440.

PBS NewsHour (2019) Why Trump is cutting El Salvador, Guatemala, and Honduras aid. See https://www.pbs.org/video/cutting-aid-1554141758/ retrieved September 29, 2019.

Povinelli, E.A. (2011) *Economies of Abandonment: Social Belonging and Endurance in Late Liberalism*. Durham, NC: Duke University Press.

Rivera-Cusicanqui, S. (2010) *Ch'ixinakax Utxiwa: Una Reflexión Sobre Prácticas y Discursos Descolonizadores*. Buenos Aires: Tinta Limón.

Romaine, S. (2007) Preserving endangered languages. *Language and Linguistics Compass* 1 (2), 115–132.

Rosa, J. (2019) *Looking Like a Language, Sounding Like a Race: Raciolinguistic Ideologies and the Learning of Latinidad*. New York: Oxford University Press.

Rosenblat, A. (1967) *La Población Indígena de América en 1492: Viejos y Nuevos Cálculos*. Mexico City: El Colegio de México.

Sepputat, F. (2000) At the frontiers of the post-modern state in Guatemala. In A. Arce and N. Long (eds) *Anthropology, Development, and Modernities* (pp. 127–140). New York: Routledge.

Trillos, M. (1986) Las Comunidades Indígenas de la Sierra Nevada y el Sentimiento de Fidelidad Lingüística. *Glota* 1 (2), 13–17.

Trillos, M. (1996) *Lenguas Aborígenes de Colombia. Memorias. Educación Endógena Frente a educación Formal*. Bogotá: Universidad de los Andes y Centro Colombiano de Estudios de Lenguas Aborígenes.

Tuhiwai-Smith, L. (2013) *Decolonizing Methodologies: Research and Indigenous Peoples*. London: Zed Books.

UNICEF y FUNPROEIB Andes (2009) *Atlas sociolingüístico de pueblos indígenas en América Latina y el Caribe*. https://www.unicef.org/lac/informes/atlas-sociolinguistico-de-pueblos-indigenas-en-ALC.

Walsh, C. (ed.) (2017) *Pedagogías Decoloniales. Prácticas Insurgentes de Resistir, (Re) Existir (Re)Vivir*. Quito: Ediciones Abya-Yala.

4 The Bumpy Journey Towards the Irish Sign Language Act: Critical Considerations and Personal Reflections of a Deaf Activist–Scholar

John Bosco Conama

Introduction

The Irish Sign Language Act was signed into law on 24 December 2017. At best, in common with sign language recognition campaigns elsewhere (Snoddon & Wilkinson, Chapter 8), the journey towards achieving this legislation can be described as long and bumpy; it took more than 30 years. As this chapter cannot cover the journey in full, I will highlight a number of challenging experiences from the campaign, which I discussed with colleagues collectively and on which I have reflected. They are the subject of critical consideration here.

The chapter begins with a brief description of what a Deaf activist–scholar is and how I became one. Based on a literature review and my personal reflections, I take a critical view of how I operate as an activist–scholar. I will summarise the campaign for the recognition of Irish Sign Language (ISL) and the act that provides recognition. I have selected some issues and incidents that occurred during the campaign, which I believe, similar to acts of racism, sexism, etc., should be called out as acts of audism or linguistic imperialism and critically discussed. Audism was first described in 1975 by Tom Humphries as 'the notion that one is superior based on one's ability to hear or to behave in the manner of one who hears' (Humphries, 1975). Linguistic imperialism was coined by Robert Phillipson as the exploitation of the ideological, cultural and elitist power of English for the economic and political advantage of dominant English-speaking cultures (Phillipson, 1992).

A Brief Account of How I Became a Deaf[1] Activist–Scholar

The youngest of 11 children, I was born into a small farming family in the West of Ireland. There was no history of *deafness* in the family and yet I was born deaf. As a result, at the tender age of three and a half, I was sent to a residential school for deaf boys in Dublin. I left formal education before completing the final set of state exams, known as the Leaving Certificate. However, I obtained this qualification a number of years later as a mature student.

In 1990 I entered the civil service. I availed of a funding scheme for staff who wished to further their education and started university as a part-time student. I progressed from a bachelor's degree, to a masters' degree and finally a doctorate. At the time, none of my immediate family had post-graduate degrees, and very few people from the Irish Deaf community were pursuing post-graduate qualifications. All in all, it was unusual for the likes of me to reach the highest levels of higher education.

My doctoral thesis was based on equality studies. Therefore, for several years I was immersed in social justice theory and its application, but I was also heavily involved in Deaf community and trade-union activities. These diverse experiences gave me a new perspective on life and I began to appreciate a second-chance approach. By any standard, I believe that I can be considered an outsider.

Since I acquired fluency in Irish Sign Language at school, and English is accessible to me only through written means, ISL naturally became my first language. Throughout my life, I have witnessed and experienced how I and others are treated unjustly at many levels because of the language culture that exists in Irish society. To access academia, a high functional level of English is required; this poses a constant *challenge* for the likes of me. Like other academics, Deaf scholars are subject to 'the publish or perish ethic of the profession [which] means that a commitment to activist-oriented endeavours which promote social justice is often difficult to sustain' (Smeltzer & Cantillon, 2015: 7). With English being my second language, writing academic articles can be a herculean task. Consequently, I am not as prolific as other, hearing academics. In academia this is seen as a liability (Smeltzer & Cantillon, 2015), leaving me vulnerable and at risk of perishing.

To paraphrase Huerta's (2018) definition, being a Deaf scholar-activist is, based on my understanding and lived experience, having a dual involvement in academia and the Deaf community (and to some extent the disabled community). My participation in both spheres bridges these asymmetric spaces. I intend to use my now privileged position in academia to serve my community. My work outside academia has seen me engage in many different roles, from campaigner to committee member.

Being a Deaf scholar in Ireland is no easy task. Neoliberalism (Morrissey, 2015) has taken a firm hold in Irish universities. At Trinity College Dublin, for example, state funding has declined significantly as a proportion of overall revenue (TCD, n.d.). The neoliberal ethos is antagonistic to small academic centres such as *Deaf Studies*, which are regularly viewed as economically unproductive (Berg *et al.*, 2016). Chatterton *et al.* (2010) believe that a deeper problem is the individualisation and de-politicisation of the work carried out by academics who more and more are subject to constraints caused by demands to meet corporate needs. Moreover, increasingly, research and teaching are commodified in order to generate a monetary return from the private investment received by universities to make up the shortfall in public funding (O'Brien, 2019).

O'Brien and Emery (2014) describe how, historically and politically, Deaf Studies have struggled to find a place within academia, and how Deaf scholars, like myself, are obliged to navigate our way through the academic system with no clear course (O'Brien & Emery, 2014; see also Kusters *et al.*, 2017).

Apple (2016: 510–513) identifies nine tasks of being an active and reflective scholar/activist, with a focus on how to counter neoliberalism in education. The list, however, is not exhaustive. The tasks are: (1) 'bear witness to negativity'; (2) be able to provide critical analysis showing possible avenues towards achieving aims; (3) serve as 'critical secretaries', i.e. bring essential knowledge to the group; (4) enable them to counter hegemonic beliefs and 'truths' to avoid cynicism and doubt; (5) maintain constant conversation about the topics; (6) demonstrate skills of discussing the same topic to different audiences/publics; (7) 'act in concert' with campaigners; (8) be excellent in the complementary roles of committed activist and researcher; and finally (9) be able to use one's privilege as an academic to bring benefits to the campaign.

At the risk of being accused of self-promotion, I am confident that I have completed all of these tasks. Regarding the first, I would assert that I have not just borne witness to negativity, but I have experienced injustices directly and indirectly and continue to do so. Cox (2015) claims that there are differences between traditional and organic intellectuals: the former is conditioned by the formal introduction to academic concepts without real-life experience, the latter develops from an understanding of the situation on the ground.

Overall, although I have certain misgivings regarding the scholar–activist role, Couture (2017: 146) reminds me that 'activist and scholarly collaborations are often productively creative and gratifying', although he also warns that 'we should be mindful of not erasing the differences between these postures and should make these distinctions an object of critical inquiry'. Additionally, Hale (2001: 13) suggests that 'there is no necessary contradiction between active political commitment to resolving a problem, and rigorous scholarly research on the problem'. O'Flynn and Panayiotopoulos (2015: 57) insist that there is space for counter-hegemonic narratives, declaring that: 'you can't be neutral on a moving train'.

Campaigning

The campaign to recognise ISL in law has its beginnings in the early 1980s (Conama, 2019). For the purposes of this chapter, however, I will focus on the last five years of the campaign (approximately 2012–2017). The starting point I have chosen is the day that the national representative organisation of Deaf people in Ireland, Irish Deaf Society (IDS), received legal advice that the campaign had to be entirely political. This was because the existing legislation offered very little scope to exercise linguistic rights. The legal advice suggested that a stand-alone Act should be the primary target for our activism (ISL Cross Community Group minutes of 13 September 2012, unpublished).

Based on this legal opinion, IDS decided to form a cross-community campaign group. The first meeting took place on 13 September 2012 and I was asked to co-chair alongside Wendy Murray, the then IDS chairperson. It is important to note that the political, social and economic climate at that time was wholly unsupportive of calls for formal recognition of ISL. The Programme for Government published in 2011, for example, blandly proposed that the new government would 'examine different mechanisms to promote the recognition of Irish Sign Language' (Government of Ireland, 2011: 54). The follow-up by the National Disability Authority and Department of Justice recommended that we accept symbolic recognition as a first step towards formal recognition (Irish Deaf Society, 2012). I vividly remember one policy advisor who favoured symbolic recognition as a way of speeding up our campaign. Rather than producing a law that would make a real difference, passing legislation seemed to be, for her, a box-ticking exercise. So, despite the testimonies we presented to the National Disability Authority and Department of Justice, describing how we face disproportionate discrimination in society, we were strongly advised to adopt a gradual and incremental approach to recognition.

The policymakers' indifference was obvious in numerous ways. The aforementioned Programme for Government objective was not referenced in other government documentation, e.g. the National Disability Strategy Implementation Plan 2013–2015. As well as that, the census commissioners chose to include the findings on the prevalence of ISL users in the report on disability and health, rather than with language, diversity and migrants (Conama, 2020).

Despite the challenges, the cross-community coordination group continued to meet. We changed our focus towards a more active campaign, which concluded in December 2017. During this phase we implemented several strategies, including:

- establishing a social media presence (Facebook, with over 3000 Likes, Twitter, etc.); Leeson (2019) has discussed this type of activism;
- meeting certain TDs (members of parliament) as often as possible;

- hosting an annual awareness week in September, including a rally outside the Irish parliament, to raise awareness of the status of ISL among the general public and politicians;
- publishing and circulating campaign leaflets as widely as possible;
- hosting conferences and giving presentations at several community locations;
- lobbying town, county and city councils to pass motions calling on the national government to recognise ISL formally;
- attending conferences organised by other organisations, such as political party conferences, constitutional conventions and UN treaty reviews, in order to identify ways to boost our campaign.

The committee also approved a proposal to employ a full-time campaign worker within IDS. However, a major economic recession started in Ireland in 2008–2009 and public expenditure decreased significantly (Curran, 2018). Consequently, the committee was unable to source funding for this post. Instead, it had to rely on voluntary community activism to sustain the campaign. Nonetheless, the remaining strategies planned by the committee were all fully or partially implemented.

The levels of activism attained over the course of the campaign brought about many desirable outcomes. The first was in 2013 when the government called a consultative meeting with the Deaf community, attended by a number of key senior civil servants. Five urgent priorities were agreed, as follows:

- A congregated settings policy affecting older Deaf people – the aim of this national health policy is to de-institutionalise disability-specific facilities; our aim was that Deaf residents would remain *within the community.*
- Procurement of government services – that government websites would be translated into ISL; that a telephone relay service would be established; and that ISL awareness training would be made available to anyone who wanted it (e.g. companies).
- A voucher system – the establishment of a scheme to fund interpretation for events and activities outside the public sector to boost participation of ISL users in wider society including culture.
- Accreditation of interpreters – to ensure the quality and regulation of interpreters.
- ISL for deaf children in schools – that there would be greater support for ISL in schools in order to increase deaf children's exposure to the language (Department of Justice and Equality, 2013).

Unfortunately, the lengthy timeframes put in place and consequent slow rate of progress in achieving these objectives proved the lack of urgency among policymakers to address the inequalities experienced by members of the Deaf community. In January 2014 Seanad Éireann (the Irish senate) rejected the original version of the Act on the advice of the then Minister for Disability, who claimed that there were insufficient practical resources, i.e. services, to support its implementation (Conama, 2019). While there was widespread disappointment at the decision, the community was galvanised into action, and there was a renewed impetus in the cross-community group which met regularly from 2014 to 2017 (Conama, 2019).

Irish Sign Language Act 2017

Eventually, the Irish Sign Language Act 2017 was passed by the Houses of the Oireachtas (the Irish parliament) and signed into law on 24 December 2017 by President Michael D. Higgins. Messages of celebration and congratulations were posted on social media, some of them describing the event as 'the best Christmas present ever!' for the Irish Deaf community (Cork Sign Language Interpreting, 2018).

Senator Mark Daly, the principal parliamentary sponsor of the ISL Bill, stated that it 'would have a major impact and would end the extreme marginalisation of the deaf community' (RTÉ News, 15 December 2017). The passing of the ISL Act marks a great achievement for the Irish Deaf community. Of the 28 private members' bills introduced in 2017, it was the only one to be enacted (Oireachtas, 2017); and in fact, in 80 years only six bills have been passed by an opposition senator (Catherine Lynch, Oireachtas Library, personal communication, 27 May 2019).

In alliance with the political movements coordinated by Deaf-led organisations internationally (see De Meulder *et al.*, 2019b), De Meulder (2015) urges Deaf communities to demand explicit recognition for their signed languages in order to strengthen, supplant or supplement the implicit recognition already in place in Ireland. The circumstances in Ireland prior to the ISL Act were not dissimilar to other countries. There was one ambiguous reference to *Irish Sign Language* included in the Education Act 1998, which resulted in no significant breakthrough in the education of deaf children through ISL (Mathews, 2017; Leeson & Saeed, 2012). A number of other statutory instruments (Conama, 2010) also made reference to sign language, but to little effect. For example, the state broadcaster, RTÉ, only broadcasts a brief daily news bulletin and a weekly weather bulletin in ISL (RTÉ, 2019), and the Centre for Deaf Studies at Trinity College, which carries out linguistic and social research into ISL, is not fully state-funded.

In her study of the international status of sign languages, De Meulder (2015) notes that explicit recognition does not necessarily bring about desirable or anticipated outcomes. Her observations are supported by Murray (2015) and McKee and Manning (2015). Despite the rhetoric used by some that ISL is now the third official language of the state, the ISL Act does not bestow any official status on the language; it merely recognises the right of deaf people to use ISL and obliges public services to serve them in this language:

(3)

(i) The State recognizes the right of Irish Sign Language users to use Irish Sign Language as their native language and the corresponding duty on all public bodies to provide Irish Sign Language users with free interpretation when availing of or seeking to access statutory entitlements and services

(ii) The community of persons using Irish Sign Language shall have the right to use, develop and preserve Irish Sign Language. (Irish Sign Language Act, 2017).

The delay in the commencement of this Act was to ensure that the infrastructure was in place before commencement (Department of Justice and Equality, 2018). There will be a review of the Act in 2023 and every five years thereafter. The Act requires public bodies to provide ISL interpretation at no cost to the user when access to statutory entitlements is being sought. The Act also makes provision for the registration and regulation of interpreters working for public services.

As for the 'voucher' system, it is too early to know if the Act will be useful for ISL users accessing the private sector. However, Ireland has ratified the United Nations' Convention on the Rights of People with Disabilities (CRPD), which has the potential to extend the Act's influence to the private sector. Daly *et al.* (2019) suggest that the Act has the practical effect of meeting one requirement of the CRPD.

Critical Considerations

Being an academic and well versed in social justice, I was able to recognise certain incidents that arose during the ISL recognition campaign as acts of linguistic imperialism (Rose & Conama, 2017) or audism. I also discussed these informally with IDS board members. The following are some critical considerations that I drew from these experiences.

Forced to negotiate or pay interpretation costs for meetings with policymakers

The ISL recognition team was consistently asked to cover the cost of interpretation when meeting ministers, politicians and key policymakers. Their rationale was that we were requesting to meet, not them. Yet it is not enough to confirm assignment details and ensure that the interpreters are properly remunerated, ascertaining that the right interpreter is booked is also key. Not all interpreters are familiar with political and legal vocabulary and infrastructure or are capable of working in complex political negotiations. Hence, only a small number of interpreters were suitable, leading to limited availability which required significant advance notice. Frequently our requests for meetings were granted at short notice and the task of securing interpreters left to us. We brought these difficulties to the attention of our political counterparts, but while they were sympathetic, they saw interpretation as our responsibility.

Payment of interpreters became a complicated issue as the campaign progressed, one we were obliged to raise since interpreters were reluctant to accept the work without assurances that they would be paid. The state often insisted that interpreters should be willing to work for free, and there were times when interpreters attending these meetings in another capacity stepped up or supported working colleagues, but it is obvious that the government negotiators failed to appreciate the principle of interpretation as a human right and interpreters' entitlement to make a living. Despite our protestations, they responded as if interpretation was a kind of auxiliary tool, and a private matter for us to resolve.

The emotional toll of this responsibility cannot be ignored. Huge efforts were required to secure interpretation services, adding considerable anxiety to an already delicate process and forcing us to consider alternative arrangements if interpreters could not be found. The politicians and civil servants never experienced or appreciated this burden. Instead, the Deaf campaign team shouldered this responsibility almost in its totality, i.e. disproportionately. This can be regarded as an advantage of hearing privilege.

While Ireland was quick to sign the CRPD, despite repeated government promises (Lee & Raley, 2015), it did not ratify the Convention until March 2018, three months after the ISL Act was passed. It is clear from my experience that Articles 9, 21 and 29 of the Convention, which entitle people with disabilities to have *equal access* to information, especially in the political arena, were continuously ignored or overlooked.

Key players' telephone conversations undocumented during negotiations

A particular behaviour emerged in the latter stages of the process, after the negotiations were expanded to include other stakeholders, such as parents' associations, service providers and other professionals. Casual conversations during negotiations revealed that these parties had established strong connections with the policymakers, for example, through telephone conversations that were neither documented nor relayed to the Deaf campaign team.

In these situations, it is easy to exclude the primary Deaf negotiators from essential, specific and technical knowledge. At one crucial point in the discussions the lack of access put us at a significant disadvantage. At other times, issues were debated briefly and agreed almost immediately on the basis of undocumented telephone conversations between the policymakers and these third parties that previously we considered to be preliminary discussions. It was not unusual for our requests to know the content of these conversations to be met with a dismissive sigh. We were reminded that time was of the essence. When we asked to be included in future conversations, for example by recording or documenting the conversations, we were ignored; on some occasions people even indicated that they were at a loss with our request. This behaviour is contrary to the spirit of the CRPD, in particular Article 4 (3) which obliges the state to consult directly with people with disabilities.

Deaf leadership side-lined or undermined

In 1991 the World Federation of the Deaf issued a recommendation (Conama, 2010; De Meulder, 2015) that members, that is national associations of the deaf, should pursue legal/official recognition of their Indigenous sign language. In reality, IDS took a position on recognition years before, and was the only national association to act on the issue for many years. In 1988, it found a sponsor in the European Parliament, Irish MEP Eileen Lemass. She tabled a resolution calling on European Economic Community member states to recognise their sign languages (Napier & Leeson, 2016). The resolution passed unanimously. It is safe to say that IDS backed ISL recognition from the 1980s, with other organisations in Ireland beginning to support the campaign around 2010 onwards.

It was well established, therefore, that IDS was directing the ISL recognition campaign. However, during the negotiation process we realised that our leadership was regularly side-lined and undermined. For example, policymakers contacted people who were not central to the IDS team to discuss crucial items. Written correspondence also caused difficulties: email communication was used to agree specific issues prior to meetings. However, the English required was deemed too complex by many Deaf ISL users on the campaign team. They felt disadvantaged because they needed time to understand these communications but, as already mentioned, our government counterparts considered time to be a scarce commodity, and so the email discussions continued apace. I regularly suggested that the emails be translated into ISL or that messages be communicated directly in ISL as it is our first language, and the subject of the legislation, but my suggestions were ignored.

When we drew attention to these incidents, they were made out to be innocuous or we were told that nothing major had been agreed. Yet to us, it was obvious that hearing privilege was at play. This enabled certain parties to gain an advantage during the process whereby they had the ear of the government negotiators. This gave them opportunities to shape and influence issues of specific interest to them with little or no input from the Deaf team, which would have offered differing perspectives.

Technology regarded as the solution

It became apparent over the course of the negotiations that the government was actively seeking out, and indeed anticipated, technological solutions. Pinning its hopes on advanced technology as the way to tackle difficult issues like the perceived high cost of interpretation, it was clear that the government was willing to invest significant time and energy into exploring these options. We were at pains to explain that, while welcome, technology should not be treated as a panacea to all of the challenges identified during the negotiations.

Remote interpreting, for instance, was mooted as the perfect solution to the shortage of qualified interpreters in rural areas. We pointed out that it is inadequate for high-risk interpreting situations like medical or legal consultations. Furthermore, research (Braun, 2015; Napier *et al.*, 2017) has shown that it is not reliable over extended periods of time and that it is highly dependent on good network connections and other practical considerations. For example, typically, educational settings like classrooms are woefully unsuitable for remote interpreting. However, despite repeatedly cautioning against reaching for overly simplistic solutions, there was a level of collective amnesia on the part of the politicians and policymakers.

Interestingly, in the wider context of Deaf accessibility, there is a public fascination with devices such as signing avatars. The World Federation of the Deaf and the World Association of Sign Language Interpreters felt obliged to issue a joint statement welcoming innovation, but warning that avatars are not adequate substitutes for professionally qualified sign language interpreters and translators (World Federation of the Deaf, 2018).

'Neutral cost'

Early in the campaign, we were left in no doubt that, given the existing political and economic climate, it would be impossible to pass legislation with a charge on the state exchequer. We were advised to pursue a 'neutral cost' approach. Considering the pros and cons of this option, especially the importance of gaining a legislative foothold, a stepping-stone towards the ultimate goal of properly legislating for and resourcing ISL, the cross-community group also understood that a 'neutral cost' option would be the equivalent of symbolic recognition. Therefore, we decided to continue to campaign for full recognition, although we did not rule out compromising on symbolic recognition if negotiations reached an impasse.

One of our arguments rested on the comparison with the Irish language (Gaelic) which, along with English, is recognised in the constitution. Irish is spoken daily as the first or mother language by less than 4% of the population (Darmody & Daly, 2015) and is supported financially by the state. Our argument made no headway, however, in illustrating the vast difference in the way politicians and policymakers perceive ISL relative to the spoken languages of the country.

Status of language in the Act

During the final debate parliamentary on the ISL Bill, Clare Daly, one of several TDs who supported the campaign and monitored its progress closely, reminded her colleagues that ISL 'is not just a vehicle for accessing information' (Daly, 2017). She referred to the following clause:

Recognition of Irish Sign Language

(3)

(1) The State recognizes the right of Irish Sign Language users to use Irish Sign Language as their native language and the corresponding duty on all public bodies to provide Irish Sign Language users with free interpretation when availing of or seeking to access statutory entitlements and services. (Irish Sign Language Act 2017)

With the end of the negotiations in sight, we came to the conclusion that this clause exemplified the government and civil-service attitude to ISL. Sharing our perspective as Deaf people, we spent hours explaining the importance of differentiating between sign languages as authentic and cultural languages from a mere communication tool, but to no avail. De Meulder *et al.* (2019a) remind us that sign languages 'are indeed *languages*, which have communicative, identity and intrinsic value' (2019a: 213). However, our efforts to amend the clause failed; it remained unchanged.

Education clauses contingent on a review, and other issues

Our attempts to establish explicit rights for deaf children to access ISL in education were met with resistance. The government claimed that it had to confirm the completion of the review on the role of Special Needs Assistants in classrooms, and whether more specific recommendations were likely to be issued. However, according to Mathews (2020), the review made no recommendations as a result of the ISL Act.

Given the critical importance of language acquisition, the team pushed for access to ISL at school for deaf children to be prioritised in the Act. Our efforts were in vain, and we had to settle for a weaker clause. It is important to remember that the political climate for the incumbent minority government was uncertain; the government could have fallen at any time. That said, we also suspected that negotiating with a future majority government would not be more favourable to the inclusion of a stronger clause.

Personal Reflection

> We cannot individually comprehend the range, depth and detail of the consequences we are collectively generating for ourselves. (Tom Atlee, 2002)

Although Atlee takes a Taoist view on participatory democracy, this quote resonates with me: it encourages me to recognise the limits of my own knowledge and the risks of self-righteousness when predicting the benefits of the ISL Act. There is early and tangible evidence that it may bring positive benefits, but it is too soon to say what the full range of outcomes will be.

Reflecting on my life and career to date, I see that the experience of being an activist–scholar has been enriching. I did not set out to be one; instead I have been moulded into this person by my experiences of linguistic discrimination. The journey has been a mental and emotional rollercoaster, jolting me from despair to exaltation and even indifference, but I enjoy being an activist–scholar thoroughly. I am inspired by the countless successes achieved through social justice campaigns, but equally I despair when they fail. I have fallen out with some friends and made a few lifelong enemies, but I have also found more friends and allies along the way.

My childhood, advice from peers (direct and otherwise) on how to navigate and survive the hearing world, as well as my social policy and equality studies, have all had a profound impact on my ability to lead this life. Leading the campaign for ISL recognition has sharpened my perspectives and beliefs. Now I draw on analysis of how language attitudes shape our stance on language rights. Armed with this analytical ability, I can recognise, name and highlight many issues, including those discussed here, in the hope that this will bring about further discussion and analysis. The primary objective of this work is to improve the capacity of Deaf ISL users to participate actively in public life.

The work done by myself and other Deaf activist–scholars is important, but we need community backing in order to bring the attention to our experiences (and their effects) that they deserve, for example, when the Minister for Disability rejected the ISL Bill, or the sadness felt in the community after the tragic deaths of two deaf brothers in 2016.[4] The multifaceted repercussions of these events are beyond the scope of this chapter. They require separate study.

My university education, pre-university trade-union activism and experience of being treated unjustly in terms of language and disability have all enabled me to be an effective activist–scholar. Through my continued involvement in the Deaf community (politically, socially and through sports), I keep up with what is going on in the wider community, i.e. trends and beliefs, and the direction in which the community is moving. Overall, it is difficult for me to imagine my life without these dual tasks of scholarship and social-justice activism.

In this chapter, I have described how I conceive the role of activist–scholar. I have outlined some challenges that I encountered during the ISL recognition campaign, for example inspiring the Deaf community (which frequently is politically apathetic especially vis-à-vis the political establishment) to support the campaign and endeavouring to avoid the campaign becoming yet another failure. I have also highlighted some of the vulnerabilities that the process exposed, and some of the risks I took, such as challenging dominant hegemonic beliefs on the status of ISL, and accepting the risk that some people whose perspectives on ISL are wildly different from mine or the Deaf community's would be alienated. However, being told that our language was not worthy of higher status had become a long-lasting ordeal for the Deaf community. Hopefully the enactment of ISL Act 2017 will be the end of it.

References

Apple, M.W. (2016) Challenging the epistemological fog: The roles of the scholar/activist in education. *European Educational Research Journal* 15 (5), 505–515.

Atlee, T. (2002) *The Tao of Democracy: Using Co-intelligence to Create a World that Works for All*. Berkeley, CA: North Atlantic Books.

Berg, L.D., Huijbens, E.H and Larsen, H.G. (2016) Producing anxiety in the neoliberal university. *The Canadian Geographer/Le Géographe Canadien* 60 (2), 168–180.

Braun, S. (2015) Remote interpreting. In H. Mikkelson and R. Jourdenais (eds) *Routledge Handbook of Interpreting*. London: Routledge.

Chatterton, P., Hodkinson, S. and Pickerill, J. (2010) Beyond scholar activism: Making strategic interventions inside and outside the neoliberal university. *Acme: An International e-Journal for Critical Geographies* 9 (2), 245–275.

Conama, J.B. (2010) Finnish and Irish Sign Languages: An egalitarian analysis of language policies and their effects. Doctoral dissertation, University College Dublin.

Conama, J.B. (2019) 'Ah, that's not necessary, you can read English instead': An analysis of state language policy concerning Irish Sign Language and its effects. *The Legal Recognition of Sign Languages: Advocacy and Outcomes Around the World*. Multilingual Matters, Bristol.

Conama, J.B. (2020) 35 years and counting! An ethnographic analysis of sign language ideologies within the Irish Sign Language recognition campaign. In A. Kusters, E.M. Green, E. Moriarty Harrelson and K. Snoddon (eds) *Sign Language Ideologies in Practice*. Mouton de Gruyter/Ishara Press.

Cork Sign Language Interpreting (2018) *Deaf Community*. See https://corkinterpreter.com/deaf-community/ (accessed 17 February 2018).

Couture, S. (2017) Activist scholarship: The complicated entanglements of activism and research work. *Canadian Journal of Communication* 42 (1), 143–147.

Cox, L. (2015) Scholarship and activism: A social movements perspective. *Studies in Social Justice* 9 (1), 34–53.

Curran, R. (2018, Jun 28) Ten years after the crash our recovery is fragile because of lessons that we still haven't learned. *Irish Independent*. Retrieved from http://elib.tcd.ie/login?url=https://www-proquest-com.elib.tcd.ie/newspapers/ten-years-after-crash-our-recovery-is-fragile/docview/2060762008/se-2?accountid=14404

Daly, C. (2017, December 14) Dáil Éireann debate – Thursday, 14 Dec 2017 [Comment on the article 'Recognition of Irish Sign Language for the Deaf Community Bill 2016 [Seanad]: Committee and Remaining Stages']. *The House of the Oireachtas – Dail Debates*. https://www.oireachtas.ie/en/debates/debate/dail/2017-12-14/43/#spk_428

Daly, A., McDermott, Y. and Curtis, J. (2019) *Enhancing the Status of UN Treaty Rights in Domestic Settings*. Liverpool: University of Liverpool.

Darmody, M. and Daly, T. (2015) *Attitudes towards the Irish Language on the Island of Ireland*. Queen's University, Belfast. https://niopa.qub.ac.uk/bitstream/NIOPA/1597/1/Attitudes-towards-Irish-2015.pdf

De Meulder, M. (2015) The legal recognition of sign languages. *Sign Language Studies* 15 (4), 498–506.

De Meulder, M., Krausneker, V., Turner, G. and Conama, J.B. (2019a) Sign language communities. In *The Palgrave Handbook of Minority Languages and Communities* (pp. 207–232). London: Palgrave Macmillan.

De Meulder, M., Murray, J.J. and McKee, R.L. (eds) (2019b) *The Legal Recognition of Sign Languages: Advocacy and Outcomes Around the World*. Bristol: Multilingual Matters.

Department of Justice and Equality (2013) Facilitator Report. Meeting with the Deaf Community, 14 November 2013. Unpublished.

Department of Justice and Equality (2018, December 11) 252. *Deputy Clare Daly Asked the Minister for Justice and Equality the Progress Made to Enact the Irish Sign Language Act 2017. [52034/18] – The Department of Justice*. http://www.justice.ie/en/JELR/Pages/PQ-11-12-2018-252

Government of Ireland (2011) *Programme for Government 2011*. https://merrionstreet.ie/en/wp-content/uploads/2010/05/programme_for_government_2011.pdf

Hale, C.R. (2001) What is activist research? *Items* (Social Science Research Council) 2 (1–2), 13–15. https://issuu.com/ssrcitemsissues/docs/i_i_vol_2_no_1-2_2001?e=24618429/35326062

Huerta, A. (2018) The importance of being a scholar–activist (opinion). *Inside Higher Ed*. See https://www.insidehighered.com/advice/2018/03/30/importance-being-scholar-activist-opinion (accessed 3 September 2019).

Humphries, T. (1975) The making of a word: Audism. Unpublished manuscript.

Irish Deaf Society (2012) *Annual Report 2012*. https://www.irishdeafsociety.ie/wp-content/uploads/2015/06/irish-deaf-society-agm-accounts-reports-2012.pdf

Irish Sign Language Act 2017 (2017) Dublin. https://data.oireachtas.ie/ie/oireachtas/act/2017/40/eng/enacted/a4017.pdf

Kusters, A., De Meulder, M. and O'Brien, D. (eds) (2017) *Innovations in Deaf Studies: The Role of Deaf Scholars*. Oxford: Oxford University Press.

Lee, G. and Raley, M. (2015, March 30) State has long neglected those with a disability: Government has still not fully ratified the UN convention eight years later. *Irish Times*, 14.

Leeson, L. (2019) Online and Kicking: Sign Language Activism via Social Media, ICMLXVII Colloquium Virtual communities a breathing space for minority languages, Leeuwarden, the Netherlands, May 2019.

Leeson, L. and Saeed, J. (2012) *Irish Sign Language*. Edinburgh: Edinburgh University Press.

Mathews, E.S. (2017) *Language, Power, and Resistance: Mainstreaming Deaf Education*. Washington, DC: Gallaudet University Press.

Mathews, E.S. (2020) Signs of equity: Access to teacher education for deaf students in the republic of Ireland. *Sign Language Studies* 21 (1), 68–97.

McKee, R.L. and Manning, V. (2015) Evaluating effects of language recognition on language rights and the vitality of New Zealand Sign Language. *Sign Language Studies* 15 (4), 473–497.

Morrissey, J. (2015) Regimes of performance: Practices of the normalized self in the neoliberal university. *British Journal of Sociology of Education* 36 (4), 614–634.

Murray, J.J. (2015) Linguistic human rights discourse in deaf community activism. *Sign Language Studies* 15 (4), 379–410.

Napier, J. and Leeson, L. (2016) Sign language in action. In *Sign Language in Action* (pp. 50–84). London: Palgrave Macmillan.

Napier, J., Skinner, R. and Turner, G.H. (2017) 'It's good for them but not so for me': Inside the sign language interpreting call centre. *Translation and Interpreting* 9 (2), 1–23.

O'Brien, C. (2019, April 4) Irish university graduates earn more from degrees than in UK. *Irish Times*. https://www.irishtimes.com/news/education/irish-university-graduates-earn-more-from-degrees-than-in-uk-1.3848600

O'Brien, D. and Emery, S.D. (2014) The role of the intellectual in minority group studies: Reflections on deaf studies in social and political contexts. *Qualitative Inquiry* 20 (1), 27–36.

O'Flynn, M. and Panayiotopoulos, A. (2015) Activism and the academy in Ireland: A bridge for social justice. *Studies in Social Justice* 9 (1), 54–69.

Oireachtas, H.O.T. (2017, December 15) *Seanad Éireann debate – Friday, 15 Dec 2017*. Seanad Eireann. https://www.oireachtas.ie/en/debates/debate/seanad/2017-12-15/3/#spk_12

Phillipson, R. (1992) *Linguistic Imperialism*. Oxford: Oxford University Press.

Rose, H. and Conama, J.B. (2017) Linguistic imperialism: Still a valid construct in relation to language policy for Irish Sign Language. *Language Policy* 17 (3), 385–404.

RTÉ (2019) *RTÉ Ireland's National Television and Radio Broadcaster*. RTE.Ie. https://www.rte.ie

RTÉ News (2017, December 15) *Dáil Passes 'historic' sign Language Legislation*. RTE.Ie. https://www.rte.ie/news/2017/1213/927259-irish-sign-language/

Smeltzer, S. and Cantillon, S. (2015) Scholar–activist terrain in Canada and Ireland. *Studies in Social Justice* 9 (1), 7–17.

TCD – Trinity College Dublin (n.d.) *Trinity College Dublin, the University of Dublin Consolidated Financial Statements Year Ended 30 September 2018*. Trinity College Dublin. https://www.tcd.ie/financial-services/external-assets/pdfs/Consol_Financial_Statements_1617.pdf

World Federation of the Deaf (2018, April 14) *WFD and Wasli Statement on Use of Signing Avatars*. https://2tdzpf2t7hxmggqhq3njno1y-wpengine.netdna-ssl.com/wp-content/uploads/2017/02/WFD-and-WASLI-Statement-on-Avatar-FINAL-14032018-Updated-14042018-1.pdf

5 'Befriending' Risks, Vulnerabilities and Challenges: Researching Sexuality and Language in Educational Sites

Helen Sauntson

Introduction

In recent years, there has been a steadily growing body of research on language and sexuality in educational settings. Research has developed in response to social, cultural and legal changes relating to sexual diversity in many places around the world. Sexuality is an important dimension of diversity and inclusion, yet in the broader field of applied linguistics, it often receives less attention than other dimensions of diversity, such as language background, nationality and ethnicity. For example, a simple search of Google Scholar for terms such as 'language', 'linguistics', 'applied linguistics' and 'diversity' in various configurations reveals a very limited focus on diversity in language(s) and in relation to race and ethnicity (see Ahmed, 2007, for a useful discussion of the limited and constrained 'language of diversity').

Drawing on some of the most recent and ongoing research in the field, this chapter proposes that one reason for the relative marginalisation of language and sexuality within applied linguistics more broadly (and in the field of human sciences as a whole) is that it is seen as a particularly 'risky' and challenging area of research for many scholars. Much language and sexuality work tends to focus on language practices as they relate to sexual minority populations. Some work does, of course, explore heterosexual language practices. However, the main dimension of heterosexuality explored in the field is the way that discourses of heteronormativity prevail in society and function to validate (certain forms of) heterosexuality as the perceived norm whilst marginalising other sexual identities. Indeed, this is a key remit of queer linguistics, an approach which has developed over the past two decades as a means of systematically exploring various aspects of the relationship between language and sexuality. The prevailing focus on sexual minorities presents numerous challenges which are explored throughout this chapter. Drawing on the concept of 'befriending' introduced by Pakuła (2018), I propose some ways of dealing with the vulnerabilities, challenges and risks relating to this area of applied linguistics, rather than seeing them as a barrier to conducting and engaging with research. Pakula recognises the negative connotations associated with 'barriers' and 'risk' and subsequently reconceptualises them as 'befriending' in an effort to create a more positive discourse of engagement in sensitive or taboo areas of applied linguistic research and practice. Pakuła's concept of befriending may ultimately be used as a way of addressing risks, vulnerabilities and challenges in other areas of applied linguistics and across the human sciences more broadly.

Researchers engaging in work exploring language and sexuality often report it as being risky and leading to them feeling vulnerable. These reports are often anecdotal, but there appear to be perhaps two key dimensions of perceived risk and vulnerability associated with conducting research in this area. The first dimension relates to riskiness in terms of engaging with a topic that is still seen as taboo in many contexts (despite the many positive social, cultural and legal changes taking place around the world). Researchers often report feeling that engaging in research on language and sexuality, as a taboo area, is potentially risky for their academic careers, particularly those who work in more conservative countries and contexts. This is particularly the case for those researchers in the field who, themselves, identify as LGBTQ+, which can already carry with it experiences of 'minority stress' (Balsam et al., 2013; Toomey, 2018). The second dimension of risk and vulnerability relates to the perceived and experienced vulnerability of research participants who identify as LGBTQ+. The vulnerability of LGBTQ+ populations in educational contexts is well documented elsewhere (e.g. Birkett & Espelage, 2015; Bradlow et al., 2017; Bryan, 2012; DePalma & Francis, 2014; Gray, 2013; Kosciw et al., 2015; Meyer, 2010; Sauntson, 2013, 2018), but less attention has been paid to those researching these populations, including those researchers who may also identify themselves as LGBTQ+. Therefore, the rest of this chapter focuses on the vulnerabilities of researchers and the perceived and actual risks they take in conducting research in the field of language and sexuality.

In the following section, I firstly present some of my own personal reflections of conducting research in the field of language, sexuality and education (and within the broader academic context in the UK) over the past two decades. I then go on to consider some examples of current academic work in the field, which are particularly effective in terms of highlighting issues of risk and vulnerability as they relate to this area of applied linguistics research. Finally, I return to Pakuła's notion of 'befriending' in order to consider how research in the area of language, sexuality and education may address some of the risks and vulnerabilities addressed in the current research.

Personal Reflections

In language and sexuality work which focuses on educational contexts, much work points to the continuing ubiquity of discriminatory behaviours towards non-heteronormativity in educational settings. Yet applied linguistics research which investigates the linguistic forms of these discriminatory practices, and why they are so prevalent, is still in its relative infancy and conducted by relatively few scholars in a limited number of geographical contexts. A key reason for this, noted by Pakuła (2018), is the risks associated with doing this research. We must acknowledge the important point that in certain geographies and temporalities educational settings constitute hazardous sites for exploring sexuality-related issues. Even in national contexts where same-sex relationships are legal (including the legalisation of same-sex marriage and civil partnerships), negative social attitudes can still prevail. Such risks include, amongst other things, putting the researcher's career in jeopardy and, thus, making ourselves professionally, as well as personally, 'vulnerable'.

This is relevant even in the UK context in which I have worked since 2000. There have been times when I have been explicitly advised not to research gender and sexuality, and times when I have been intimidated and even overtly bullied for being a gay woman and for pursuing social justice research. I have experienced environments characterised by hyper-competitiveness, aggression and fear. And, as Pakuła stresses, both gender and sexuality are taboo concepts in the public discourse of some cultural contexts owing to a politics of fear which, although subtle, is pervasive. This has manifested in a number of ways as I have been openly engaging in research projects which explore language and sexuality in educational settings, including schools.

For example, I have been advised on more than one occasion to not have language, gender and sexuality as my only or primary research area – as this is generally considered a 'risky' research area (in that it is potentially taboo) and is also not taken as seriously as other areas of applied linguistics. This of course is a result of classic anti-feminist backlashes against any work which strives to expose inequality and injustice (Faludi, 1991; Silva & Mendes, 2015). Even though I still have much respect for the people who have advised me to maintain a more 'mainstream' research specialism alongside language and sexuality (e.g. language and education or discourse analysis), I have, for the large part, continued to openly maintain language, sexuality and education as my research specialism. Interestingly, although this advice continued to be issued to me by different people throughout the early years of my career, they ended when I took up my position at my current institution. This suggests that there is variability around different levels of acceptance of the field of language and sexuality across different institutions even within the same country. For myself, a way of addressing the risks that had been presented very explicitly to me by colleagues early in my career was to simply move to a more liberal and social justice-focused institution. However, it has to be acknowledged that this is not a viable option for many scholars for a variety of reasons.

Even within social justice-oriented institutions, challenges do remain. One of the biggest challenges I continue to experience is that audit is an inescapable feature of life as a university academic to the extent that many feel their primary purpose is to provide measures and validation of their work over and above the performance of the work itself. This happens even within the most liberal and progressive higher education contexts (for a discussion of the reasons for this, see, for example, Hall, 2018; Morrish & Sauntson, 2020). Within the overwhelmingly neoliberal context of British higher education, 'success' as an academic often becomes linked to these proxy measures. As Peseta et al. (2017) argue:

> The demand to count, measure, rank, quantify, evaluate and judge the work of universities (along with those who labour and study in them) haunts virtually all aspects of our work: from the quality of research, to targets for income generation, counts of patents, citations of articles and public testimonies of policy impact made visible and likeable online; from the quality of curriculum, to teaching with technology, responding to student feedback, watching the employment destinations and salaries of graduates as a comment on the value of their education; to whether a university is healthy, sustainable, sufficiently globalized or doing enough to position itself as the world leader in this or that discipline. (Peseta et al., 2017: 453–454)

As individual scholars, we need to decide whether to go along with this, or try to navigate an alternative path to 'success' which is more collegiate, less individualised and more balanced with other aspects of life. These proxy measures of academic success can exacerbate the risks felt by researching particular topics in applied linguistics which are seen as marginal (and therefore less likely to be widely cited, achieve widespread and measurable 'impact', etc.) and this is certainly something I have experienced as a challenge (and continue to experience) in my own professional life, particularly in relation to language and sexuality as a 'marginal' area within applied linguistics more broadly.

In some ways, this chapter is, in itself, risky. In addition to focusing on the taboo topic of sexuality (especially in educational settings), it may be read as critical of applied linguistics, and of higher education more broadly. And, in other national and geographical contexts, this chapter simply could not be written. For example, colleagues in areas of South America are currently experiencing unprecedented amounts of pressure and prejudice since the emergence of the political far right which has effectively 'closed down' social-justice focused research, especially that which is seen to potentially destabilise ideas of normative gender and (hetero) sexuality. However, progress in any human endeavour can only happen if brave people take risks and if they prioritise human advancement over their own personal safety and wellbeing. And this is precisely what has happened (and continues to happen) in the field of language and sexuality, especially in relation to education.

Language, Sexuality and Education: Key Issues in Applied Linguistics Research

It is not the intention to provide a comprehensive overview of work on language, sexuality and education here. Reviews of work in this area can be found in Pakuła (2021) and Sauntson (2017, 2018). In this section, I simply highlight some issues in this area of research which have prompted the need for more attention to be paid to elements of risk and vulnerability and which, therefore, are more directly relevant to the concerns of the present chapter.

A key issue which has emerged in the field in recent years is that, despite some context-specific claims that homophobia in schools is on the decline (e.g. McCormack, 2012), discriminatory behaviours, both verbal and non-verbal, in educational settings with reference to non-heteronormativity seem to continue to be ubiquitous (e.g. Bloomfield & Fisher, 2016; Connell, 2014; Meyer, 2010; Pascoe, 2011; Sauntson, 2018). This observation especially applies to secondary schools where maturing individuals enter the (hetero)sexual marketplace (Eckert, 1996). Moreover, it is a finding which spans a range of international school contexts.

These findings have led to an examination of homophobic language and behaviour in schools from a range of disciplinary perspectives. Within applied linguistics, a valuable element of work in the field is that it does not exclusively focus on homophobic language and bullying (although this does, of course, continue to be an important element of research). There is acknowledgement that to focus exclusively on homophobic bullying and explicit homophobic language can only get us so far and often 'misses the point' about how and why heteronormative discourse prevails in educational contexts. The case studies of current research discussed in the following section shed light on why this may be the case, as well as revealing some of the risks associated with engaging with research that addresses these issues.

A shortcoming of existing work which focuses exclusively or overwhelmingly on homophobic language and homophobic bullying is that the field can become dominated by discourses about homophobia. Monk (2011) observes that homophobic bullying has become a legitimate object of social concern in recent years (to the point where it has become 'mainstreamed'), and this has become reflected in much sexualities and education research outside linguistics. Monk notes how, from the late 2000s in the UK, all three major political parties expressed concerns about homophobic bullying. A result of this mainstreaming is that homophobic bullying has been enabled to become a harm that can be spoken of with a concurrent breaking of taboos around sexual diversity which can mitigate the risk of researching it. However, Monk goes on to explain how homophobic bullying is a complex phenomenon and is actually a productive process contingent on various cultural and political factors. The dominant discourse of bullying in schools is one which is largely individualised – bullies are pathologised and victims are held responsible for the effects of bullying through having and displaying 'resilience'. Thus, homophobic bullying becomes situated within a broader 'law and order' discourse where there are clear 'perpetrators' and 'victims'. Monk argues that, within this discursive conceptualisation of bullying, *structural* forms of homophobia (and other forms of sexuality-based discrimination and harassment) get largely overlooked. Bullying at school (and in other contexts) is, in fact, the end point – it is what happens when sexuality and gender are not understood and when they are presented in constrained and highly limited ways. The examples of research discussed in the next section all explore this lack of understanding of how certain sexual identities become 'minoritised' from a linguistic perspective in different educational settings – in schools, children's picturebooks, language textbooks, and ESOL classrooms. These examples of current research all highlight different kinds of vulnerability and risk in their approach to researching language and sexuality in educational contexts. In drawing attention to these issues, I hope to emphasise the important contribution that applied linguistics can make to developing understanding of sexual diversity in educational settings and, ultimately, how to create more inclusive environments for both researchers and participants.

'Taxonomies of Risk' in Researching Language and Sexuality

Pakuła (2018) importantly observes that, since language is conceived as a conduit of ideologies, which pertain to sexuality just as to other forms of social identity (see King, 2015), what is somewhat baffling to many is the fact that 'much current work on sexuality and education lacks [...] an explicit focus on the role that language plays in constructing discourses around sexuality in schools' (Sauntson, 2017: 147). Pakuła offers several possible reasons for this. One reason is that the field is in its relatively early stages of development when compared with other areas of applied linguistics which have a much longer history. Related to this temporal issue, Pakuła suggests that the role of language more broadly has been underestimated in certain contexts. In Poland, for example, language has frequently been perceived merely as a medium of instruction and not in terms of its constitutive functions, i.e. as a conduit of constructing, deconstructing, normalising and othering social relationships, identities and behaviours.

Another related reason, according to Pakuła, is the risks associated with conducting research in this area. As I suggested earlier in my reflections on my own early career, such risks may concern putting the researcher's career in jeopardy. If this is the case even in the UK, which is generally liberal in its attitudes towards sexual diversity, then in other geographies and temporalities, educational settings constitute extremely hazardous sites for exploring sexuality-related issues. Both gender and sexuality are taboo concepts in the public discourse of some cultural contexts (for example, Pakuła *et al.*, 2015) owing to a politics of fear (Wodak, 2015). Pakuła posits that a further type of risk regards exploring innovative paradigms which may, or may not, enable the researcher to arrive at a fuller role that language plays in shaping, constructing and negotiating sexuality in and out of educational settings.

Pakuła (2018) goes on to propose the idea of a 'taxonomy of risk' relating to the study of language and sexuality in educational settings. In doing so, he begins to theorise 'risk' from an applied linguistic perspective. Importantly, Pakuła encourages researchers to be self-reflexive in asking whether the 'risk' is perceived or real, and in 'locating' the risk. He notes that language and sexuality are both *overtly* and *covertly present* in educational contexts and reviews work which has examined different linguistic manifestations of this and the ways that these manifestations may impact the researcher and their perceptions of 'risk' and 'feelings of vulnerability'. In incorporating these issues into a taxonomy of risk, Pakuła draws on the work of Renn and Klinke (2004), who conceptualise risk and risk management from a scientific perspective. Pakuła draws specific attention to the opening paragraph of Renn and Klinke's paper where they posit that 'risks must be considered as heterogeneous phenomena that preclude standardised evaluation and handling' (Renn & Klinke, 2004: S41). What this means in practice is that, although broad criteria for risk management can be drafted at a very general level, each research project should take on board not only theoretical perspectives of risk but also the project-specific practical applications of such theorisations. An overriding principle is that applied linguists engaging in language, sexuality and education research (and other areas of research that entail risk and vulnerability) need to see themselves as risk managers. A first step in dealing with risks in any research project is firstly their identification, followed by analysis of them and then coming up with ways of tackling them. Within this overarching framework, Pakuła proposes two stages in applying a 'taxonomy of risk' to a research project in language, sexuality and education. The first stage involves assessing whether the risk is perceived or real. For example, as researchers (especially those who identify as LGBTQ+), are we mapping our own fears onto the research process or is it a potential risk predicated on real-life social attitudes, political situations or the culture of the issue(s) under research? If the latter is the case, are we able to minimise the likelihood of such risks to enable the feasibility of the project?

The second stage in the taxonomy proposed by Pakuła asks the question 'where is the locus of risk?' Pakuła proposes that there are three potential loci of risk in applied linguistics research on language, gender and sexuality: existential risk; linguistic and conceptual risk; and risk that involves experimenting with research paradigms. The first of these loci, existential risk, may be internal or external, according to Pakuła. Internal existential risk involves engaging in research which has the potential to jeopardise the researcher's own career (see Weeks, 2006, for a discussion of how this is a particularly pertinent issue in sexuality-focused research). External risk refers to the research participants and their feelings of possibly feeling uncomfortable or endangered through their involvement in the research.

Linguistic and/or conceptual risks are the second locus of risk identified by Pakuła. These risks relate to the use of particular words or concepts within a research project which may be perceived as taboo in the context under scrutiny. Pakuła refers to his own work on analysing sexuality in English Language textbooks in Poland as an example of this locus of risk. Within this research project (Pakuła et al., 2015), the researchers experienced resistance from participants in relation to the use of words which overtly describe non-heterosexual identity categories (e.g. gay, lesbian). This hostility can feel threatening for the researchers and may limit what they feel they are able to do or say in the research.

The third locus of risk in Pakuła's approach focuses on experimenting with research paradigms. Language and sexuality has provided a platform for the development of new methodologies in applied linguistics research (e.g. queer linguistics and queer applied linguistics – see Leap, 2013; Motschenbacher, 2011; Motschenbacher & Stegu, 2013) as well as being known as a welcoming field for experimenting with innovative approaches and methods. In fact, a tenet of queer linguistics (and the queer theory that informs it) is that it resists methodological constraint, dominance or categorisation. It is, rather, characterised by what Leap (2020) terms a 'scavenger methodology' which allows for a great amount of variety in methodological approaches as well as encouraging experimentation with new approaches. However, this can still feel risky to the researcher and leave them feeling vulnerable and open to criticism. Even if no criticism is forthcoming, Pakuła argues that researchers can still experience vulnerable feelings about whether their methods and approaches will 'catch on' with the wider scholarly community.

These issues can be further explored through references to examples of current work that examines different dimensions of language, sexuality and education, which have in common a shared focus on analysing manifestations of the overt and covert presence of heteronormativity in education. All of the projects go beyond a simple focus on language and bullying, and they also entail addressing various issues within Pakuła's taxonomy of risk outlined above.

Firstly, work by McGlashan (2018) examines children's picturebooks featuring same-sex parents/caregivers and their use in UK schools. McGlashan notes that these books have become some of the most requested-to-be-banned books of modern times. This strongly suggests that, even in relatively liberal national contexts such as the UK, homosexuality and its representations in public life continue to be arguably the most controversial aspect of identity representation. Homosexuality is perceived as extremely threatening relative to other aspects of identity such as race and disability. This is probably due largely to problematic but pervasive discourses of sexuality as a 'choice'. McGlashan's research is innovative and risk-taking not just in terms of the topic, but also in its ambitious but extremely valuable use of corpus-assisted multimodal critical discourse analysis.

McGlashan's findings suggest that the representations of same-sex parent families (SSPFs) in his picturebook corpus are underpinned by discourses of homonormativity and attempt to position families with same-sex parents as 'a different kind of family' rather than as something radically different from families with heterosexual parents. So SSPFs are still marked and therefore non-normative in the books comprising McGlashan's corpus. Normativity is premised upon things being *unmarked* in discourse. Despite this, McGlashan posits that provision of SSPF picturebooks in primary schools could provide educators with a vital resource for talking about familial and sexuality diversity.

Therefore, children's picturebooks containing SSPF representations may be one way of 'befriending the risks' associated with addressing sexual diversity through language practices in schools. The use of particular language teaching textbooks may be another way. In contrast to the huge number of analyses of gender representation in language textbooks, Sunderland (2018) observes that there have been very few on the representation of sexuality. Moreover, she notes that the lack of critical commentary on heteronormativity in language textbooks has been notable (some exceptions are Thornbury, 1999; Gray, 2013; Pakuła *et al.*, 2015; Sunderland, 2015). Sunderland claims that this is particularly surprising given Thornbury's accurate observation that '[g]ayness is about as omitted [from foreign language textbooks] as anything can be' (Thornbury, 1999: 15).

To partially address this, Sunderland's research considers and exemplifies the notion of 'degrees of heteronormativity'. She contends that language textbook heteronormativity is not a monolithic entity, but can be 'more' or 'less'. An example provided by Sunderland to illustrate this idea is as follows. A highly heteronormative text/image combination would be a two-parent nuclear family, mother and father, who are sitting down to dinner with their teenage son and daughter, who are talking about the son's girlfriend and the daughter's boyfriend. Much less heteronormative would be a text/image concerning a group of female and male friends – no 'pairings' specified – enjoying a 'gender-neutral' activity such as hillwalking, which allows a range of readings in class about the different possible relationships between these people. Sunderland argues that textbook analysts can then consider a given textbook and look at the range and degrees of heteronormativities represented. Publishers themselves also have a degree of choice over what representations to include. Texts themselves may legitimately be considered as discriminatory under the 2010 Equality Act in that they can omit representation of particular identities and relationships, and/or misrepresent certain groups and identities, or present them in a negative way. Aldridge-Morris (2016: 80) highlights this issue and draws attention to the following specific paragraph in the *Equality and Diversity UK Post-16 Education Toolkit* document:

> Equality and diversity have to be embedded into all aspects of the curriculum: [...] from inclusive resources and materials to teaching which explores the nature and impact of discrimination, harassment and victimisation because of disability, race, sex, sexual orientation, transgender, religion or belief, age and so on.

Given this legal context, Sunderland, perhaps optimistically, concludes that publishers can make a choice about what degrees of heteronormativity they want (or do not want) to represent. Like the picturebooks discussed by McGlashan, Sunderland importantly reminds us that language textbooks and children's picturebooks are, of course, guided by market forces and financial imperatives. It is arguably for this key reason that international textbooks are unlikely to feature non-heterosexual characters. Publishers will have to be willing to take (financial) risks if things really are to change in the future. However, considering 'degrees of heteronormativity' may help publishers. Sunderland suggests that one strategy they may implement is simply to move away from representations of extreme heteronormativity towards lower or lesser degrees of heteronormativity. Rather than directly including overt representations of same-sex romantic relationships, this may include, for example, more portrayals of single parents, same-sex friends and friendship groups (which allow a range of readings) and the inclusion of fewer explicitly heterosexual interest narratives.

This approach is potentially less risky to publishers in terms of the market forces they are driven by. The risks to researchers may also be reduced by this approach – analysing degrees of heteronormativity may open up possibilities which are more liberating than setting out to analyse language textbooks in ways which focus only on the exclusion of non-heterosexual identities.

A final case study of current research on language, sexuality and education considered here is Baynham's ongoing work which explores

LGBTQ+ inclusion issues in ESOL (English for speakers of other languages) classrooms. Baynham (2018) argues, quite rightly, that this issue arises in the UK as a consequence of the 2010 Equality Act. This act consolidated nine previous pieces of legislation to create the UK's first unified equalities legislation. The Equality Act places a new duty on public services to: 'have due regard to the need to':

(a) eliminate discrimination, harassment and victimisation;
(b) advance equality of opportunity between persons who share a relevant protected characteristic and persons who do not share it;
(c) foster good relations between persons who share a relevant protected characteristic and persons who do not share it. (Equality Act, 2010: 96)

These legal edicts, Baynham argues, are relevant to the highly diverse ESOL student population in the UK. In considering ESOL classrooms as a specific educational setting within this legal framework, Baynham discusses three ways of understanding the positioning of LGBTQ+ teachers and students in a sexually normative world:

(1) Invisibility/visibility – within this dimension of the positioning of LGBTQ+ subjects, Baynham asks how visible LGBTQ+ lives are in the activities, practices and artefacts of the ESOL classroom.
(2) Silencing and voice – this dimension of Baynham's work focuses on how audible LGBTQ+ voices (including both teachers, students and representations) are in ESOL classrooms and artefacts, or to what extent there is a culture of silence around manifestations of non-normative sexuality.
(3) Space – in this third dimension, Baynham considers whether ESOL classrooms are safe, inclusive spaces for students and teachers whose sexuality is non-normative.

Baynham considers the ESOL classroom as an element of the queer migration process, and students' narratives of migration and adaptation to life in the UK as part of a process of 'queering' the ESOL classroom. The ESOL classroom, of course, is an educational site in which LGBTQ+ asylum seekers have access to learning English. Given that asylum seekers may have escaped severely traumatic and potentially life-threatening situations when coming to the UK, it may well be quite alarming (and possibly trauma triggering) for these populations to then experience, at best, invisibility of LGBTQ+ identities and, at worse, explicit discrimination from others in the ESOL classroom. This may be confounded by parallel instances of implicit and overt racism and other forms of discrimination (see, for example, Motha, 2006, 2014).

Against this backdrop, Baynham considers a number of important questions pertaining to issues of vulnerability and risk in relation to sexuality issues in ESOL classrooms. He asks who should be responsible for addressing these issues and what ethical and political issues (which may themselves be considered 'risky') are involved. A further question centres around how to protect the privacy of LGBTQ+ teachers and students, including their right not to be out if they do not want to be. Baynham also draws explicit attention to research situations in which the classroom conversation may turn hostile, threatening and revealing of homophobic attitudes and behaviour.

More positively, and as a potential way of befriending these risks, Baynham makes reference to the creative arts and their place in ESOL and in applied linguistics more broadly. This particular befriending strategy resonates with some of my own research data from UK secondary schools, in which LGBTQ+-identified young people, who often report feeling ignored and invisible in school, also report making use of creative arts to increase their visibility and to authenticate themselves, especially through literature, music, drama and art. Other scholars, too, have identified the use of creative arts in schools as a means of befriending the risks associated with LGBTQ+ visibility and positive inclusion. Kjaran *et al.* (2020), for example, explore the use of drama in schools in Iceland and South Africa to examine issues around sexual diversity. Calvelhe Panizo examines young gay men's aesthetic experiences of engaging with media texts in schools in Spain and finds that such an approach can be transformative (2020) and effective in terms of producing a 'queer counter-space' in schools.

Ways Forward? Strategies of 'Befriending'

The illustrative case studies on current and ongoing work in the field of language, sexuality and education discussed above reveal a number of possible 'befriending' strategies that could be explored and implemented as a means of addressing the frequent risks, vulnerabilities and challenges which pervade this area of applied linguistics research. These strategies could be of benefit to both researchers and participants (as well as to those participating in education beyond specific research projects). Within the educational contexts studied, the strategies identified include: the use of creative arts in classrooms (Baynham, 2018); the use of children's books containing representations of same-sex families (McGlashan); and greater exploitation of degrees of heteronormativity (and its concurrent alternatives) in language (and other kinds of) textbooks in schools. Beyond the educational research contexts themselves, I suggest a number of wider befriending strategies, all of which require varying acts of bravery not just from researchers themselves, but also from allies and colleagues working in other areas of applied linguistics.

Firstly, as argued by Sunderland, publishers must be willing to take more risks in terms of including positive representations of diverse gender and sexual identities in their materials, including books for both children and adults (e.g. adult learners of English). While publishers are generally supportive of publishing research work in the field of language, sexuality and education, this has yet to translate into publishers' pedagogic material for use in schools and other kinds of educational settings.

My own personal reflections also reveal a need for institutional support for those conducting research in the field of language, sexuality and education (and, arguably, language and sexuality more broadly). The institutions in which researchers are employed must be willing to befriend the inevitable risks associated with the research field, in ways that ensure their employees and students are fully supported. This may entail a straightforward checking in with practices that already take place, such as ensuring colleagues engaged in sexuality-based research are being supported through conference funding, the fair allocation of research leave and so on. But beyond this, institutions could also consider ways of providing spaces and systems of support whereby researchers can 'offload' after and during engagement with risky research. This is already established practice in some professional areas such as psychology and counselling. Extending this to researchers in linguistics, and in any other discipline, who may be engaged in research that exposes risks and vulnerabilities could help to create a context which is less isolating for those researchers. There may be a case to be made for additional support to be made available to LGBTQ+ researchers which takes into account experiences frequently associated with 'minority stress' as well as the vulnerabilities which may be exposed through the research being conducted. Another suggestion for institutions may be for issues around researcher risk and vulnerability to be explicitly addressed through ethics processes and practices, if this is not currently the case.

As well as individual institutional support, researchers in this area would benefit from organisational support from professional organisations such as the British Association for Applied Linguists (and parallel organisations in other countries) and International Association of Applied Linguistics (AILA). Professional organisations may therefore be asked to befriend the risks and vulnerabilities associated with their members conducting research in the area of language, sexuality and education. Practical suggestions for achieving this may include organisations including sections on 'vulnerable populations' in their ethics guidelines. Organisations could operate peer support networks for researchers engaging in risky research, along similar lines to the way that some professional organisations already operate mentoring schemes for researchers. It may even be possible for organisations to hold specific events (e.g. workshops, conferences) dedicated to exploring these kinds of issues.

Beyond institutional and professional organisational befriending practices, we should also consider the wider higher education context. As briefly discussed earlier, we know that in a neoliberal era, academic freedom, ethics, social justice, democracy and humanitarian practices are all increasingly under threat. However, within the neoliberal system, there are, arguably, small pockets of resistance that can be found in places such as co-operative universities, liberal arts colleges, small specialist universities and some Cathedrals group universities in the UK (which have an avowed commitment to faith and social justice values as part of their mission). Can these kinds of educational contexts provide safer platforms from which research on language, sexuality and education can truly develop, flourish and make a real difference? This final question perhaps embodies an appeal to vice-chancellors to be brave and to befriend the risks involved in applied linguistics (and other) research driven primarily by an emancipatory and social justice agenda.

References

Ahmed, S. (2007) The language of diversity. *Ethnic and Racial Studies* 30 (2), 235–256.

Aldridge-Morris, K. (2016) *How to Write ESOL Materials*. Oxford: ELT Teacher 2 Writer.

Balsam, K., Beadnell, B. and Molina, Y. (2013) The daily heterosexist experiences questionnaire: Measuring minority stress among lesbian, gay, bisexual, and transgender adults. *Measurement and Evaluation in Counseling and Development* 46 (1), 3–25.

Baynham, M. (2018) Queer voices in the ESOL classroom. Paper presented at the *British Association of Applied Linguistics Annual Meeting*, York St John University, UK, 6–8 September 2018.

Birkett, M. and Espelage, D. (2015) Homophobic name-calling, peer-groups, and masculinity: The socialization of homophobic behaviour in adolescents. *Social Development* 24 (1), 184–205.

Bloomfield, V. and Fisher, M. (2016) *LGBTQ Voices in Education: Changing the Culture of Schooling*. London: Routledge.

Bradlow, J., Bartram, F., Guasp, A. and Jadva, V. (2017) *School Report: The Experiences of Lesbian, Gay, Bi and Trans Young People in Britain's Schools in 2017*. London: Stonewall.

Bryan, J. (2012) *From the Dress-up Corner to the Senior Prom*. Plymouth: Rowman and Littlefield.

Calvelhe Panizo, L. (2020) Gay teenage boys' experiences and usages of the media in Spain: Educational implications. In J.I. Kjaran and H. Sauntson (eds) *Schools as Queer Transformative Spaces: Global Narratives on Sexualities and Genders* (pp. 178–188). London: Routledge.

Connell, C. (2014) *School's Out: Gay and Lesbian Teachers in the Classroom*. Berkeley, CA: University of California Press.

DePalma, R. and Francis, D. (2014) The gendered nature of South African teachers' discourse on sex education. *Health Education Research* 29 (4), 624–32.

Eckert, P. (1996) Vowels and nail polish: The emergence of linguistic style in the preadolescent heterosexual marketplace. In N. Warner *et al.* (eds) *Gender and Belief Systems* (pp. 183–190). Berkley, CA: Berkley Women and Language Group.

Equality Act (UK) (2010) http://www.legislation.gov.uk/ukpga/2010/15/contents

Faludi, S. (1991) *Backlash: The Undeclared War Against Women*. London: Vintage.

Gray, J. (ed.) (2013) *Critical Perspectives on Language Learning Materials*. Basingstoke: Palgrave.

Hall, R. (2018) *The Alienated Academic: The Struggle for Autonomy Inside the University*. Basingstoke: Palgrave.

King, B. (2015) Language and sexuality in education. In P. Whelehan and A. Bolin (eds) *The International Encyclopedia of Human Sexuality* (pp. 649–719). New York: Wiley-Blackwell.

Kjaran, J.I., Francis, D. and Oddsson, A.H. (2020) Creating a queer counter-space in high schools in Iceland and South Africa: A drama-inspired pedagogical approach. In J.I.

Kjaran and H. Sauntson (eds) *Schools as Queer Transformative Spaces: Global Narratives on Sexualities and Genders* (pp. 17–34). London: Routledge.

Kosciw, J., Greytak, E., Giga, N., Villenas, C. and Danischewski, D. (2015) *The 2015 National School Climate Survey: The Experiences of Lesbian, Gay, Bisexual, Transgender, and Queer Youth in Our Nation's Schools.* New York: GLSEN.

Leap, W. (2013) Commentary II: Queering language and normativity. *Discourse and Society* 24 (5), 643–648.

Leap, W. (2020) *Language Before Stonewall: Language, Sexuality, History.* Basingstoke: Palgrave.

McCormack, M. (2012) *The Declining Significance of Homophobia. How Teenage Boys are Redefining Masculinity and Heterosexuality.* Oxford: Oxford University Press.

McGlashan, M. (2018) Same-sex parents in children's picturebooks: Examining representations and their place in the curriculum. Paper presented at the *British Association of Applied Linguistics Annual Meeting*, York St John University, UK, 6–8 September 2018.

Meyer, E. (2010) *Gender and Sexual Diversity in Schools: An Introduction.* London: Springer.

Monk, D. (2011) Challenging homophobic bullying in schools: The politics of progress. *International Journal of Law in Context* 7 (2), 181–207.

Morrish, L. and Sauntson, H. (2020) *Academic Irregularities: Language and Neoliberalism in Higher Education.* London: Routledge.

Motha, S. (2006) Racializing ESOL teacher identities in US K–12 public schools. *TESOL Quarterly* 40 (3), 495–518.

Motha, S. (2014) *Race, Empire, and English Language Teaching: Creating Responsible and Ethical Anti-Racist Practice.* New York: Teachers College Press.

Motschenbacher, H. (2011) Taking queer linguistics further: Sociolinguistics and critical heteronormativity research. *International Journal of the Sociology of Language* 212, 149–179.

Motschenbacher, H. and Stegu, M. (2013) Queer linguistic approaches to discourse: Introduction. *Discourse and Society* 24 (5), 519–535.

Pakuła, Ł. (2018) Befriending the risk(s): Exploring sexuality and language in educational sites. Paper presented at the *British Association of Applied Linguistics Annual Meeting*, York St John University, UK, 6–8 September 2018.

Pakuła, Ł. (ed.) (2021) *Linguistic Perspectives on Sexuality in Education: Representations, Constructions, and Negotiations.* Basingstoke: Palgrave.

Pakuła, Ł., Pawelczyk, J. and Sunderland, J. (2015) *Gender and Sexuality in English Language Education: Focus on Poland.* London: British Council.

Pascoe, C.J. (2011) *Dude, You're a Fag: Masculinity and Sexuality in High School.* Berkeley, CA: University of California Press.

Peseta, T., Barrie, S. and McLean, J. (2017) Academic life in the measured university: Pleasures, paradoxes and politics. *Higher Education Research and Development* 36 (3), 453–457.

Renn, O. and Klinke, A. (2004) Systemic risks: A new challenge for risk management. *EMBO Reports* 5 (Supplement 1): S41–S46.

Sauntson, H. (2013) Sexual diversity and illocutionary silencing in the English National Curriculum. *Sex Education: Sexuality, Society and Learning* 13 (4), 395–408.

Sauntson, H. (2017) Language, sexuality and education. In S. Wortham *et al.* (eds) *Encyclopedia of Language and Education: Discourse and Education* (pp. 147–159). New York: Springer.

Sauntson, H. (2018) *Language, Sexuality and Education.* Cambridge: Cambridge University Press.

Silva, K. and Mendes, K. (eds) (2015) *Feminist Erasures: Challenging Backlash Culture.* Basingstoke: Palgrave.

Sunderland, J. (2015) Gender (representation) in foreign language textbooks: Avoiding pitfalls and moving on. In S. Mustapha and S. Mills (eds) *Gender Representations in Learning Materials: International Perspectives* (pp. 19–34). London: Routledge.

Sunderland, J. (2018) Exploring the representation of sexuality in foreign language textbooks. Paper presented at the *British Association of Applied Linguistics Annual Meeting*, York St John University, UK, 6–8 September 2018.
Thornbury, S. (1999) Window-dressing vs. cross-dressing in the EFL sub-culture. *Folio 5* (2), 15–17.
Toomey, R. (2018) Coping with sexual orientation-related minority stress. *Journal of Homosexuality 65* (4), 484–500.
Weeks, J. (2006) The social construction of sexuality. In S. Seidman, N. Fischer and C. Meeks (eds) *The Handbook of the New Sexuality Studies* (pp. 14–20). London: Routledge.
Wodak, R. (2015) *The Politics of Fear: What Right-wing Populist Discourses Mean*. London: Sage.

Part 2
Policy

6 Challenging Constitutional Bilingualism with 'What if ...': Counterfactual Histories and At-risk Minorities in Finland

Johanna Ennser-Kananen and Taina Saarinen

Introduction: At-risk Minorities in Different Language Policy Scenarios

This chapter analyzes language ideologies in Finnish language policy through a lens of risk. More specifically, it presents a meta-analysis of Finnish language policy spanning a 100-year period since 1917, discusses this policy against the concept of risk (Beck, 1992) and examines the implications for language minoritized groups since the establishment of Finnish constitutional bilingualism in 1919, when Finnish and Swedish were designated equal status as national languages. In our discussion we utilize the analytical tool of counterfactual histories (see Villstrand & Karonen, 2017 for a discussion), a form of historiography that attempts to answer 'what if' questions known as counterfactuals (Rodwell, 2013; Bunzl, 2004). Through this, we attempt to illuminate the risks of language policy for different minoritized speaker groups by presenting an alternative to the mainstream analysis and thus opening historical developments and processes for critical scrutiny from a new perspective.

At the heart of our counterfactual alternative is an imaginary constitution declaring Swedish a (regional) minority language rather than a national language, a viable scenario in the geopolitical situation of the post-independence and post-civil-war Finland of 1919 (Saarinen & Ihalainen, 2018). By discussing this counterfactual, we aim at problematizing the often assumed and self-evident language policies, particularly from the point of view of vulnerable minoritized speaker groups.

We continue by first discussing the concept of risk and the ways in which it features in language policy research, particularly in 'majority' and 'minority' frames. While doing this, we acknowledge the problematic nature of these concepts: we do not wish to essentialize or normalize majorities and minorities (see Laihonen & Halonen, 2019) and recognize that minoritizing a particular population is never a politically innocent process. When we use these concepts and terms that are common in language policies and legislation and have very material consequences, we do so with the aim of unpacking the ideologies behind them. We conclude the theoretical part of our chapter by discussing the merits of counterfactual history for our topic.

Theoretical Framework

Risk as future-oriented, partly fictional and inequitable

Risk has maybe been most prominently theorized by Ulrich Beck (e.g. 1992, 2006), who describes its nature as an anticipation of the future with an awareness of the past (see also Giddens & Pierson, 1998). Therein lies, Beck explains, also the great irony of risk:

> The irony of risk here is that rationality, that is, the experience of the past, encourages anticipation of the wrong kind of risk, the one we believe we can calculate and control, whereas the disaster arises from what we do not know and cannot calculate. (Beck, 2006: 330)

The future orientation of risk as an 'attempt to anticipate what cannot be anticipated' (2006: 329) has two important implications for this chapter: First, it invites and encourages a counterfactual approach that foregrounds untrodden paths of history to uncover new aspects and elements of risk and vulnerability. Second, it acts as a social stratifier: the ability to anticipate and minimize risk is not equally distributed. In Beck's words, risk is a 'socially constructed phenomenon, in which some people have a greater capacity to define risks than others' (2006: 333). Thus, Beck concludes, '[r]isk definition, essentially, is a power game' (2006: 333).

Although Beck points to power as an important aspect of risk management, his understanding of risk has also left room for criticism (e.g. Mythen, 2007). For instance, Beck's binary view of 'natural' vs 'manufactured' risks, his assumption of the universality of risk, and his failure to allow for heterogeneous risk perceptions have been brought up as weak points of the theory. In this paper, we concur with Mythen's point that risk perception and avoidance are 'informed by a range of social factors including class, gender, age, ethnicity and location' (2007: 800). Thus, risk and how it is perceived and addressed can serve as an indication of social inequities and as a tool to identify and initiate steps to challenge such inequities.

As indicated above, Beck's (2006) concept of risk is deeply tied to a future-oriented society and a fundamental sense of not-knowing. Consequently, risk as understood by Beck always contains an element of fiction, which may compel people and institutions to react (sometimes hastily) to a perceived risk. He explains that 'it is irrelevant whether we live in a world which is in fact or in some sense "objectively" safer than all other worlds; if destruction and disasters are anticipated, then that produces a compulsion to act' (2006: 332). Whether and how such partial fictitiousness of risk can potentially create new risks is one focus point of this chapter.

Owing to these characteristics of risk – its future orientation, its partial fictionality and its potential to highlight inequality – the concept lends itself to closer consideration in language policy and planning, particularly in our particular context of nation building and the role of official languages there (Tollefson & Pérez-Milans, 2018). Throughout the text, we will be using language policy as an overarching concept to refer to the various, multilevel and layered activities that may include explicit legislation and planning or *de facto* ideological practices, produced intentionally or unintentionally (Johnson, 2013: 24). While the early 20th century Finnish language regulation followed the optimistic 'problem solving' ethos of earlier language-planning approaches of a newly founded nation state, we also acknowledge the potential of these approaches to reproduce and generate language inequalities that ultimately imply social inequalities (Tollefson, 1991), thus emphasizing the political and ideological aspects of language policy.

We will next examine the assumed risks behind the current language policy situation in Finland and continue then to analyze a counterfactual situation to explore possible alternative explanations for the position of minoritized languages in Finnish language policy.

Language policy literature from the perspective of risk

Language policy efforts tend to have as their declared purpose the goal of improving or maintaining a sociolinguistic situation, be it, for instance, through the creation of national or regional unity, the protection of minoritized groups or the promotion of linguistic rights and statuses. In all, the management and minimization of risks such as language loss or linguistic and societal marginalization can be described as the goal of language policy. Less often, language policies are viewed as also inducing risk. We want to explore this aspect of language policy, particularly from the perspective of minoritized language populations.

Our approach draws on existing scholarship that has analyzed and illustrated the complicated role of language planning and policies between inducing and minimizing risks and rights. For instance, Hult (2004) examined the situation of Swedish and Sweden's five recognized minority languages and showed how languages can simultaneously be at risk and induce risk for others. The status of languages varies in different situations and when in touch with different languages, thus also affecting the dynamic between them. For instance, in our case, both Finnish and

Swedish can be construed as being both vulnerable and hegemonic in the same historical situation.

In his book *Planning Language, Planning Inequality*, Tollefson (1991) explains how language policy efforts can perpetuate social inequalities in different national contexts, for instance through insisting on linguistic standards, reinforcing linguistic hierarchies, creating linguistic barriers and dismissing or ignoring a variety of linguistic resources. Takam and Fassé (2019) give a recent example of harmful language policymaking in Cameroon, where unvetted bilingual (English and French) programmes are spreading and undermining public education and standards, and, one might add, run the risk of disregarding many other languages and perpetuating colonial language ideologies.

The vulnerability or stability of a speaker community is never something fixed or stable but can change when new risks are introduced through socio-political or ideological developments. In their article, De Silva and Heller (2009) analyze a shift in discourse about minoritized languages, specifically French in Canada, from protecting rights toward providing economic opportunities, which, as they point out, goes hand in hand with a shift from welfare to neoliberalism as main paradigms. The complex relationship between minoritized languages, language policy efforts and state policy that De Silva and Heller describe, reminds us that even nationally recognized and supported minoritized languages remain in a precarious and ever-shifting situation that is subject to global trends and discourses (see also Murillo's discussion of discursive constructions of social inequalities in Chapter 3). Given that risks and vulnerabilities can be introduced or increased even unintentionally and unexpectedly, an examination of risks, especially those that lie in rarely studied alternative histories, seems justified and valuable.

Counterfactual histories as frame for language policy analysis

Counterfactual histories offer alternatives to actual historical storylines and, in our chapter, help us understand what the situation for minoritized speaker groups could have been in a different historical scenario. Such studies offer a way of looking at history through the eyes of the contemporaries as a window of several possibilities rather than an inevitable historical development from a retrospective position. As such a framework presents an alternative to the mainstream analysis, it has the potential to open up historical interpretations for critical discussion and scrutiny, make us more receptive toward historical contingencies and act as a countermeasure against historical determinism (Rodwell, 2013). The intention of such an approach is not to 'counter facts', but to offer plausible alternate readings of historical events and help us tease out the often-unarticulated assumptions that our historical interpretations rest on (Lebow, 2007).

A counterfactual history approach allows us to foreground cases in which the dominant and minoritized language speaker groups are positioned differently. Lebow's example from a different context is illustrative: while the 'corporate boardrooms and corridors of power' in Paris, London and Washington may have been happy with the outcome of World War I, from the point of view of Polish Jews, Germany winning World War I might have led to the scenario of no Hitler and no Holocaust (Lebow, 2007). Counterfactual analysis helps us overcome traditional paths of thought and 'zoom out, refocus and contemplate a fresh perspective' (Wenzlhuemer, 2009: 30), or create a Spielraum (Wenzlhuemer, 2009: 35) where the alternate possibilities can be examined in a less constrained way.

In the historical setting this chapter is concerned with, the existence of certain events is relatively unquestioned (e.g. Finland gaining independence in the beginning of December 1917). However, the interpretations and contextualizations of those events are more open to debate and discussion. As Lebow (2007) points out, historical events are not analytically taken for granted but analyzed against several, often conflicting data, and there is rarely any factual evidence that leaves no room for alternative analyses (see also Wenzlhuemer, 2009).

Analytically, a study on counterfactual history first identifies a potential case for scrutiny (in our chapter, the constitution with two national languages and no provision for minority languages). The role of this case in a causal chain will then be manipulated as part of a counterfactual reality (Wenzlhuemer, 2009) As limitations of this approach, Lebow (2007) mentions the statistical improbability of multistep counterfactuals, the interconnectedness of effects and counterfactuals leading to second-order counterfactuals, all of which might interfere with the logic of counterfactual realities. While we acknowledge these limitations, we believe they are outweighed by the opportunities of looking at vulnerable language minorities through a counterfactual lens.

Questioning assumptions in our history is an exercise in juxtaposing causality and correlation. In our present-day analysis, we may assume a particular development as a causal consequence of an earlier development; taking an alternative view with counterfactuals, we may find the developments coincidental and not linked to the assumed events (Wenzlhuemer, 2009). The assumption of the bilingual constitution being at the root of Finnish minority language policy can be tested by taking a counterfactual event as a starting point. If the constitution of two national languages indeed causes a particular position for minority languages, a different constitution would either lead to a different status for minority languages and speakers, or alternatively help us see that the root of the vulnerability of minoritized language status is elsewhere (see also Severo & Makoni, Chapter 2, as well as Murillo, Chapter 3, on alternative epistemologies in discussing vulnerable groups).

Policies that have established or supported constitutional bilingualism have gone hand in hand with the discourse of protecting Finnish and Swedish. Counter to this master narrative, we explore whether and how this effort has caused other languages, such as Sámi languages, Roma, Karelian or Sign Languages, to be at risk, or added to their at-risk status. What if Finland's language policymakers had anticipated different risks? What risks did they not see? (How) would Finland's language policy landscape differ from that of today if they had seen them? What other blind spots might that, in turn, have created?

We answer the questions by conducting a meta-analysis of existing literature and expanding on existing literature on historical language policy. Our data is thus primarily existing research literature on Finnish language policies from which we construct the counterfactual history of Swedish as a minority language.

The 1919 Constitution with Two National Languages and the Position of Minorities

Finland was part of the kingdom of Sweden from the late 13th century until 1809 and a Grand Duchy under the Russian Empire between 1809 and 1917. During the Swedish reign, developments in the Lutheran Church and the need to develop local administration led to gradual strengthening of the Finnish language alongside Swedish in the 17th and 18th centuries, amplified by Herderian, national romantic nation-building efforts in the 19th century. Finland's formal legislative bilingualism was slowly established during the late 19th century, first in municipal administration and then gradually in education and state administration. For a while, between 1902 and 1917, Finland was even administratively trilingual (Finnish–Swedish–Russian), for example, with compulsory Russian being taught at schools. However, the role of Russian language remained small, and the two-decade-long Russification of the society ended with independence (Engman, 2016; Ihalainen *et al.*, 2019).

After independence in late 1917 and following the Civil War of 1918, Finland became a republic with the first bilingual (Finnish–Swedish) constitution taking effect in 1919. In the first constitution and the consequent 1922 Language Act, the two languages were positioned as equal national languages, with no mention of other linguistic or ethnic minorities. The first constitution, as well as the renewed one of 1999/2000 did, however, represent a monoglot ideology (Silverstein, 1996), stressing individual monolingualism (assuming first languages to be 'either Finnish or Swedish'), combined with administrative practices allowing the registration of only one so-called mother tongue for individuals. In that sense, the Finnish constitution still today combines state bilingualism with individual monolingualism.

The solution of two equal national languages has often been described both as 'model bilingualism' and as problematic (for a discussion, see Salo, 2012), applauded and criticized for giving a minority of less than 10% a legislative status beyond the share of the population.

Constitutional debate 1919

The decision on a constitution with two national languages took place in the intersection of various political debates, highlighting the fact that 'language' emerged as proxy for different policies (Engman, 2016; Saarinen & Ihalainen, 2018). Discourses on language and ethnicity, economic and political class distinctions, and certain active politicians came together in the parliamentary debate (Saarinen & Ihalainen, 2018), which was further contextualized by the bloody and traumatic civil war that took place immediately after independence in the spring of 1918. Class conflict relating to population growth, industrialization and the rise of a labor movement also unearthed some of the social tensions between different language groups, which were then reflected in the polarized political discourses between the 'elites' and 'common people' (Saarinen & Ihalainen, 2018).

A larger backdrop to the constitutional debate was provided by international developments during and after World War I. After the civil war, the monarchist rump parliament (the Social Democrats as the losing party had been excluded) declared Finland a monarchy, selecting the German Prince Friedrich Karl of Hesse as its first king in October 1918. However, after Germany's defeat in World War I and Karl Friedrich stepping down, negotiations for a republican constitution resumed in 1919. In these debates, the mainly monarchist Swedish People's Party's support was sought by proposing a constitution with two national languages as well as other language regulations (Ihalainen, 2017).

From a language ideological viewpoint, the bilingual constitution was also in part an outcome of the 19th-century nationalistic discourses idealizing the connection between a language and a political unit (Hobsbawm, 1992). This ideology manifested itself in the debates as the dominant discourse of 'two languages, one nation', and the alternative discourses of 'two languages, two nations' and 'one language, one nation'. For the Swedish MPs, the bilingual proposal was, while not completely satisfactory, still acceptable as a protection of minority rights, as witnessed by a turn in the debate by Swedish People Party's MP Georg von Wendt on 3 June 1919. Finnish MPs, in turn, saw the legislation that guaranteed equal rights to the Swedish- and Finnish-speaking communities as making sure the 'eternal complaining about the supposed oppression of the Swedish speakers would finally end', as Mikko Erich, MP for the conservative National Coalition Party, declared (3 June 1919). The proposal was first overturned in mid-June 1919 but accepted a week later, and without the Swedish votes in the end (Saarinen & Ihalainen, 2018).

From the perspective of anticipated risks, for proponents of Finnish, the risk was that to the unity and stability of a new state and potential international damage to the newly independent country's reputation. Swedish speakers were accused of separatism (Saarinen & Ihalainen, 2018) and of harming Finland's reputation internationally. For the proponents of Swedish, in turn, the expected risk was that of being in a minority position, without adequate protection for the rights of the Swedish language population (Engman, 2016).

The debates of two nations took place until World War II (Meinander, 2016: 30–31), but after that, with the comprehensive school reform in 1960s, the focus of the debate turned on the position of Swedish as a compulsory language in education. The national language status of Finnish and Swedish did not fundamentally change in the renewed current (1999) constitution, while political institutions were essentially unaware or ignorant of Indigenous and autochthonous minorities in the first decades of independence.

Minorities and the 1919 constitution

The constitutional debate of 1919 focused completely on Finnish and Swedish; no mention of other languages took place. Ideologically, both the representatives of Swedish and Finnish speakers referred to Swedish as a minority language, but with very different undertones. In other words, a minority legislative status for Swedish was not discussed in the constitutional debate, but the debate on the bilingual constitution revolved around the rights of the Swedish-speaking minority population. Thus, the constitution can be seen as a set of minority provisions intended to secure parliamentary and societal normalcy after a crisis (Saarinen & Ihalainen, 2018).

On occasion, Finnish was also construed as a regional minority language, interestingly mixing the question of hegemonic minorities and majorities and making visible the possibilities of differing dynamics in the situation. Both the debate on administrative regions and the final version of the regional administration paragraph included a direction that referred to both Finnish and Swedish in minority terms. The outcome also regulated that administrative regions should be, when possible, monolingually Finnish- or Swedish-speaking, and that minority populations in bilingual areas should be as small as possible. In other words, even if these minorities (Finnish and Swedish) were eagerly discussed, the aim was to promote as much administrative monolingualism as possible.

Minority languages, specifically Sámi, Romani, Sign Language and Karelian, began to receive formal recognition only in the 1990s. Sámi, Romani and Sign languages were added to the Constitution in an amendment in 1995 and kept in similar form in the renewed Constitution of 1999. Additionally, Karelian was named as a minority language in 2009 following the European Charter for Regional or Minority Languages of 1992, a status which has no legislative but rather a symbolic effect in Finland. All of the above are generally referred to as 'minority languages', although their status is based on different arguments, and Finnish legislation does not as such include minority provisions. The three Sámi languages spoken in Finland derive their rights from their Indigenous status. Romani is mentioned in the constitution among 'other groups' who are granted the right to maintain their language and culture, and Sign Language rights are derived from their users' disability rights, rather than referring to individual Finnish or Swedish Sign Languages. The Sámi Language Act was accepted in 2003 and the Sign Language Act in 2015. However, the position of minority languages, particularly the Romani and Karelian language as well as some Sámi languages, remains vulnerable, with little support and low status within education. For further reading on Indigenous rights, see Murillo (Chapter 3), and on sign language rights see Conama (Chapter 4) and Snoddon and Wilkinson (Chapter 8).

The Counterfactual Constitution and At-risk Minorities

A potential counterfactual: Swedish as minority language

How then, would a counterfactual constitution have taken shape and what would it have looked like? As Lebow (2007: 156–157) points out, 'every good counterfactual (...) rests on multiple "factuals", just as every factual rests on counterfactual assumptions – and these assumptions too often go unexamined'. The outcome of the bilingual constitutional debate was tied in many ways to the outcome of World War I. Had Germany emerged as winner, the German Prince Friedrich Karl of Hesse may have become king under the monarchist constitution. This would have rendered obsolete the recognition of Swedish as a national language, the trade-off for a republican constitution with the Swedish People's Party.

Already prior to independence and immediately after its declaration, strong opinions existed in the parliament and media both about making Finnish the only official language and about granting Swedish a minority status (Engman, 2016; Saarinen & Ihalainen, 2018). As the language of the political elites and education, an equal position was the political goal for Swedish until 1906, when the change in the electoral system and universal suffrage replaced the old estates system that had favored the Swedish population with education and capital (Engman, 2016: 365–367). From then on, the Swedish speakers went from requiring an equal position toward considering a minority position, or even a regional minority position (Ihalainen *et al.*, 2019; also Engman, 2016). Thus, a regional minority status for Sweden would have been a viable counterfactual.

A minority status for Swedish would also have been in line with developments in Central and Eastern Europe after World War I. According to Ruiz Vieytez (2001: 10–11), the first international treaties protecting minority languages were drafted after World War I, with the newly founded League of Nations monitoring the situations. The position of Swedish in Finland was brought to the attention of the Paris Peace Conference of 1919, much to the irritation of several Finnish language advocates (members of a nationalist movement named Fennomans, as opposed to the Swedish language activists or Swekomans) who found the development problematic.

Legislation that protects linguistic minorities is relatively new in Europe, starting with (often religious) minority provisions in the Congress of Westphalia in the early 17th century and continuing with international treaties in early 19th century on the protection of ethnic minorities. While these treaties rarely mentioned languages except by implication, the early 20th century Paris Peace Treaty provisions explicitly considered linguistic minorities (Ruiz Vieytez, 2001). International protection of Central and Eastern European minorities was set up to be monitored by the newly established League of Nations, and the position of Swedish might have followed these (often territorial) minority provisions. The Swedish Assembly of Finland Folktinget which had been founded in 1919 to represent Swedish speakers in Finland would have developed from a consultative into a regional legislature for the Swedish region.

Thus, the position of Swedish might have been organized much along the lines of developments in the other new states of Poland, Czechoslovakia and Yugoslavia (Fink, 1995). Swedish speakers might have been supported by Sweden (which had already taken part in the real-life dispute over the status of Åland Islands between Finland and Sweden), much as Germany appeared as the protector of German speakers in other European countries (Mazower, 1997) or Russia of the present-day Russian diaspora (Lähteenmäki & Pöyhönen, 2015).

Minority languages in the counterfactual scenario

It seems, however, that less well organized autochthonous or Indigenous minorities did not get the same kind of attention after World War I as more established languages. Also in Finland, languages like Sámi and Karelian did not have nationally or internationally recognized institutions or status, but they nonetheless had different situations, as did Russian, our third example.

Lehtola (2012) describes the Sámi history around the turn of the 20th century extensively. The multilayeredness of Sámi society, dealing with questions of livelihood and landowning as well as the linguistic and cultural aspects, points to alternative historical outcomes, had the Swedish counterfactual minority position opened a door for a different kind of Sámi policy.

The Finnish way of handling Sámi affairs seemed to be that of passive oppression, i.e. ignoring their needs while focusing on the whole population, as opposed to more actively oppressive measures in Sweden and Norway (Lehtola, 2012: 16–17). This passivity gave some room for activities promoting Sámi rights. There were bilingual Finnish–Sámi practices in schools in the early 20th century as well as some political organization (Lehtola, 2012), and although from the end of the 19th century, Nordic administrations tightened their hold of the Sámi areas, there was increasing political activity in the first decades of the 20th century together with an increasing Sámi population. The first inter-Scandinavian Sámi conference was organized in February 1917, demanding several practical actions to improve the education of civil servants and clergy, as well as to enable Sámi representation in the parliaments (Lehtola, 2012: 193).

Thus, there is some potential for a Sámi national awakening that could have led to a more explicit status for the minority. With Sámi, anticipation of danger to national security and unity was smaller than with Russian or Karelian minorities, who lived closer to the potentially volatile Soviet Russian border (Lehtola, 2012). However, recognition as a regional minority language would have required strong intergovernmental cooperation between the Nordic states, and the Sámi issue was neither a priority for them at that point, nor did the Sámi push for regional autonomy (Lehtola, 2012).

It could be speculated that had Sámi been granted minority status, there might have been more push for a Sámi nation across the Cap of the North. Had this happened, it is possible that Sámi assimilation would not have taken place after World War II to the extent that it did. However, post-war foreign policy developments, combined with population transfers between countries to ensure homogenous populations, might nevertheless have caused a push toward an assimilation policy of the Sámi after World War II regardless of a minority status, were the institutions not strong enough. It is thus debatable whether the counterfactual outcome by the 1990s would have been much different from the historical one.

Had the Civil War not broken out in 1918, there might have been less pressure on the national unity front, giving more space to more established minorities like the Sámi and perhaps Russian speakers. While some of the arguments used for supporting the position of Swedish in Finland would also apply to Russian (e.g. a long common history), Russian has traditionally been construed as a threat for several reasons (for a discussion, see Lähteenmäki & Vanhanen-Aniszewski, 2012 and Lähteenmäki & Pöyhönen, 2015). Part of this is due to a historical representation of Russia as a primordial enemy. Interestingly, in an analysis of name changes in the Helsinki Jewish community in the 1930s, Ekholm and Muir (2016) argue that Jewish names were changed not only because of antisemitism but also because of Russophobia and anti-Bolshevism. As the Fennified names in the Jewish community were generally associated with Russia and Russian language, name changing ultimately served as avoiding belonging to multiple minorities, i.e. Swedish-speaking Jews with Russian names. This example illustrates the fluidities and complexities of minority group belonging and the multiple sources of vulnerabilities behind it.

Another explanation concerns events closer to independence. The first and second periods of Russification between 1899–1905 and 1901–1917, i.e. Russian governmental policies of limiting the autonomous position of the Grand Duchy of Finland, were still fresh in the memory of Finnish people. In addition, the Soviet threat was deliberately propagated to create fear of communism before and during the Civil War (Lähteenmäki & Pöyhönen, 2015; Lähteenmäki & Vanhanen-Aniszevski, 2012). Thus, the prevailing image of a 'Russian threat' stood in the way of recognition of Russian and its speakers.

Karelian only received formal recognition as a minority language in 2009, when Finland added it to the languages protected by the European Charter. Before that, Karelians were mostly viewed as Finns by Finnish institutions and policies, making Karelian invisible in Finnish education, culture and political life. As opposed to Sámi, Karelian educational systems were already assimilated into Finnish and Russian ones at the beginning of the 20th century (Sarhimaa, 2017). An additional obstacle for the Karelian community was their diaspora situation, as the population was somewhat split in 1809 between Russia and the Grand Duchy of Finland, and more effectively in 1920 in the Tartu Treaty between Finland and Soviet Russia. Teaching in Karelian might have been possible in the mid-19th century on the basis of the 1866 education act, but lack of organization and Karelian activists prevented this from happening (Sarhimaa, 2017). In this, Karelians differ from the Sámi, who had at least some access to Sámi language education, albeit sporadic and dependent on local clerics and the availability of teachers (Lehtola, 2012). As for Karelian, the linguistic and societal activism of early 20th century led toward a Finnish nationalist rather than Karelian orientation, leading to a diminishing institutional position of Karelian (Sarhimaa, 2017: 104–110). Thus, the position of Karelian, compared with that of Sámi, was less secure both linguistically and institutionally and thus would have probably remained marginalized.

One tiny opportunity for minority languages to gain traction may have been the formulation in the Education Act of 1921, which talked about the pupils' language of tuition choice as being the language that the child 'either exclusively or best knows'. This is an exceptional conceptualization in Finnish language legislation as it indicates the possibility of individual bi- or multilingualism instead of the individual monolingualism of 'either Finnish or Swedish' implied elsewhere in legislation. Had this formulation transferred into the language policy, and had Sámi, Karelian or Russian been declared a minority language, minority populations would have had legal ground to claim their right to use their languages at school more extensively and systematically. However, this is an unlikely scenario, as the wording was probably read (and intended) to refer to Finnish and Swedish as they were discussed in the constitutional debate.

Whose risks matter in minority language legislation?

The hegemonic narrative of 1919 was largely that of a new bilingual nation in need of constitutional legislation that protects the national languages, which were being depicted as vulnerable. Finnish and Swedish occupied the center stage until the 1990s. The discussion of risks and vulnerabilities until the end of the 20th century mostly focused on these two languages. In other words, the languages with the most solid societal status ended up being most protected, at the cost for languages that did not and still do not possess the societal status that Swedish had at the turn of the 20th century.

The counterfactual narrative would have been to constitutionally recognize other national minorities and languages, such as Sámi, Russian and Karelian. With several languages having minority status, Finland would have looked very different with regional autonomous areas in Western, Northern and Eastern Finland. However, even our counterfactual consideration of (a few) minoritized speaker groups in Finland does not even begin to address how migrant languages might and should factor into this equation. With the absence of historical (documented or recognized) presence, their status remains the most vulnerable.

One sobering interpretation of our analysis is that language policy efforts are rather likely to perpetuate privilege to some degree. Thus, in order to even be considered for language planning and support, linguistic groups need to have gained some visibility and agency and have become part of the discourse. Differently put, those whose language are most endangered are most likely not to have a seat at the table, which further increases their marginalization. In our case, Swedish and for instance Karelian were in completely different situations in our counterfactual 1919 constitutional debates. This, of course, is related to questions of legitimacy in methodology and epistemology, but also of policymaking: how do we know who is at risk? Who decides? Who is being heard and by whom?

Secondly, the position of minority languages is legally regulated from the language perspective, while it is the social, political, cultural and economic status of not the language itself but its speakers that ultimately has an effect on how the language has been positioned. Looking at our three sample minority languages of Sámi, Karelian and Russian, this is clear. Sámi, while having fewer speakers than Karelian, seems to have had at least a marginal economic status and political institutions at the turn of the 20th century, with active assimilation policies starting more pronouncedly only after World War II. The Karelian speakers, in turn, were actively assimilated either into the Russian or Finnish educational and societal institutions, with no formal political representation. Russian might have had the economic, educational and social status, but was politically considered a threat. The status and position of none of these minorities can be explained by the number of speakers alone. Consequently, the fact that looking beyond minorities as numbers is paramount is one lesson to learn from our analysis.

Thirdly, it seems that international legislation has worked to provide some attention and protection to linguistic minorities. Despite differences in practices in the post-World War I League of Nations policy and the approach promoted by the European Council, it needs to be recognized that these policies made many minority populations and languages (more) visible, first as collectives and later from an individual human rights perspective.

In order for such positive initiatives not to run into risks, language policymakers are called to engage in constant self-reflective processes. Attention to multiple contexts can mitigate the risk of pushing populations to a legal or social offside, and self-reflection has to have as its aim to minimize our social, political, linguistic and cultural blind spots. Maybe it is time that language policymakers and influencers learn to routinely ask questions in Beck's (2006) sense, such as: what future are we not imagining? What risk are we not anticipating?

It is further crucial to recognize that hegemonies are not stable, monodirectional or fixed. In the hegemonic narrative, those at risk today can exert risk for others tomorrow or be presented in this way. Close and critical attention to discourses in the media and in academic and political contexts is needed to understand the intricacies of multidirectional and contextually shaped risk and to discern, for instance, populist overstatements of risks from situations that demand language policy intervention and support.

Conclusion

Seen through a counterfactual lens, one might come to the conclusion that minoritized languages of populations that may be white or non-white, European or non-European, and Indigenous, autochthonous or migration based, would have been disenfranchised in Finland regardless of the status of Swedish in Finland. Even a minority provision for Swedish in the 1919 constitution might not have made a significant difference to new minority languages in Finland.

However, a counterfactual perspective can compel us to look beyond language toward the speakers of the language and consider factors such as race, ethnicity, class, culture and others that impact our language policy foci and risk discourses consciously or subconsciously. Raising such issues requires the acknowledgment of the vulnerability of minoritized individuals and populations, which in turn forces scholars of a social majority (such as us, the authors of this chapter) to acknowledge our privileged positions and become aware of hegemonic processes that we are otherwise blind to, yet complicit in. The idealized notion of Finland as a model of bilingualism is one of the normalized discourses that requires unpacking. Counterfactual histories may turn out to be a helpful tool for other contexts too, to understand multilingualism and language policymaking in our societies more deeply and more honestly.

Acknowledgements

We would like to thank Tuomo Kondie, a Karelian activist, and Senior Researcher Heli Valtonen, for their insightful comments on the first draft of this paper.

References

Beck, U. (1992) *Risk Society: Towards a New Modernity in 1992*. London: Sage.
Beck, U. (2006) Living in the world risk society: A Hobhouse Memorial Public Lecture given on Wednesday 15 February 2006 at the London School of Economics. *Economy and Society* 35 (3), 329–345.
Bunzl, M. (2004) Counterfactual history: A user's guide. *American Historical Review* 109 (3), 845–858.
De Silva, E. and Heller, M. (2009) From protector to producer: The role of the State in the discursive shift from minority rights to economic development. *Language Policy* 8, 95–11.
Ekholm, L.K. and Muir, S. (2017) Name changes and visions of 'a new Jew' in the Helsinki Jewish community. *Scripta Instituti Donneriani Aboensis* 27, 173–188. https://doi.org/10.30674/scripta.66574
Engman, M. (2016) *Språkfrågan. Finlandssvenskhetens uppkomst 1812–1922*. Finlands Svenska Historia 3. Helsingfors: Svenska Litteratursällskapet i Finland.
Fink, G. (1995) The League of Nations and the minorities question. *World Affairs* 157 (4), 197–205.
Giddens, A. and Pierson, C. (1998) *Conversations with Anthony Giddens: Making Sense of Modernity*. Stanford University Press.
Hobsbawm, E.J. (1992) *Nations and Nationalism Since 1780. Programme, Myth, Reality* (2nd edn). Cambridge: Cambridge University Press.
Hult, F.M. (2004) Planning for multilingualism and minority language rights in Sweden. *Language Policy* 3, 181. https://doi.org/10.1023/B:LPOL.0000036182.40797.23
Ihalainen, P. (2017) *The Springs of Democracy: National and Transnational Debates on Constitutional Reform in the British, German, Swedish and Finnish Parliaments, 1917–1919*. Studia Fennica Historica 24. Helsinki: Suomalaisen Kirjallisuuden Seura.
Ihalainen, P., Nuolijärvi, P. and Saarinen, T. (2019) Kamppailua tilasta ja vallasta: kieli- ja kielikoulutuspolitiikan historiallisesti kierrätetyt diskurssit. In T. Saarinen, P. Nuolijärvi, S. Pöyhönen and T. Kangasvieri (eds) *Kieli, Koulutus, Politiikka: Monipaikkaisia Käytänteitä Ja Tulkintoja* (pp. 27–59). Tampere: Vastapaino.
Johnson, D.C. (2013) *Language Policy*. London: Palgrave.
Lähteenmäki, M. and Pöyhönen, S. (2015) Language rights of the Russian-speaking minority in Finland: Multi-sited historical arguments and language ideologies. In M. Halonen, P. Ihalainen and T. Saarinen (eds) *Language Policies in Finland and Sweden: Interdisciplinary and Multi-sited Comparisons* (pp. 90–115). Bristol: Multilingual Matters.

Lähteenmäki, M. and Vanhala-Aniszewski, M. (2012) Hard currency or a stigma: The Russian–Finnish bilingualism among young Russian-speaking immigrants in Finland. In J. Blommaert, S. Leppänen, P. Pahta and T. Virkkula (eds) *Dangerous Multilingualism* (pp. 121–141). London: Palgrave Macmillan.

Laihonen, P. and Halonen, M. (2019) Vähemmistöt ja enemmistöt kieli-ideologisina käsitteinä In T. Saarinen, P. Nuolijärvi, S. Pöyhönen and T. Kangasvieri (eds) *Kieli, Koulutus, Politiikka : Monipaikkaisia Käytänteitä Ja Tulkintoja* (pp. 61–90). Tampere: Vastapaino.

Lebow, R.N. (2007) Counterfactual thought experiments: A necessary teaching tool. *The History Teacher* 40 (2), 153–176.

Lehtola, V.-P. (2012) *Saamelaiset Suomalaiset. Kohtaamisia 1896–1953*. Helsinki: SKS.

Mazower, M. (1997) Minorities and the League of Nations in interwar Europe. *Daedalus* 126 (2), 47–63.

Meinander, H. (2016) *Nationalstaten. Finlands svenskhet 1922–2015*. Finlands svenska historia 4. Helsingfors: Svenska Litteratursällskapet I Finland.

Mythen, G. (2007) Reappraising the risk society thesis: Telescopic sight or myopic vision? *Current Sociology* 55 (6), 793–813.

Rodwell, G. (2013) Counterfactual histories and the nature of history. In *Whose History?: Engaging History Students through Historical Fiction* (pp. 81–98). Adelaide: University of Adelaide Press.

Ruiz Vieytez, E.J. (2001) The protection of linguistic minorities: A historical approach. *International Journal on Multicultural Societies* 3 (1), 5 – 14.

Saarinen, T. and Ihalainen, P. (2018) Multi-sited and historically layered language policy construction: Parliamentary debate on the Finnish constitutional bilingualism in 1919. *Language Policy* 17 (4), 545–565.

Salo, O. (2012) Finland's Official Bilingualism — a Bed of Roses or of Procrustes? In J. Blommaert, S. Leppänen, P. Pahta and T. Räisänen (eds) *Dangerous Multilingualism. Northern Perspectives on Order, Purity and Normality* (pp. 25–40). Basingstoke: Palgrave.

Sarhimaa, A. (2017) *Vaietut Ja Vaiennetut – Karjalankieliset Karjalaiset Suomessa*. Helsinki: Suomalaisen Kirjallisuuden Seura.

Silverstein, M. (1996) Monoglot 'standard' in America: Standardization and metaphors of linguistic hegemony. In D. Brenneis and R. Macaulay (eds) *The Matrix of Language: Contemporary Linguistic Anthropology* (pp. 284–306). Boulder, CO: Westview Press.

Takam, A. and Fassé, I. (2019) English and French bilingual education and language policy in Cameroon: The bottom-up approach or the policy of no policy? *Language Policy*. Online first: https://link.springer.com/article/10.1007/s10993-019-09510-7

Tollefson, J. (1991) *Planning Language, Planning Inequality*. London: Longman.

Tollefson, J. and Pérez-Milans, M. (2018) *The Oxford Handbook of Language Policy and Planning*. Oxford: Oxford University Press.

Villstrand, N.E. and Karonen, P. (2017) Tirkistysaukkohistoriaa vai avoimia tulevaisuuksia? [Peep hole history or open futures?] In N.E. Villstrand and P. Karonen (eds) *Kulkemattomat Polut. Mahdollinen Suomen Historia* [Untrodden Paths. A Possible History of Finland] (pp. 7–21). Gaudeamus.

Wenzlhuemer, R. (2009) Counterfactual thinking as a scientific method. *Historical Social Research* 34 (2), 27–54.

7 UK Language Policy Quo vadis? Language Learning in the UK post Brexit

Ursula Lanvers

Introduction

As the popularity of English as global lingua franca is increasing steadily, the disinterest, in Anglophone countries, in learning any foreign languages is rising, both in formal school education and beyond (Lanvers, 2017a). Consequently, in many Anglophone countries, we observe students leaving education with poor language competencies, developed via formal study. The UK exemplifies the 'linguaphobia' we find in Anglophone countries, in the sense that the combination of liberal language education policies, poor learner motivation at school and little interest among the general public in developing language skills all contribute to poor language proficiency, among both school students and the general public.

Enter Brexit into this scenario, and we observe that discussions around language learning have been politicised to unprecedented levels (Lanvers *et al.*, 2018). Brexit heightens the danger of the UK becoming an increasingly monoglot country, in terms of formally acquired language skills (HEPI Report 123, 2019). Simultaneously, among promoters of language learning, Brexit has triggered a range of – often uncorroborated – predictions and hypotheses regarding the UK's future language needs.

This chapter analyses discussions around language education in the UK in the politically volatile context, addressing the following questions:

- How is UK language education policy and practice discussed, in all four UK nations, within the current contexts of Brexit and global English?
- How are the risks and opportunities of following different language policies positioned within this context?

Thus, this chapter offers a meta-review of the – by now, quite considerable – published literature on the above issues: no systematic review exists to date. Both the global English and Brexit agendas have been linked to a range of claims regarding language learning in the UK: these rationales will be scrutinised here.

The next section presents facts about the UK's language learning crisis, the language education policies in the four nations in relation to Brexit and the UK's economic needs for language skills. The subsequent section scrutinises a range of claims regarding links between Brexit and language learning in particular, asking if the above-described 'linguaphobia' could, in itself, be described as a sign of Europhobia. This section will also consider claims made regarding the future of English in the EU, post Brexit. The conclusion returns to the issue of politicisation of language policy since Brexit, and asks what dangers and vulnerabilities on the one hand, and opportunities on the other, Brexit offers. By common consent, UK language learning is in crisis (HEPI Report 123, 2019), so might a Brexit-induced shape-up of language learning provide an opportunity to revitalise the dire situation?

Language Learning in the UK

Languages among the general population

Foreign language proficiencies among the UK adult population are reported as either the worst or, on some measures, second-worst (after Ireland) in the EU (British Council, 2013; Eurobarometer, 2012b). Furthermore, 4% of UK citizens were of the opinion that no language learning is useful, compared with an EU average of 2% (Eurobarometer, 2012b). In sum, we see both a greater reluctance to learn languages among the general UK population than in other EU countries and much poorer second language proficiencies resulting from formal education. The UK also has the lowest percentage of tertiary students studying abroad in another EU country (Eurostat, 2015). These facts seem to support the notion that the British are indeed 'linguaphobes' but tell us little about why this might be so. One argument relates English 'linguaphobia' to the global 'ideology of (English) monolingualism' (Wiley, 2000), found across Anglophone countries. After all, the global status of English has led to a decreased interest in learning languages other than English (LOTE; Busse, 2017), potentially leading to foreign language monolingualism. The decrease in the study of languages other than English is matched by an increase in the learning of English: 94% of secondary and 83% of primary school students in the EU are learning English (Eurobarometer, 2012b). Viewed in this light, learners in Anglophone countries might simply be following the global trend for a disinterest in LOTE, with the unfortunate consequence that Anglophone countries end up with monolingualism pure and simple (at least, developed via formal learning). A brief glance at language education policies and practices in other Anglophone countries, such as the USA, Australia and New Zealand, confirms that education systems in these countries equally demand very little by way of formal compulsory language learning or proficiency outcomes (Lanvers, 2017a).

In sum, the phenomenon of global English may be responsible for 'linguaphobe' or 'English is enough' attitudes, which can arguably be found among the UK population. Thus, care should be taken not to confound this phenomenon with current political agendas such as Brexit or purported 'intrinsic' national characteristics such as xenophobia or Europhobia. We shall return to this issue.

Language policies in the four UK nations

Education policies are devolved to the four nations (England, Scotland, Wales and Northern Ireland) which make up the UK. Before discussing the different nations' stances on language learning post-Brexit, we provide a brief reminder of the voting outcomes of the 2016 Referendum: both England and Wales voted to leave with a c. 52% majority, while Northern Ireland and Scotland strongly voted to remain in the EU. For those seeking to explain UK 'linguaphobic' attitudes with reference to Brexit, it may be a surprise that two nations have committed – in principle, at least – to the European aim of 1 + 2 (mother tongue plus competency in two other languages), but these are not the same two who voted to remain: they are Scotland and Wales.

Scotland is committed to the EU's '1 + 2 model' (Scottish Government, 2012). The plan is to introduce a first language in the first year of primary school and continue this language up to age 15. A second additional language is to be introduced no later than age 9. There was a rise in post-16 language examinations between 2014 and 2017, but owing to funding cuts, it is not clear whether this trend can be sustained. Scotland's 'mother tongue plus two' policy is supported by – to date – £18 million in investment (Gorrara, 2018); however, funding for the policy is not guaranteed beyond 2021. Currently, Scotland has a higher success rate regarding participation in language education after the age of 14, with nearly 90% of 16 year olds learning a language, but this does not translate into increased uptake of languages (compared with other nations) beyond this, for instance in higher education or adult education (Doughtly & Spöring, 2018). Doughtly and Spöring remind us that language learning outcomes to date have not exceeded those in the rest of the UK, despite more EU-friendly policies overall (Bieri, 2014). The ultimate success of Scotland's ambitious multilingual policy depends much more on continual funding than any Brexit-related developments. Thus, care must be taken not to over-interpret the fact that, in this nation, the Brexit vote and an ambitious language policy both seem to support a 'more Europhile' outlook. This link is nonetheless made frequently in the Scottish press (Lanvers et al., 2018). Other political agendas, such as the long-standing debate around devolution or independence from the rest of the UK, might equally explain Scotland's desire to set themselves apart.

In Wales, there is no requirement to teach a language at primary school. However, Welsh is compulsory in the first three years of secondary school, and a further language is 'encouraged'. The aim of the Welsh Government is to achieve 'Bilingualism plus 1' by 2020 (Global Futures, 2020). Wales has a long tradition of poor language learning results. In response, the Global Futures initiative of 'Bilingualism + 1' was announced in 2015 but is not a compulsory policy to date (Donaldson, 2015). A specific Welsh problem is that, while Wales promotes Welsh–English bilingualism relatively well, other languages are squeezed out of the curriculum timetable by Welsh (Gorrara, 2018). Monolingual mindsets also contribute to particularly low learner motivation. Ultimately, the success of both the Scottish and Welsh ambitious policy initiatives will depend on continuous funding and support for schools to implement the policies. Ultimately, the risk of these ambitious policies failing resides mainly with national policy and is not directly related to Brexit. Notwithstanding, the Welsh media praise their policy, with references to anti-Brexit stances (Lanvers *et al.*, 2018).

Northern Ireland voted overwhelmingly to remain in the EU. Nonetheless, their current language education policy, as well as Northern Ireland's learning outcomes, might be described as weakest among the four nations. A short-lived initiative for Primary Languages was scrapped in 2015, so that currently, only three years of language learning are compulsory for all. Language proficiencies among the general population are also poor (Carruthers & Mainnín, 2018), hampering economic success (Northern Ireland Chamber of Commerce, 2014). Similarly to Wales – but to a lesser extent – the teaching of the heritage language Irish 'eats into' the time available for the teaching of other languages. One positive trend is that language continuation beyond the compulsory phase at school level has not declined in recent years, while it did in England. The provision for Irish remains a strongly politicised and contentious issue and is implicated in the 'Irish question' of Brexit: this is indeed a language problem exacerbated by Brexit. The overall progress (or otherwise) in the learning of any language, however, will depend on the nation's success in implementing and supporting stronger language policies (such as Primary Languages; see Collen *et al.*, 2017). Thus, a particular Northern Irish risk is that the Brexit-induced stalemate over the Irish language will hamper progress in the learning of other languages.

Some 85% of all UK school students reside in England. Here, schools must teach a language to pupils aged 7–11 in primary school and aged 11–14 in secondary school. The discontinuation of compulsory languages for all up to the age of 16 (in 2004) has led to a continual drop in those learning languages beyond the compulsory phase. The last three years have seen the percentage of students aged 16 with a language qualification stagnating around 42% (Tinsley, 2018), with little sign of improvement. There is also a stark social divide between those who learn languages beyond the compulsory phase and those who do not (Lanvers, 2017b): this fact is significant in that incentivisations and initiatives to increase language learning uptake should focus on those students currently disenfranchised from language study and likely to come from comparatively disadvantaged backgrounds. However, there are no indications of initiatives or policy directions focusing on this Widening Participation goal: thus, the risk is that well-intended policy initiatives will not impact on language uptake. One such example is the introduction of the English Baccalaureate (Ebacc) in 2011. The Ebacc is a qualification which students aged 16 receive automatically if they score good grades in five subjects, including a foreign language. It was hoped that the promise of obtaining the Ebacc would increase language uptake. However, the Ebacc did not lead to the expected increase, mainly because the educational benefit of receiving this qualification remains unclear, both to individual students and to schools. Language learning beyond the age of 16 continues to fall year on year, as does uptake of language degrees at higher education levels. Furthermore, governmental focus to improve language learning is currently not changing to increase uptake, but to invest in a new national centre of excellence for language pedagogy. Thus, the focus is set on improving pedagogy, in the hope that these improvements ultimately filter though into greater uptake. There are no specific aims for future uptake, nor are there strategies to incentivise those learners from less advantaged backgrounds (see Introduction), in order to increase uptake.

Quo vadis: Brexit-related risk in UK language learning?

To sum up, all four nations currently make language learning compulsory for the ages 11–14. UK provision for language education is particularly poor compared with European countries (second lowest; Eurostat, 2016), with only 4.2% of students studying two or more languages, compared with the EU average of 51%. Each UK nation has their own agenda and policy for improving language provision and uptake: some focus more on fostering early plurilingualism, such as the Scottish initiative; others, such as England, rely on improving pedagogy for the secondary sector. The initiatives have in common that: (a) they either do not set clear targets for the percentage of students with language qualifications at age 16 or 18, or, if clear targets are set, do not specify how they are to be achieved; and (b) long-term funding, needed to support a school year's cohort progress in language learning, from one year to the next, is not guaranteed. In these policy developments, no clear links to the Brexit agenda emerge. However, Brexit might impact negatively on UK language learning and teaching for reasons unrelated to education policies: schools might find future travel to the EU more difficult (Tinsley, 2018), for instance, because students lose the right to European Health insurance when travelling abroad (both UK students visiting the EU and vice versa). Rules and regulations, e.g. regarding safeguarding rules of minors, are likely to increase the efforts and costs of school exchanges. Current political Brexit decisions make it likely that students might lose access to the Erasmus exchange. Such disincentives might encourage European students and exchange partners to visit Ireland rather than UK partner schools. The language teacher shortages across the UK is a further worry in that a third of language teachers currently are from the EU (Tinsley, 2018): the teaching sector relies on EU nationals. It is difficult to foresee how the UK will manage to retain, let alone attract, future EU nationals to teach in UK schools.

The future of the above-described ambitious policies of Scotland and Wales remains uncertain, as it depends on sustained funding. The next section addresses the UK's future needs for languages, and critically asks if the current policy plans are fit to address these needs.

The UK's economic needs for languages

Currently, the UK already loses about 3.5% of its GDP annually owing to its language deficit (Foreman-Peck, 2007). The largest contributor to this loss is the lack of export activities in medium-sized and small businesses, because they lack language skills (Hogan-Brun, 2018). The continuing and future importance of small and medium-sized enterprises for the UK (Rhodes, 2016) makes the UK especially vulnerable to further disbenefit from the lack of language skills. The problem is confounded by the fact that larger companies are better situated to invest and prepare for new language skills than smaller and medium-sized ones.

International business is, of course, also often conducted in English. However, in this respect, the importance of the US, as both the largest English-speaking country and the largest economic power, cannot be understated. The UK is susceptible to suffering the consequences of any changes that the US might implement in their international trade activities. For instance, the 'America first' policy favoured by the last US administration might lead to a decrease in English used in international trade (Hogan-Brun, 2018). This would negatively affect countries such as the UK, which rely strongly on using English as an international trading language.

Economists have turned to the question of whether Brexit will change the UK's future language needs, or if the UK might want to continue to rely largely on the English language for their exporting activities. The languages most frequently used in exporting businesses are German, French, Italian and Spanish, reflecting the currently largest trading partners of the UK. In addition, Foreman-Peck and Wang (2014: 34) predict that the UK's future language demands will be more diverse, and include, on the one hand, Japanese and Arabic, and on the other, the languages of the fast emerging economies of the BRICS countries (Brazil, Russia, India, China and South Africa).

Given that the UK currently offers very little formal language provision in these languages, and that developing language skills in a cohort of young learners takes a minimum of 5–7 years, the UK is unlikely to meet such language skills demands from 'homegrown' sources. However, to date, no economic linguist has been able to predict with any certainty if, for instance, the languages of the BRICS countries will be prioritised, or other world languages, or indeed languages of the UK's European neighbours. After all, the UK's most important trading partners, France, Germany, Spain and Italy, are likely to remain in this position post-Brexit for some time, and the UK is already severely disadvantaged by language skills shortages in European languages (see above). A further dimension influencing the UK's post-Brexit language needs concerns the current trade agreements that the EU has with 164 different countries: will the UK somehow be able to build upon, or retain, these relations, or will it need to start its own trade negotiations?

In sum, whatever the precise language needs post-Brexit might be, the UK's linguistic skills are likely to be stretched to their limits, or indeed beyond (Holmes, 2018). In the light of (a) the current economic loss owing to a language skill shortage, (b) increased need for skillful negotiations with a host of both EU and non-EU countries and (c) uncertainty as to which languages a post-Brexit UK might need most desperately, this chapter will not add to speculation regarding the 'most wanted' languages. Instead, this section will conclude with the observation that the national policy plans outlined in the previous sections cannot, even under most felicitous conditions, provide the UK with language needs post-Brexit, for the following reasons:

- There is a considerable lead-in phase in any new language teaching phase to equip a new cohort with new sets of language skills. Newly trained generations would not be ready for any immediate needs resulting from the UK's departure from the EU.
- The existing strong policy initiatives in some of the UK's four nations are not secured by long-term funding.
- The initiatives and policies do not address the need to increase competencies at higher levels (age 16 and beyond).
- Current policies do not address diversification of the languages that schools currently offer to meet the likely post-Brexit demands for more diverse language skills (regardless of which languages exactly they might diversify to).
- There are no detailed strategies for incentivising students from lower socioeconomic backgrounds: to increase overall uptake, this group must be targeted, as students from more advantaged backgrounds already study languages post-14.

Europhobia and Linguaphobia – Two Sides of the Same Coin?

The long-standing concerns over the UK's poor language learning record span three decades and predate any Brexit discussions. Even before the referendum, academics had hypothesised that Britons' reluctance to learn languages is due to their mentality of Euroscepticism, insularism and xenophobia (Coleman, 1997). Understandably, this rationale has received heightened attention since the Brexit vote, with pedagogues expressing concern that Euroscepticism will reinforce the nation's general disinterest in languages. Prognostications and opinions on the issue are by no means unanimous: among school learners and their parents, Brexit has led to a further 'entrenchment of monolingualism' (Tinsley, 2018: 129), and further deterioration of motivation among learners and their parents (Tinsley & Board, 2018; Tinsley, 2018). Some linguists take such attitudes as evidence that the UK's disinterest in language learning does indeed stem from the same mentality of insularity, xenophobia and heightened nationalism (Lanvers *et al.*, 2018). Indeed, this rationale, purporting a link between Euroscepticism and poor language learning, gained in popularity very soon after the referendum. In this rationale, the British are variously essentialised as having 'a national mentality', insularity, xenophobia and/or Europhobia (Lanvers *et al.*, 2018), resulting in either an incapability or an unwillingness to learn languages. In this rationale, other, for instance educational, factors or the negative effect of Global English on UK language learning are ignored.

Rationales linking anti-Europeanness to unwillingness to learn languages have little relation to actual language needs: the above section has discussed how Brexit, if anything, will increase Britain's needs for language skills (Hogan-Brun, 2018), both in the diversity of languages to be mastered and in fluency levels. The questions, at this (late) stage in the Brexit process, is thus not if the UK could indeed afford to learn even fewer European languages post-Brexit than currently is the case (it cannot), but (a) how this rationale holds up to scrutiny and (b) if it is beneficial to the agenda of promoting languages. In order to scrutinise the rationale in these respects, we must consider several factors, namely (a) Europhobia in the EU generally, (b) language policy and practice in the UK and (c) global English.

Concerning the first, Europhobia does, of course, exist in the UK, as it does in other EU countries, and is reported as being higher in some countries (strongest among the newest and smaller EU member states) than in the UK (Eurobarometer, 2012a). Concerning the second, poor language learning policies and practices might explain the UK's disappointing learner outcomes, compared with other EU nations (Milton & Meara, 1998; Mitchell, 2010). Thirdly, the language crisis is shared by many Anglophone countries (see Introduction). A disinterest in language learning has been observed elsewhere, such as in the US and other Anglophone countries: the spread of English has led native speakers to lose motivation to learn other languages. The 'English is enough' fallacy has been described widely among learners with English as (one of) their first language(s) (e.g. Graham, 2004; Lo Bianco, 2014). Thus, the 'English is enough' or 'monolingual mindset' rationale to explain the UK's reluctance to learn languages is supported by evidence. However, care must be taken not to confound this phenomenon with purported 'intrinsic' or 'inherent' national characteristics such as an essential inability to learn languages. The UK's disinterest in learn languages needs to be understood as a parallel phenomenon to the European (and global) trend of English as the dominant Modern Foreign Languages (MFL) supressing the learning of other languages (e.g. Busse, 2017), i.e. 'foreign language monolingualism'.

One danger of essentialising the British as 'inherently incapable' or 'too lazy to learn' is that all of those who are currently demotivated, and living in 'English monolingual bubbles', are further discouraged. In this manner, such rationales may – unwittingly – reproduce the social segregation in language learning that we currently witness. Such arguments might undermine poor learner self-efficacy further (Graham & Santos, 2015) and provide reasons for the current motivational crisis among learners, fuelled by the 'English is enough' attitude. For these reasons, such negative framing, although often started with the best intentions to address the language crisis, might do more harm than good to the future of language learning in the UK.

Other views on language needs post-Brexit are very different in tone. Commercial language providers, for instance, speculate about the UK's future language needs in a very proactive manner (Lanvers *et al.*, 2018). In their interest to attract future clients (i.e. language learners), commercial language learning providers frame Brexit as an opportunity rather than a threat, linking the political change to their vested interest ('Get your Brexit negotiation language skills with us'). Such opportunistic stances offer empowering messages to those currently not engaged with languages and offer avenues to foster self-efficacy in language learners, in particular among those currently lacking this most, i.e. those from disadvantaged backgrounds. Furthermore, commercial provisions for language learning, for example for the adult professional market, need not be expensive and/or addressed to privileged students: the ubiquity and low cost of language learning apps in particular has made language learning accessible for many. Thus, opportunistic stances are one example of a positive avenue to address the crisis of demotivation.

Of course, UK citizens may well harbour Europhobe, linguaphobe and 'English is enough' rationales concurrently. The rationales are not contradictory: they can complement each other. Nonetheless, as discussed above, the current UK context dictates that we should tackle 'English is enough' mindsets first and foremost to enthuse learners across the whole socioeconomic spectrum for languages.

Is English in Europe Vulnerable post-Brexit?

A further element to mix into the debate of languages post-Brexit is the concern over the future of English as a working language within the EU economy, as well as within EU institutions. A continuing dominance of English within the EU would be in the UK's interest but the Brexit process has given rise not only to speculation regarding the future of English in the EU but also what forms of English (if any) might emerge and what effects there may be on the future of other European languages.

Economic linguists as well as policy researchers (e.g. Chriost & Bonotti, 2018; Gazzola, 2016; Ginsburgh *et al.*, 2016) argue that English is very likely to remain the most spoken language in EU after Brexit, and that a continuation of a wide use of English would ensure greatest fairness and least linguistic disenfranchisement of the EU population. Different ranking methods to predict the position of English in the EU post-Brexit lead to similar conclusions, namely that English will continue to be of high ranking, as it is the most spoken language in the EU, combining first and second language proficiencies (Gazzola, 2016; Ginsburgh *et al.*, 2016).

However, much disagreement exists concerning (purported) future varieties of English in Europe, as well as the likelihood of the EU further diversifying their plurilingual practices (e.g. more translations from/into smaller languages). Some (Modiano, 2017) predict that the departure of the UK leaves a 'linguistic vacuum', in the EU, which will (should?) be appropriated by the continental Europeans, creating an English 'European variant' form. Modiano postulates that, although the position of English remains central, a new EU variant, different from UK English, will emerge. Others (e.g. Phillipson, 2017) contest the notion of a 'European English', pointing out the continuing plurilingual practices of all EU communications, as well as the global hegemony of the English language. Others still predict a diminishing importance of English, in line with a rise in other languages in the EU. The French nationalist party Front National, for instance, has been vying for some time to use Brexit as launchpad for their long-standing ambition to increase the use of French in the EU (Bolton & Davis, 2017).

However, much of the above remains based on wishes and assumptions, not facts. The 'no great change for English in the EU' thesis can be said to stand on firmer empirical – both economic and linguistic – evidence than the two competing predictions, that of increased use of other big European languages and that of increased plurilingual practices (Gazzola, 2016). Evidence supporting the 'no great change' view stems from the fact that Europeans have developed their (mostly formally acquired) English language competencies at a fast rate. Continuing to use English across the EU at its current rate would result in lower percentages of linguistic disenfranchisement (relative to other solutions). Furthermore, ideological stances for the prediction that UK varieties will continue to be more attractive than any (purposive) EU varieties align with notions of linguistic imperialism and hegemony (Phillipson, 2017).

We conclude with Seargeant (2017) that, currently, there is little certainty about the future of the English language in the EU, but we note with interest how politicians utilise symbolic functions in political debates. Just as the National Front has seized the Brexit moment to boost the EU position of French in a post-Brexit EU (Bolton & Davis, 2017), others position the future of English in line with their ideological stances towards both English and/or languages in general.

Conclusion

Just as Ennser-Kananen and Saarinen (Chapter 6) describe for the Swiss language-learning context, the challenges the UK language-learning crisis faces reach beyond language education policy. Brexit has politicised the debate around the UK language crisis to unprecedented levels. This chapter scrutinised this politicisation, addressing topics as diverse as language education policy in the four UK nations, explanations for the UK population's reluctance to learn languages and languages in the UK post-Brexit. Within each of these debates, we find examples of political appropriation of the language debate, for parochial interests (similar to Ennser-Kananen & Saarinen, Chapter 6). For instance, looking at policies in the for UK nations, the framing of the Scottish policy initiative as 'pro-European' exemplifies a politicisation that is not supported by evidence (as far as the Scottish record of language learning is concerned). The 'essentialising' of the British as both bad language learners and anti-Europeans unduly confounds political and linguistic agendas. Commercial providers of language learning, for their part, interpret the UK's language needs to suit their agenda, and finally, the efforts of the French to increase the use of their language post-Brexit constitutes an example of appropriating language for patriotic and nationalistic agendas.

Such appropriations of languages and language policy are not new (Rampton, 1999). However, the risk of 'essentialising' the British as lazy learners shows how political appropriation can – in this case, unwittingly – do harm rather than good to incentivisations to learn. Other stances, such as the opportunistic one exemplified by language providers, offer novel avenues to tackle the current demise of language learning. Regardless of the (yet unspecified) precise Brexit-related language needs for the UK, the main future challenge is to seize the opportunity that Brexit might offer to rejuvenate language learning, tackle monolingual mindsets and engage all citizens in language learning. At the time of writing (March 2020), policy initiatives across all nations, and especially in England, are vulnerable to not tackling the crisis at its core, most often because of a lack of sustained funding and long-term planning. In addition, as in the case of England, the planned changes do not tackle all challenges and aspects of the language crisis. To increase learner uptake we mainly need to engage those groups currently most underrepresented in language uptake; in the UK, that means those from the lower socioeconomic spectrum – no policy initiative yet has addressed this challenge.

References

Bieri, M. (2014) Separatism in the EU. ETH-Zürich. See http://www.css.ethz.ch/content/dam/ethz/special-interest/gess/cis/center-for-securities-studies/pdfs/CSSAnalyse160-EN.pdf (accessed 10 January 2017).
Bolton, K. and Davis, D.R. (2017) Brexit and the future of English in Europe. *World Englishes* 36 (3), 302–312.
British Council (2013) *Languages for the Future Which languages the UK needs most and why*. See https://www.britishcouncil.org/sites/default/files/languages-for-the-future-report-v3.pdf (accessed 10 January 2017).
Busse, V. (2017) Plurilingualism in Europe: Exploring attitudes toward English and other European languages among adolescents in Bulgaria, Germany, the Netherlands, and Spain. *The Modern Language Journal* 101 (3), 566–582.
Carruthers, J. and Mainnín, M.B.Ó. (2018) Languages in Northern Ireland: Policy and practice. In M. Kelly (ed.) *Languages after Brexit* (pp. 159–172). Cham: Palgrave Macmillan.
Chriost, D.M.G. and Bonotti, M. (2018) *Language Policy and Linguistic Diversity*. London: Palgrave Macmillan.
Coleman, J.A. (1997) Why the British do not learn languages: Myths and motivation in the United Kingdom. *Language Learning Journal* 37 (1), 111–127.
Collen, I., McKendry, E. and Henderson, L. (2017) *The Transition from Primary Languages Programmes to Post-Primary Language Provision*. Belfast: QUB, NICILT.
Donaldson, G. (2015) Successful futures. Independent Review of Curriculum and Assessment Arrangements in Wales. Cardiff: Welsh Government. See http://gov.wales/topics/educationandskills/schoolshome/curriculum-for-wales-curriculum-forlife/why-we-are-changing/successful-futures/?lang=en (accessed 10 October 2019).
Doughty, H. and Spöring, M. (2018) Modern languages in Scotland in the context of Brexit. In M. Kelly (ed.) *Languages after Brexit: How the UK Speaks to the World* (pp. 137–147). London: Palgrave Macmillan.
Eurobarometer (2012a) European Citizenship Report. See http://ec.europa.eu/public_opinion/archives/eb/eb77/eb77_citizen_en.pdf (accessed 2 January 2017).
Eurobarometer (2012b) Europeans and their languages. See http://ec.europa.eu/public_opinion/archives/ebs/ebs_386_en.pdf (accessed 2 January 2017).
Eurostat (2015) Tertiary Education statistics. See http://ec.europa.eu/eurostat/statistics-explained/index.php/Tertiary_education_statistics (accessed 10 January 2017).
Eurostat (2016) Foreign language learning statistics. See http://ec.europa.eu/eurostat/statistics-explained/index.php/Foreign_language_learning_statistics (accessed 10 January 2017).
Foreman-Peck, J. (2007) Costing Babel: The contribution of language skills to exporting and productivity. *Quarterly Economic Bulletin* 28 (4), 20–28.
Foreman-Peck, J. and Wang, Y. (2014) The costs to the UK of language deficiencies as a barrier to UK engagement in exporting. See https://www.gov.uk/government/uploads/system/uploads/attachment_data/file/309899/Costs_to_UK_of_language_deficiencies_as_barrier_to_UK_engagement_in_exporting.pdf (accessed 10 January 2017).
Gazzola, M. (2016) Multilingual communication for whom? Language policy and fairness in the European Union. *European Union Politics* 17 (4), 546–569.
Ginsburgh, V.A., Moreno Ternero, J.D. and Weber, S. (2016) Ranking languages in the European Union: Before and after Brexit. CEPR Discussion Papers, 11529.

Global Futures (2020) A plan to improve and promote modern foreign languages. See https://gov.wales/global-futures-plan-improve-and-promote-modern-foreign-languages (accessed 10 May 2021).
Gorrara, C. (2018) Speaking from Wales: Building a modern languages community in the era of Brexit. In M. Kelly (ed.) *Languages after Brexit: How the UK Speaks to the World* (pp. 149–158). London: Palgrave Macmillan.
Graham, S.J. (2004) Giving up on modern foreign languages? Students' perceptions of learning French. *The Modern Language Journal* 88 (2), 171–191.
Graham, S. and Santos, D. (2015) Language learning in the public eye: An analysis of newspapers and official documents in England. *Innovation in Language Learning and Teaching* 9 (1), 72–85.
HEPI Report 123 (2019) A language crisis? (Megan Bowler). See https://www.hepi.ac.uk/wp-content/uploads/2020/01/HEPI_A-Languages-Crisis_Report-123-FINAL.pdf (accessed 16 March 2020).
Hogan-Brun, G. (2018) This post-Brexit linguanomics. In M. Kelly (ed.) *Languages after Brexit: How the UK Speaks to the World* (pp. 49–59). London: Palgrave Macmillan.
Holmes, B. (2018) Speaking to a global future: The increasing value of language and culture to British business post-Brexit. In M. Kelly (ed.) *Languages after Brexit: How the UK Speaks to the World* (pp. 61–74). London: Palgrave Macmillan.
Lanvers, U. (2017a) Contradictory others and the habitus of languages: Surveying the L2 motivation landscape in the United Kingdom. *The Modern Language Journal* 101 (3), 517–532.
Lanvers, U. (2017b) Elitism in language learning in the UK. In D. Rivers and K. Kotzmann (eds) *Isms in Language Education* (pp. 50–73). Berlin: De Gruyter.
Lanvers, U., Doughty, H. and Thompson, A.S. (2018) Brexit as linguistic symptom of Britain retreating into its shell? Brexit-induced politicization of language learning. *The Modern Language Journal* 102 (4), 775–796.
Lo Bianco, J. (2014) Domesticating the foreign: Globalization's effects on the place/s of languages. *The Modern Language Journal* 98 (1), 312–325.
Milton, J. and Meara, P. (1998) Are the British really bad at learning foreign languages? *Language Learning Journal* 18 (1), 68–76.
Mitchell, R. (2010) Policy and practice in foreign language education: Case studies in three European settings. *European Journal of Language Policy* 2 (2), 151–180.
Modiano, M. (2017) English in a post-Brexit European Union. *World Englishes* 36 (3), 313–327.
Northern Ireland Chamber of Commerce (2014) Exporting the challenge. See http://www.northernirelandchamber.com/wp-content/uploads/2014/02/Exporting-the-Challenge-February-2014.pdf (accessed 11 August 2020).
Phillipson, R. (2017) Myths and realities of European Union language policy. *World Englishes* 36 (3), 347–349.
Rampton, B. (1999) Deutsch in inner London and the animation of an instructed foreign language. *Journal of Sociolinguistics* 3 (4), 480–504.
Rhodes, C. (2016) Business statistics. House of Commons Library. Briefing Paper Number 06152, 23 November 2016.
Scottish Government (2012) Language Learning in Scotland: A 1 + 2 approach. See https://www.gov.scot/publications/language-learning-scotland-12-approach/ (accessed 10 May 2021).
Seargeant, P. (2017) The symbolism of English on the Brexit battleground. *World Englishes* 36 (3), 356–359.
Tinsley, T. (2018) Languages in English secondary schools post-Brexit. In M. Kelly (ed.) *Languages after Brexit: How the UK Speaks to the World* (pp. 127–136). London: Palgrave Macmillan.

Tinsley, T. and Board, K. (2017) Language trends 2016/17. Language teaching in primary and secondary schools in England. Survey Report. London: British Council. See https://www.britishcouncil.org/sites/default/files/language_trends_survey_2017_0.pdf(accessed 20 October 2017).

Wiley, T. (2000) Continuity and change in the functions of language ideologies in the United States. In T. Ricento (ed.) *Ideology, Politics and Language Policies: Focus on English* (pp. 67–86). Amsterdam: John Benjamins.

8 Vulnerabilities, Challenges and Risks in Sign Language Recognition in Canada

Kristin Snoddon and Erin Wilkinson

Introduction

This chapter explores the theme of vulnerabilities, challenges and risks in applied linguistics research from the perspective of sign language recognition in the Canadian context, where a national policy of official bilingualism in English and French has neglected so-called allophone (or immigrant) and Indigenous language speakers (Churchill, 2003), as well as deaf sign language users (see Conama, Chapter 4). On 21 June 2019, Bill C-81, An Act to Ensure a Barrier-Free Canada (also known as the Accessible Canada Act) received royal assent, the last step before a bill becomes law in Canada (Canada, 2019a). The version that passed into law featured several amendments to the bill that had earlier passed in the House of Commons and proceeded to the Senate. These amendments by the Senate included the addition of the following clarification to the section titled 'Purpose of the Act':

> 5.1 (2) American Sign Language, Quebec Sign Language and Indigenous sign languages are recognized as the primary languages for communication by deaf persons in Canada.

In the context of the Accessible Canada Act, sign language recognition takes place within a framework of communication barriers and the prevention and removal of such barriers by way of accessibility accommodations (i.e. sign language interpreters). In contrast, Bill C-91, An Act Respecting Indigenous Languages, which received royal assent on the same day as Bill C-81, includes Indigenous sign languages within the purpose and direct scope of the Act to support and promote the use of Indigenous languages and support the efforts of Indigenous peoples to reclaim, revitalize, maintain and strengthen Indigenous languages (Canada, 2019b).

These two different laws that, in different ways, recognize sign languages offer two distinct and contradictory perspectives on sign language rights, and as a corollary, on deaf people themselves as members of sign language communities. As this chapter argues, the vulnerabilities, challenges and risks inherent in viewing sign languages as disability accommodations include individualizing sign language rights to deaf persons as single disabled individuals rather than members of cultural and linguistic communities and reducing sign language rights to interpreter provision and funding. In contrast, the recognition of Indigenous sign languages offers promise for sign language rights that encompass language education initiatives and teaching materials, research, funding and monitoring by way of a Commissioner of Indigenous Languages. We discuss the diverse frameworks and processes of activism leading up to the passage of each bill, along with potential alignments and misalignments between the goals of deaf people and sign language policymakers in Canada and how these disparities may present vulnerabilities, challenges and risks in terms of advancing sign language rights. The next section provides more information about the context for the Accessible Canada Act.

Background: A Barrier-free Canada

In December 2016, media reports stated that official recognition of American Sign Language (ASL) and Langue des signes québécoise (LSQ) had emerged in the context of federal government consultations regarding the drafting of national accessibility legislation (Press, 2016). These reports and consultations took place following the Canadian government's 2007 signature and 2010 ratification of the United Nations Convention on the Rights of Persons with Disabilities (CRPD) and the 2016 ratification of the CRPD's Optional Protocol (Council of Canadians with Disabilities, 2016). Article 21 of the CRPD, regarding freedom of expression and opinion, and access to information, calls on governments to recognize and promote the use of sign languages. The media reports also referred to sign language recognition in other countries, namely 'New Zealand, Scotland, Finland, and Sweden as part of research about how the government could enact a similar federal law here' (Press, 2016). The Canadian Association of the Deaf–Association des Sourds du Canada (CAD-ASC), the country's main national deaf advocacy organization, which successfully lobbied for the Senate amendments to Bill C-81, has viewed federal accessibility legislation as a path toward granting ASL and LSQ recognition (The Daily Moth, 2018). On social media, CAD-ASC representatives made frequent references to sign language recognition legislation in other countries but not to the framing, scope or effectiveness of such legislation, which may have lent greater consideration to different possible pathways toward sign language recognition. This omission was perhaps due to the desire to capitalize on the federal government's consideration of sign language recognition during consultations leading up to the drafting of Bill C-81. However, most sign language recognition has been unsuccessful in terms of furthering the aims of deaf communities to promote deaf children's right to learn sign language from early childhood (Snoddon & Wilkinson, 2019).

On 20 June 2018, Bill C-81 was introduced in the House of Commons. The original text of Bill C-81 that was introduced and passed third reading in the House of Commons on 27 November 2018 made no mention of sign language. However, the bill that was eventually passed by the Senate on 13 May 2019 featured several amendments, including the addition of s. 51(2) that recognizes ASL, LSQ and Indigenous sign languages as primary languages for communication by deaf persons in Canada (Canada, 2019a). This subsection clarifies s. 5 regarding the purpose of the act 'to benefit all persons, especially persons with disabilities, through the realization … of a Canada without barriers, particularly by the identification and removal of barriers, and the prevention of new barriers'. The following areas fall under the scope of Bill C-81, with subsection c.1 as an amendment by the Senate:

(a) employment;
(b) the built environment;
(c) information and communication technologies;
(c.1) communication, other than information and communication technologies;
(d) the procurement of goods, services and facilities;
(e) the design and delivery of programs and services;
(f) transportation; and
(g) areas designated under regulations made under paragraph 117(1)(b).

The addition of subsection c.1 is said in government publications to relate to 'barrier-free services and spaces for persons with communication disabilities' (Employment and Social Development Canada, 2019). In our previous work, we speculated that the following provisions may be entailed by the bill:

- the translation of federal government documents into sign languages;
- the right of receiving federal services in ASL or LSQ via sign language interpreters;
- potentially increased provision of and funding for sign language interpreting for public institutions and services under federal jurisdiction; and
- sign language accessibility features in public transportation, broadcasting and telecommunications (Snoddon & Wilkinson, 2019).

However, the Senate amendments to s. 5.1 include the clarification that the area of communication referred to in paragraph 5(c.1) 'does not include broadcasting as defined in subsection 2(1) of the Broadcasting Act or telecommunications as defined in subsection 2(1) of the Telecommunications Act'. This means that sign language accessibility features in broadcasting and telecommunications, which occur with such provisions as video relay services that allow deaf individuals to make phone calls via sign language interpreters, do not fall under the remit of Bill C-81. Instead, these features may be covered by the Canadian Radio-television and Telecommunications Commission (CRTC) in separate regulations and statutes. The Canadian Transportation Agency, like the CRTC, is responsible for certain accessibility issues which otherwise would fall under the scope of the Accessible Canada Act. On the same day that Bill C-81 received royal assent, the Canadian Transportation Agency issued a news release about its enhanced enforcement powers and development of new regulations 'to help advance the accessibility of the national transport system' (Canadian Transportation Agency, 2019), although it did not address sign language accessibility features. However, a similar release regarding telecommunications and broadcasting was not issued until January 2020, when an external Broadcasting and Telecommunications Legislative Review Panel presented their report (Canada, 2020).

The panel's report, Canada's Communications Future: Time to Act (Minister of Industry, 2020), makes reference to 'sign language' in two sections dealing with video relay services as a mandated service by the CRTC (2020: 181). This acknowledgement of sign language in the panel's report is a step forward given that neither the Canadian Broadcasting Act (Canada, 1991a) nor the Telecommunications Act (Canada, 1993), which are part of the body of acts governing the CRTC, refer to sign languages (Canadian Radio-television and Telecommunications Commission, 2018). Canada's Communications Future recommends bringing both the Broadcasting and Telecommunications Acts together into a new framework under the jurisdiction of the CRTC, which would oversee all media content services (Minister of Industry, 2020: 11–12). This leads to the question of how media content services may be implemented for signing populations within the framework of sign language recognition. Article 21 of the UN CRPD, which deals with sign language recognition, refers to the following with specific reference to sign languages:

- providing information for the general public in accessible formats;
- urging private entities that provide services to the general public, including through the internet, to provide information and services in accessible formats; and
- encouraging the mass media to make their services accessible to persons with disabilities.

The CAD-ASC has presented for the Standing Committee responsible for rewriting the Broadcasting and Telecommunications Acts to request the inclusion of requirements for sign language interpretation in all publicly transmitted programming (J. Roots, personal communication, 19 June 2019). However, Canada's Communications Future refers to closed captioning and text message alerts for deaf and hard of hearing people rather than to providing information in sign language. Given the apparent prioritization of English or French text over sign language to ensure accessibility for deaf and hard of hearing people, this suggests some challenges of using a disability framework for advancing sign language rights. The exclusion of broadcasting and telecommunications from the scope of the Accessible Canada Act, with specific reference to sign language recognition, and the pending overhaul of legislation governing the CRTC that will presumably take up these responsibilities, therefore raises the question of how the Canadian government will meet its obligations under Article 21. However, it is possible that some deaf ASL/LSQ users and their advocacy organizations will be content with an increased visibility of sign language interpreters in public programming as evidence of the effectiveness of sign language recognition. This may in turn risk limiting future deaf community advocacy for more impactful sign language rights.

At the same time as CAD-ASC has focused on the inclusion of ASL and LSQ recognition in the Accessible Canada Act and on the provision of sign language interpreters, the Indigenous Languages Act has been regarded as a vehicle for recognition of Indigenous sign languages (Crescenzi, 2018). This point speaks to the differential treatment and understanding of sign languages used by Indigenous peoples vs those perceived to be used by non-Indigenous Canadians, as well as to the framing of ASL and LSQ in contrast to other minority languages. The next section of this chapter further outlines these issues.

The Legal (Mis)recognition of Indigenous Sign Languages

The framing of Indigenous sign languages in the debates leading up to the passage of the Accessible Canada Act raises several issues regarding Canadian deaf communities' and the Canadian public's understandings of these languages and language varieties. This lack of understanding may leave Indigenous deaf signers doubly vulnerable in terms of achieving their sign language rights. Little research exists that documents the language and communication practices of Indigenous deaf peoples in Canada. Data from the 2016 Canadian Census indicates that nearly half of signers view their language as neither ASL nor LSQ, which suggests there may be multiple undocumented sign language varieties (Snoddon & Wilkinson, 2019). However, little information is available regarding Indigenous sign languages as compared with research involving national sign languages, which typically emerged from schools for deaf children (Bickford & McKay-Cody, 2018). Exceptions are MacDougall (2001) and Schuit (2013), who describe an Indigenous sign language variety named Inuit Sign Language. Bickford and McKay-Cody (2018) and others describe Plains Indian Sign Language as an endangered, shared sign language historically used by non-deaf and deaf peoples. McKay-Cody (2019) discusses several other North American Indian Sign Language varieties, or hand talk, that are thousands of years old. However, these older, tribal shared sign languages were historically rejected by deaf residential schools and are not commonly passed down by elders to Indigenous deaf children today (McKay-Cody, 2019).

In addition, Indigenous sign languages were not originally included in CAD-ASC's activism. This omission can be seen in, for example, the bilingual logo adapted by CAD-ASC to 'recognize ASL/reconnaître LSQ', in a May 2019 vlog, and in the template letter provided by CAD-ASC for deaf communities to individual senators about including ASL and LSQ recognition in Bill C-81 (Canadian Association of the Deaf, 2019, n.d.). CAD-ASC's promotion of ASL and LSQ as sign languages of Canada in parallel with the official languages of English and French is reminiscent of efforts in other countries, such as Belgium, to mirror federal government spoken language policy in furthering the cause of sign language recognition (Snoddon & Wilkinson, 2019; Van Herreweghe *et al.*, 2016). In Belgium, the multiple sign language varieties used by deaf communities in Flanders and Wallonia have been reduced and distinguished by naming (as Flemish Sign Language, or VGT, and Langue des signes de Belgique francophone, or LSFB) and by separate sign language recognition legislation in the Flanders and Wallonia for the respective named varieties (Van Herreweghe *et al.*, 2016). Like in Canada, the coexistence of multiple sign language varieties has been overridden by political efforts to emulate spoken-language policies. In one sense, this can be seen as political expediency to promote the cause of sign language recognition, but these efforts may threaten the vitality of other sign language varieties (Skutnabb-Kangas, 2008).

Canadian official bilingualism policies also reinforce 'a specific racial and linguistic order' that marginalizes other languages, especially Indigenous languages (Kim *et al.*, 2019: 1) and maintains 'a white-settler nation' (Haque & Patrick, 2015: 27). This marginalization occurs in spite of the 1988 Canadian Multiculturalism Act (Canada, 1988a) and 1991 Canadian Heritage Languages Institute Act (Canada, 1991b) that recognize Indigenous languages as non-official but 'part of the linguistic heritage of Canada' (Site for Language Management in Canada, n.d.; Snoddon & Wilkinson, 2019). As Haque and Patrick (2015) note, the erasure of Indigenous languages can be traced to the 19th- and 20th-century Canadian residential school system for Indigenous children that sought to eradicate their languages. The Canadian government's Royal Commission on Bilingualism and Biculturalism, which led to the 1969 Official Languages Act (Canada, 1969) and subsequent multiculturalism policies, made no reference to Indigenous peoples in the Commission's terms of reference and reinforced 'a white-settler racial order based on English and French communities' (Haque & Patrick, 2015: 30).

The CAD-ASC's emulation of Canadian official bilingualism policies for framing sign language recognition has raised the challenge of how deaf Indigenous peoples and their sign languages are at risk of being rendered peripheral to ASL and LSQ users. This point relates to CAD-ASC's suggestion of separate legislation for recognizing ASL and LSQ under the Accessible Canada Act, and for recognizing Indigenous sign languages under the Indigenous Languages Act (The Daily Moth, 2018). If Bill C-81 was seen by a national deaf advocacy organization as an appropriate venue for the perceived mainstream recognition of sign languages aligned with white settlers, this suggests an underlying colonial framework where disability as a medical and colonial concept is centered (Ineese-Nash *et al.*, 2018). As Friedner (2019) notes, in disability frameworks such as the CRPD 'disability rights are largely individualized, abstracted, and devoid of interpersonal and providential bonds, and there is a focus on individual independence, accessibility, and inclusion without considering whether or not these concepts are salient in specific contexts' (2019: 407–408). Following this framework, sign language recognition is defined in terms of deaf individuals' access to communication and managing the provision of interpreters as a disability accommodation, rather than to Indigenous languages and cultural practices that are often viewed as sacred. In practice, a disability framework for sign language access rights may risk meaning only the right to an interpreter. Disability frameworks such as the CRPD have been less successful in promoting sign language-medium early childhood education or other initiatives that relate to sign language vitality. This is arguably in part because of how inclusive education has been interpreted by governments as mainstreaming deaf children (Snoddon & Murray, 2019), and in part because disability frameworks view early identification and intervention in medical terms and as tied to diagnoses of individual characteristics of the child (Underwood *et al.*, 2018). This is seen in the CRPD's classification of early intervention under Article 25 – Health instead of Article 24, which deals with education and calls on governments to facilitate the learning of sign language and promote the linguistic identity of the deaf community. This classification of early intervention in solely medical terms may place young deaf children's early sign language learning at risk since an optimal intervention for many deaf children includes parents' learning of sign language.

In contrast to the above framework, many Indigenous languages may have no word for 'disability' (Ineese-Nash *et al.*, 2018). Indigenous worldviews see disabilities as gifts and view individuals in relation to the community they inhabit (Ineese-Nash *et al.*, 2018). Following this, Indigenous sign languages have been used by, and viewed as belonging to, both deaf and hearing members of Indigenous communities (Flynn, n.d.). Indigenous sign languages may be discussed in terms of 'shared sign languages' or 'village sign languages' in communities that have different perspectives on deafness as compared with communities that use 'national sign languages' such as ASL and LSQ, which have typically been transmitted in schools for deaf children (Bickford & McKay-Cody, 2018). Thus, the recognition of Indigenous sign languages along with ASL and LSQ in the Accessible Canada Act as 'primary languages for communication by deaf persons' may be a misnomer and may place the ecologies of these languages at risk. These diverse community worldviews and challenges regarding the characterization of sign languages and deaf people are perhaps reflected in the different legislative timelines for including sign language recognition in Bill C-81 and C-91.

Timelines for Sign Language Recognition

The addition of Indigenous sign languages to Bill C-81 occurred following a 2 May 2019 motion by Senator Forest-Niesing, a Franco-Ontarian lawyer who has advocated for access to justice in both official languages (Trudeau, 2018) during a meeting of the Standing Senate Committee on Social Affairs, Science and Technology. As the Senator stated:

> You will see that although the testimony dealt mainly with American Sign Language and LSQ as the sign languages of communication by deaf persons in Ontario, my amendment proposes the addition of Indigenous sign language, whose existence I did not know of until recently. Given that it is the language of a significant and important component of our population, I believe it's important to recognize that language as well and to add it, in equal standing, to American Sign Language and LSQ as communication languages of deaf persons in Canada. (Canada, Parliament, Senate, 2019)

Similar references to a single 'Indigenous Sign Language' recurred in discussions surrounding the Senate amendments to Bill C-81 and led to speculation that some senators may have believed that Indigenous deaf people use a uniform sign language variety. As with our previous discussion of gaps in knowledge surrounding sign language use in Canada, based on 2016 Canada Census data, this may point to Canadian government officials' general lack of understanding of sign languages (Snoddon & Wilkinson, 2019).

Sign languages were added to Bill C-81 nearly one year after the bill's first reading in the House of Commons. In contrast, sign languages were added to Bill C-91 respecting Indigenous languages during its second reading in the House of Commons, which took place two months after this bill's first reading. Possible variables that expedited or prolonged the inclusion of sign languages in both bills may include CAD-ASC's desire to have ASL and LSQ recognized as official languages. Official language recognition that gives legal imperative to sign languages equal to that given to English and French is different from a resolution that recognizes sign languages as languages of deaf people (Snoddon & Wilkinson, 2019). Official recognition on this level has also been sought by Indigenous language activists (All Points West, 2015). However, neither Bill C-81 nor Bill C-91 confers official recognition on a par with the Official Languages Act's recognition of English and French. As stated by Carla Qualtrough, Minister of Public Services and Procurement and Accessibility, during the

Senate Standing Committee on Social Affairs, Science and Technology's first meeting to study Bill C-81 on 3 April 2019, recognizing sign languages as official languages was both beyond the scope of Bill C-81 and required changes to be made to the Canadian Charter of Rights and Freedoms (Barrier-Free Canada, 2019), which constitutionalizes the principle of equality between French and English, as well as to the Official Languages Act (Snoddon & Wilkinson, 2019). In its current form, the Official Languages Act (Canada, 1988b) ensures the equality of French and English in all federal institutions; supports the development of English- and French-minority communities and advances the status and use of English and French in Canadian society; and outlines the powers and duties of federal institutions with respect to official languages (Canada, 2009). Adding sign languages to the Official Languages Act requires broad consensus in the legislature and raises the need to address the fragmented nature of Canadian legislation that divides oversight of public services among various government departments (Roots, 2014).

Therefore, Bill C-81's recognition of sign languages not as official languages but as 'primary languages for communication by deaf persons' may be most meaningful as symbolic recognition within the framework of the Accessible Canada Act. In contrast, while the first reading of the Indigenous Languages Act on 5 February 2019 did not mention sign languages, on 1 April 2019 s. 5(a) regarding Purposes of Act was amended to 'support and promote the use of Indigenous languages, including Indigenous sign languages'. A letter dated 9 March 2019 from the Indigenous Sign Language Council under the British Columbia Hummingbird Society for the Deaf and addressed to the Standing Committee on Canadian Heritage attests to activism by Indigenous deaf communities regarding the inclusion of Indigenous sign languages in the Indigenous Languages Act (Indigenous Sign Language Council, 2019). This letter referred to two separate resolutions approved at the 2018 Annual General Assembly of the Assembly of First Nations regarding advocacy 'for disabilities as a central issue in all policy and program sectors ... as integral to restoring the human rights of First Nations persons with disabilities' (Resolution no. 24/2018) and regarding making future meetings and events accessible to all First Nations participants (Resolution no. 38/2018). While the CAD-ASC did not participate in lobbying for Indigenous sign language recognition in the Indigenous Languages Act, the letter from the Indigenous Sign Language Council (2019) attests to the organization receiving support from CAD-ASC. The letter also refers to both the 2007 United Nations Declaration on the Rights of Indigenous People's mention of 'the rights and special needs ... of persons with disabilities' (s. 21–22) and to the CRPD. In addition, Marsha Ireland, an Indigenous deaf elder and member of the Turtle clan from Oneida Nation of the Thames, played an instrumental role in the addition of Indigenous sign languages to the Indigenous Languages Act through her 19 February 2019 presentation to the Standing Committee on Canadian Heritage (Beatty, 2019).

The relatively rapid addition of Indigenous sign languages to the Indigenous Languages Act suggests that Indigenous organizations actively sought to accommodate sign languages and their users within the entire scope of Bill C-91, which is focused on revitalization of Indigenous languages. In the next section, we discuss how these diverse frameworks for recognizing sign languages may in turn impact sign language users in Canada and vulnerabilities, challenges and risks that these frameworks pose in terms of achieving sign language rights.

The Right to Use Sign Languages

In the context of the Accessible Canada Act, sign language recognition may not safeguard deaf Canadians' right to use sign language in the home (where some family members may not know sign language, since most deaf children have hearing parents and sign language tuition is not often readily available to the latter), school or other settings. This is aside from provisions and funding to ensure sign language interpretation in the context of the federal government and federal government services. Since Canadian provinces have jurisdiction over areas not under federal sovereignty, such as education, the impact of these provisions may be less influential than hoped (Canada, 2017). Moreover, this impact may be felt mainly by deaf adult signers, whose Charter rights are ostensibly fulfilled by sign language interpretation accommodations (Paul & Snoddon, 2017). On the other hand, Canadian deaf children's sign language rights in the home, child-care, education and recreation are unlikely to fall under the remit of the Accessible Canada Act.

In contrast, as legislation aimed at revitalization of what, owing to colonial policies and practices, are often highly endangered languages, the Indigenous Languages Act supports and promotes the right to learn and use Indigenous sign languages in various domains, including education. The federal government funds education for on-reserve First Nations students, while provincial governments are responsible for education for off-reserve Indigenous students. However, federal government funding for on-reserve First Nations education is not equal to that provided by provincial governments (Blackstock, 2019). Section 10(1) of the Indigenous Languages Act states that federal institutions may provide access to services in Indigenous languages if there is capacity and demand for access to these services. The law may therefore be most impactful on Indigenous deaf signers of all ages and may possibly have implications for non-Indigenous deaf signers through a trickle-up effect. However, it is less clear how Indigenous sign languages will be introduced in education for Indigenous deaf children given the history of colonial governments oppressing sign languages in Canadian deaf children's education. In the present day, ASL and LSQ are languages of instruction mainly in the small number of provincial schools for the deaf and are largely not provided for deaf children in mainstream classroom settings where most deaf students are enrolled (Snoddon, 2016). In our previous work, we raised the question of whether the Accessible Canada Act and its recognition of sign languages will apply to federally funded reserve schools to implement sign language-in-education policy for Indigenous deaf students (Snoddon & Wilkinson, 2019). With the passage of the Indigenous Languages Act, it is now an open question of whether Indigenous deaf students have the right to learn and use Indigenous sign languages in school regardless of whether their education falls under federal or provincial jurisdiction. However, because the Indigenous Languages Act falls under the remit of the Department of Canadian Heritage rather than Indigenous Services Canada, the Act faces challenges in terms of reaping immediate changes in Indigenous education (Leitch, 2019). This issue is timely since Indigenous Deaf students who have attended provincial schools for the deaf have 'experienced more acute cultural disjuncture in institutions that lacked any reflection of their home culture' (Smiler & McKee, 2007). This point regarding cultural dislocation is potent given the legacy of Canadian residential schools for Indigenous children and the contemporary need for some Indigenous deaf children to stay in residence at schools for the deaf owing to the remote location of their home communities.

The history of colonialism has rendered many Indigenous peoples more fluent in the white settler languages of English and French than Indigenous languages. Among Indigenous deaf signers, this may also be true of ASL and LSQ. Distinct ASL (and LSQ) varieties have been reported to be used by some Indigenous deaf people (J. Weber, personal communication) and may possibly be considered to fall under the mantle of Indigenous sign languages. This issue raises the additional challenge of whether the Indigenous Languages Act may provide for ASL and LSQ in Indigenous education for deaf learners, insofar as ASL and LSQ varieties as used by Indigenous deaf people are seen as Indigenous sign languages. The Act supports Indigenous language learning activities, programmes and research, and cooperation across governments and other entities to implement Indigenous language programmes and services (s. 8).

However, Canada has a grave shortage of deaf teachers (as well as non-deaf teachers fluent in sign languages) who can transmit sign languages in education for deaf learners (Snoddon, 2020). Indigenous deaf teachers are rare. If the Indigenous Languages Act were utilized to support Indigenous sign languages in teacher education for Indigenous deaf learners at Canadian post-secondary institutions, this could potentially revitalize and reorient teacher-of-the-deaf education, which in Canada has rarely supported teachers' sign language proficiency or the recruitment of deaf teachers (Snoddon, 2020). The next section of this chapter further outlines vulnerabilities, challenges and risks in applied linguistic research related to challenges in Indigenous sign language revitalization.

Revitalizing Indigenous Sign Languages

The Indigenous Languages Act will ensure that provisions are made for raising awareness and supporting the revitalization of Indigenous sign languages. On the same day that the Act received royal assent, the Minister of Canadian Heritage and Multiculturalism announced a budget of $330 million over five years and $115 million annually thereafter to support the Act's implementation (Canadian Heritage, 2019). There will also be an Office of the Commissioner of Indigenous Languages to fulfill the Act's mandate and 'support innovative projects and the use of new technologies in Indigenous language education and revitalization, in cooperation with Indigenous governments and other Indigenous governing bodies, Indigenous organizations, the Government of Canada and provincial and territorial governments' (s. 23[1][e]). However, given the limitations on funding provided by the Act, there are vulnerabilities and challenges involved in decision-making since sign language research has traditionally been neglected in terms of funding and resources. In addition, it is possible that, owing to a lack of access to information and participation in Indigenous communities (McKee *et al.*, 2006), Indigenous deaf peoples may not realize that funding is available for community-driven projects to revitalize Indigenous sign languages. Therefore, additional consideration may be needed for ensuring that Indigenous deaf communities have opportunities to participate in sign language research and teaching initiatives.

A common practice in language revitalization processes is developing partnerships between Indigenous communities and theoretical and/or applied linguistic researchers. However, this practice may carry additional challenges and vulnerabilities for Indigenous sign language revitalization since, to date, there are few Indigenous applied linguists in Canada who specialize in sign languages. Indigenous signing communities may therefore be in a position of seeking partnerships with either non-Indigenous sign language applied linguists with minimal background in Indigenous languages or linguists who specialize in Indigenous languages but have little knowledge of sign languages. These challenges may be reflected in other research regarding the development and promotion of Māori sign language in the context of New Zealand, where Māori and New Zealand Sign Language (NZSL) both enjoy official language status but Māori has more legal protections than NZSL (McKee *et al.*, 2006). The latter authors situate 'Māori signs' within the NZSL lexicon since 'there is no tradition of manual signs used by hearing Māori people as an alternate or complementary form of verbal communication' (McKee *et al.*, 2006: 31). McKee *et al.* (2006) describe processes of lexical borrowing from Māori into NZSL that are negotiated by hearing Māori speakers and deaf Māori signers of NZSL; interpreter-mediated communication by trilingual interpreters of Māori, NZSL, and English; and sign coinage by hearing Māori speakers. These accounts invite further reflection regarding ways to bridge gaps between Indigenous deaf signers, Indigenous non-deaf people, and applied linguists as community outsiders in order to revitalize endangered sign languages. This reflection should focus on strategies that respectfully include and enable Indigenous deaf signers to reclaim and revitalize sign languages.

One such community-driven project involves Oneida Sign Language, led by Marsha Ireland of the Turtle clan from Oneida Nation of the Thames as an Indigenous deaf elder with five deaf adult children and four deaf grandchildren (Albert, 2018). Ireland described feeling left out of community meetings when Oneida was spoken, even when a sign language interpreter was present. She also expressed the desire to transmit Oneida culture to her children and grandchildren (Albert, 2018). With support from the Oneida Language and Cultural Centre, Ireland and her partner as an interpreter worked with a master Oneida speaker to create signs corresponding to spoken Oneida words and work toward developing an Oneida Sign Language guidebook (Albert, 2018). She also discussed her hearing granddaughter, Grace Elijah, as a trilingual speaker and possible future interpreter of Oneida, sign language and English (Albert, 2018). While Ireland described making reference to Plains Indian Sign Language as a shared sign language historically used by non-deaf and deaf peoples, the effort to document and revitalize Oneida Sign Language holds promise for supporting Indigenous deaf peoples in reclaiming their Indigenous identities as inseparable from their identities as deaf signers (Smiler & McKee, 2007).

Conclusion

As in Māori communities and other Indigenous communities around the world, the proportion of Indigenous children and adults in Canada who are deaf is higher than in non-Indigenous communities (Smiler & McKee, 2007; Snoddon & Wilkinson, 2019). There is a corresponding need for more research regarding Indigenous deaf peoples' educational and linguistic practices and experiences (Snoddon & Wilkinson, 2019). The growth in Indigenous deaf populations and promise of greater support for Indigenous sign languages, as evidenced by the Indigenous Languages Act, suggests a potential revitalization of sign languages in a manner that may in some ways be distinct from macro-sign language communities that historically emerged from deaf residential schools established by white settlers. However, as the Indigenous Languages Act also attests, Indigenous language revitalization needs to work in tandem with new educational initiatives that account for Indigenous deaf children's sign language learning needs.

As this chapter has attempted to show, when mainstream deaf communities and their organizations fail to consider diverse deaf people's identities, cultural needs and experiences, they can reproduce power differentials from dominant cultures (Smiler & McKee, 2007). This chapter has outlined some vulnerabilities, challenges and risks in applied linguistics research related to sign language recognition in the Canadian context. These vulnerabilities include assumptions that the inclusion of sign language recognition in accessibility legislation will greatly impact and improve the life chances of deaf Canadians. This assumption seems tied to references to sign language recognition in other countries that fail to take into account the lack of success of this legislation in terms of securing educational linguistic rights (De Meulder & Murray, 2017). In this context, unexpectedly strong potential protections for Indigenous sign languages in Indigenous language legislation appear as a happy accident that may inadvertently have a trickle-up effect on non-Indigenous deaf peoples and their associated sign languages.

Unanswered questions include how the Indigenous Languages Act may be utilized to enforce sign language rights for deaf peoples given what appears to date to be the failure of the CRPD and other national sign language recognition legislation to enforce meaningful sign language rights that uphold deaf children's right to acquire and use sign languages in the home and school from early childhood. These questions are pervasive in the context of historical and ongoing educational inequities for both Indigenous and non-Indigenous deaf children in Canada. Further research should investigate possible mechanisms and initiatives that may optimize the efforts of Indigenous signing communities to reclaim, revitalize and preserve their sign languages.

References

Albert, A. (2018) Oneida sign language created to connect deaf community with their culture. *CBC News*. See https://www.cbc.ca/news/canada/london/oneida-sign-language-culture-deaf-1.4605295 (accessed 10 August 2020).

All Points West (2015) Indigenous languages in Canada can and should be made official, expert says. CBC News, 11 July. See http://www.cbc.ca/news/canada/british-columbia/Indigenous-languages-in-canada-can-and-should-be-made-official-expert-says-1.3147759 (accessed 10 August 2020).

Barrier-Free Canada (2019) Senate Standing Committee on Social Affairs, Science and Technology first meeting to study Bill C-81, 4 April. See http://barrierfreecanada.org/senate-standing-committee-on-social-affairs-science-and-technology-first-meeting-to-study-bill-c-81-april-3-2019/ (accessed 10 August 2020).

Beatty, J. (2019) Standing Committee on Canadian Heritage (CHPC): Marsha Ireland and Max Ireland as individuals: Oneida Nation and Turtle Clan, 14 May. See https://www.facebook.com/jeffrey.beatty.94/posts/10156833771850862 (accessed 10 August 2020).

Bickford, A. and McKay-Cody, M. (2018) Endangerment and revitalization of sign languages. In L. Hinton, L. Huss and G. Roche (eds) *The Routledge Handbook of Language Revitalization*. New York: Routledge.

Blackstock, C. (2019) When will Ottawa end its willful neglect of First Nations children? *The Globe and Mail*, 16 July. See https://www.theglobeandmail.com/opinion/article-when-will-ottawa-end-its-willful-neglect-of-first-nations-children/ (accessed 10 August 2020).

Canada (1969) Official Languages Act, SC 1969.
Canada (1988a) Canadian Multiculturalism Act, SC 1988, c 31.
Canada (1988b) Official Languages Act, RSC 1988, c 38.
Canada (1991a) Canadian Broadcasting Act, S.C. 1991, c. 11.
Canada (1991b) Canadian Heritage Languages Institute Act, SC 1991, c 7.
Canada (1993) Telecommunications Act, S.C. 1993, c. 38.
Canada (2009) 40 Years of the Official Languages Act, 9 September 9. See https://www.canada.ca/en/news/archive/2009/09/40-years-official-languages-act.html (accessed 10 August 2020).
Canada (2017) Creating new federal accessibility legislation: What we learned, 10 August. See https://www.canada.ca/en/employment-social-development/programs/accessible-people-disabilities/reports/consultations-what-we-learned.html (accessed 10 August 2020).
Canada (2019a) An act to ensure a barrier-free Canada, SC 2019 c 10.
Canada (2019b) An act respecting Indigenous languages, SC 2019 c 23.
Canada (2020) Broadcasting and telecommunications legislative review. See https://www.ic.gc.ca/eic/site/110.nsf/eng/home (accessed 10 August 2020).
Canada, Parliament, Senate (2019) Standing Senate Committee on Social Affairs, Science and Technology. SOCI Meeting no. 136, 2 May. http://senparlvu.parl.gc.ca/XRender/en/PowerBrowser/PowerBrowserV2/20190502/-1/8882 (accessed 10 August 2020).
Canadian Association of the Deaf (2019) Last Steps of Bill C-81 (ASL) – Les dernières étapes du projet de loi C-81 (LSQ) [video file], 14 May 14. See https://youtu.be/pefz-kVmq-bM (accessed 10 August 2020).
Canadian Association of the Deaf (n.d.) *Senate of Canada – Template Letter.* See http://cad.ca/senate-of-canada-template-letter/?fbclid=IwAR2I9e7UcxTW7_W945Smbce EdvNNwZ0gnslHNwldes-zQ4oTMqILgJfsH4w (accessed 10 August 2020).
Canadian Heritage (2019) The Indigenous Languages Act receives royal assent, 21 June. See https://www.canada.ca/en/canadian-heritage/news/2019/06/the-indigenous-languages-act-receives-royal-assent.html (accessed 10 August 2020).
Canadian Radio-television and Telecommunications Commission (2018) Statutes and regulations. See https://crtc.gc.ca/eng/statutes-lois.htm (accessed 10 August 2020).
Canadian Transportation Agency (2019) Canadian Transportation Agency announces plans to enhance accessibility of Canada's national transportation system, 21 June. See https://www.otc-cta.gc.ca/eng/content/canadian-transportation-agency-announces-plans-enhance-accessibility-canadas-national (accessed 10 August 2020).
Churchill, S. (2003) *Language Education, Canadian Civic Identity, and the Identities of Canadians.* Strasbourg: Council of Europe Language Policy Division.
Council of Canadians with Disabilities (2016) Canada to Ratify CRPD's Optional Protocol, 23 December. See http://www.ccdonline.ca/en/international/un/canada/CRPD-OP-23Dec2016 (accessed 10 August 2020).
Crescenzi, N. (2018) BC deaf community wants different sign languages on federal accessibility act. Castelgar News, 22 September. See https://www.castlegarnews.com/news/b-c-deaf-community-wants-different-sign-languages-on-federal-accessibility-act/ (accessed 10 August 2020).
De Meulder, M. and Murray, J.J. (2017) Buttering their bread on both sides? The recognition of sign languages and the aspirations of deaf communities. *Language Problems & Language Planning* 41 (2), 136–158.
Employment and Social Development Canada (2019) Making an accessible Canada for persons with disabilities, 28 June. See https://www.canada.ca/en/employment-social-development/programs/accessible-people-disabilities.html?fbclid=IwAR1JDV_HAbXUgnaHiEMe5ln9iW-6oiRqIdUw-gPrcdHyez_5srFS_mtdJEo (accessed 10 August 2020).
Flynn, D. (n.d.) Indigenous sign languages in Canada. See https://www.ucalgary.ca/dflynn/sign (accessed 10 August 2020).

Friedner, M. (2019) Praying for rights: Cultivating deaf worldings in urban India. *Anthropological Quarterly* 92 (2), 403–426.

Haque, E. and Patrick, D. (2015) Indigenous languages and the racial hierarchisation of language policy in Canada. *Journal of Multilingual and Multicultural Development* 36 (1), 27–41.

Indigenous Sign Language Council (2019) Letter to the Standing Committee on Canadian Heritage Re: Support for Indigenous sign languages, 9 March. See https://www.ourcommons.ca/Content/Committee/421/CHPC/Brief/BR10366021/br-external/BCHum mingbirdSocietyOfTheDeaf-e.pdf?fbclid=IwAR0_mCBMlGhEJrjcjteGxbDRp4m-8e 5828NMQcxM3d1_1KBoLxiQdIQIyqY (accessed 10 August 2020).

Ineese-Nash, N., Bomberry, Y., Underwood, K. and Hache, A. (2018) Raising a child with early childhood disability supports. *Indigenous Policy Journal* 28 (3), 1–14.

Kim, H., Burton, J.L., Ahmed, T. and Bale, J. (2019) Linguistic hierarchisation in education policy development: Ontario's Heritage Languages Program. *Journal of Multilingual and Multicultural Development* 41 (4), 320–332. DOI: 10.1080/01434632.2019.1618318.

Leitch, D.G. (2019) Indigenous language rights: Moving beyond C-91. Paper presented at the *National Colloqium on Canada's Indigenous Languages Policy in the Wake of Bill C-91*, Glendon College, York University, Toronto.

MacDougall, J.C. (2001) Access to justice for deaf Inuit in Nunavut: The role of 'Inuit sign language'. *Canadian Psychology/Psychologie canadienne* 42 (1), 61–73.

McKay-Cody, M.R. (2019) Memory comes before knowledge – North American Indigenous Deaf: Socio-cultural study of rock/picture writing, community, sign languages, and kinship (unpublished doctoral dissertation). University of Oklahoma, Norman, OK.

McKee, R., McKee, D., Smiler, K. and Pointon, K. (2006) Māori signs: The construction of Indigenous deaf identity in New Zealand Sign Language. In D. Quinto-Pozos (ed.) *Sign Languages in Contact. Sociolinguistics in Deaf Communities Series* 13 (pp. 31–81). Washington, DC: Gallaudet University Press.

Minister of Industry (2020) *Canada's Communications Future: Time to Act*. Ottawa, ON: Innovation, Science and Economic Development Canada. https://www.ic.gc.ca/eic/site/110.nsf/eng/00012.html (accessed 10 August 2020).

Paul, J.J. and Snoddon, K. (2017) Framing deaf children's right to sign language in the Canadian Charter of Rights and Freedoms. *Canadian Journal of Disability Studies* 6 (1), 1–27. https://doi.org/10.15353/cjds.v6i1.331.

Press, J. (2016) Sign language being considered as third official language: Documents. Maclean's, 1 December. See http://www.macleans.ca/politics/sign-language-being-considered-asthird-official-language-documents/ (accessed 10 August 2020).

Roots, J. (2014) Sign language rights. Presentation for *ALDS 3903: Sign Language Planning and Policy*, 9 November, Carleton University, Ottawa, Ontario.

Schuit, J. (2013) Signs of the Arctic: Typological aspects of Inuit Sign Language. (Unpublished doctoral dissertation.) University of Amsterdam, The Netherlands.

Site for Language Management in Canada (n.d.) Legal framework. See https://slmc.uottawa.ca/?q=native_legal (accessed 10 August 2020).

Skutnabb-Kangas, T. (2008) Bilingual education and Sign Language as the MT of deaf children. In C.J.K. Bidoli and E. Ochse (eds) *English in International Deaf Communication* (pp. 75–96). London: Routledge.

Smiler, K. and McKee, R.L. (2007) Perceptions of Māori deaf identity in New Zealand. *Journal of Deaf Studies and Deaf Education* 12 (1), 93–111.

Snoddon, K. (2016) Whose ASL counts? Linguistic prescriptivism and challenges in the context of parent sign language curriculum development. *International Journal of Bilingual Education and Bilingualism* 21 (8), 1004–1015.

Snoddon, K. (2020) Sign language planning and policy in Ontario teacher education. *Language Policy*. https://doi.org/10.1007/s10993-020-09569-7.

Snoddon, K. and Murray, J.J. (2019) The Salamanca Statement and sign language education for deaf learners 25 years on. *International Journal of Inclusive Education* 23, 7–8, 740–753, DOI: 10.1080/13603116.2019.1622807.

Snoddon, K. and Wilkinson, E. (2019) Problematizing the legal recognition of sign languages in Canada. *Canadian Modern Language Review* 75 (2), 128–144.

The Daily Moth (2018) Deaf Canadians rally for sign language recognition, 28 September. See https://www.youtube.com/watch?v=SBNtb7LtvGY (accessed 10 August 2020).

Trudeau, J. (2018) Prime Minister announces the appointment of two senators, 11 October. See https://pm.gc.ca/eng/news/2018/10/11/prime-minister-announces-appointment-two-senators (accessed 10 August 2020).

Underwood, K., Frankel, E., Spalding, K. and Brophy, K. (2018) Is the right to early intervention being honoured? A study of family experiences with early childhood intervention services. *Canadian Journal of Children's Rights* 5 (1), 56–70.

Van Herreweghe, M., De Meulder, M. and Vermeerbergen, M. (2016) From erasure to recognition (and back again?): The case of Flemish sign language. In M. Marschark and P.E. Spencer (eds) *The Oxford Handbook of Deaf Studies in Language* (pp. 45–61). New York: Oxford University Press.

Part 3
Research

9 From the Outside Looking in: The Risks and Challenges of Analysing Extremist Discourses on Far-right and Manosphere Websites

Kate Barber

Introduction

The use of the internet by extreme right-wing groups is nothing new (see, for example, Conway *et al.*, 2019; Hale, 2012) although its use by extremists has traditionally been in conjunction with activity organised on the ground (e.g. marches, meetings or organised events; Mudde, 2000). While some far-right organisations still operate in this way, the emergence of the Alternative Right (Alt-Right), which operates predominantly online, has redefined far-right extremism and enabled radical white male nationalists to unify (Neiwert, 2017: 258). The affordances of the online environment have similarly united a range of men's rights groups: from those campaigning against the repression of traditional gender roles to those which define themselves through extreme misogyny, blaming feminism for the perceived emasculation and degradation of men. These collectives are together known as the *manosphere* (a term coined in 2009 on the blog *The Manosphere*). Through a series of online campaigns, the Alt-Right and the manosphere are growing closer in their expression of 'hostile sexism', a term Mudde uses to describe the combination of 'toxic masculinity' – in which manhood is defined by violence, sex, status and aggression – and misogyny (Mudde, 2019: 150). This expression often takes the form of hate speech, sexually explicit reframing of rape and sexual assault and recontextualised news reports on rape cases and is reported through various blogs, websites, mainstream social media platforms and forums.

This chapter contains sensitive and potentially offensive content in order to discuss the challenges and risks associated with doing research on extreme discourses found online. These risks include those posed to researchers on an emotional level but also risks connected to contravening established ethical protocols for research, and those which may infringe the rights of the extremists themselves. These insights are based on my experiences collecting data for a corpus-assisted critical discourse analysis of Alt-Right and manosphere blogs, which examines the indexing of identity and use of narratives within these online, Anglophone spaces. The chapter starts off by giving an overview of these two extremist groups, more accurately referred to as 'factions' (DiSalvo, 2012), and the challenges of collecting data from such fluid, amorphous online communities. The remainder of the chapter looks at the personal and professional risks and challenges of analysing extremist discourses online, beginning with a focus on the ethical issues surrounding this type of research and how meeting future ethical requirements in the long-term may be problematic. The difficulties of analysing communities with values at the opposite end of the spectrum from my own – addressing the *emic* and *etic* debate – will also be discussed. The chapter ends with an honest reflection on the value of studying the discourses of extremist organisations and whether the risks of studying such pernicious texts are worth taking.

The Discourses of the Alt-Right and the Manosphere

Before outlining the type of discourses associated with the extremism of the Alt-Right and the manosphere, it is perhaps worthwhile clarifying what is meant by *extremism* in the context of this study. The official, and somewhat sanitised, definition put forward by the UK government's counter-extremism policy paper is that it includes 'the vocal or active opposition to our fundamental values, including democracy, the rule of law, individual liberty and the mutual respect and tolerance of different faiths and beliefs' (H.M. Government, 2015: 9). The manifestation of this opposition is often exhibited in terms of an in-group's belief that hostile action, violence or discrimination is necessary against an out-group for the in-group's survival (Berger, 2018: 44). Conway *et al.* conceptualise Western right-wing extremism as 'a racially, ethnically, and/or sexually defined nationalism, which is typically framed in terms of white power and/or white identity (i.e. the in-group) that is grounded in xenophobic and exclusionary understandings of the perceived threats posed by some combination of non-whites, Jews, Muslims, immigrants, refugees, members of the LGBTQI+ community, and feminists (i.e. the out-group(s))' (Conway *et al.*, 2019: 3). This definition of extremism can be mapped onto a range of ideologies promoted by far-right factions, as will be seen below.

The Alternative Right (Alt-Right)

Having remained very much on the fringe of public and political consciousness until 2015 and only emerging into mainstream discussions in

2016, very little academic research has been published on the Alt-Right. Hawley, one of the first academics to write on this movement, points out that getting any reliable information on such a loosely defined faction, whose default is to cause chaos, confusion and deliberate distortion of the truth, makes even what is supposedly known about the Alt-Right fallible (Hawley, 2017: 75). The movement was defined by American White Nationalist Richard Spencer in 2009 (Neiwert, 2017: 236) and has been influenced by historical ideologies from far-right European movements and as well as those in the US. Defining its current policies and updated ideologies, however, is particularly difficult. Unlike traditional right-wing organisations which may have dedicated websites and/or literature (e.g. *The Daily Stormer* for the White Nationalists or *The Klansman* for the White Separatists), the Alt-Right has no written manifesto, no clear structure and defines itself more by what it does than by what it says (Wendling, 2018). This is often in the form of online trolling and being in it *for the lulz* (an adulteration of *laugh out loud*), encompassing unrestrained amusement at the expense of others, which forms the key element of transgressive humour aimed at celebrating 'the anguish of the laughed at victim' (Phillips, 2015: 27). Much of this reactionary trolling originated on the anonymous message board, 4chan – a site synonymous with internet memes, pranks and an 'anything goes' ethos (Neiwert, 2017: 232) and which is home to neo-Nazi and white supremacist material, pornography and homophobic hate speech, and is a sanctuary for paedophiles (Neiwert, 2017).

Despite its amorphous form and lack of discernible policy, repeated rhetorical discourses often surface on Alt-Right sites, with immigrants and feminists as their main targets. Rhetoric relating to rape and sexual assault includes opposing the concept of rape within marriage (Nagle, 2017: 93); men being deliberately targeted by '"systemic" false rape allegations' (Burley, 2017: 84); and denying that date rape exists (Wendling, 2018: 70). Looking through online sites which identify as Alt-Right, readers are also presented with the regular tropes of the sexually deviant and dangerous immigrant (most often referred to as a 'rapefugee') and the sexually frustrated feminist who is asking to be raped.

The Manosphere

Also argued to have been influential on 4chan (Neiwert, 2017: 232), particularly for its misogynistic trolling (Ging *et al.*, 2020: 841), the manosphere mirrors the Alt-Right in its lack of coordinated form. Described as 'a loose confederacy of interest groups' (Ging, 2019: 639) made up of men's rights activists, the Pick Up Artist (PUA) community, men identifying as involuntary celibates (incels) and the men's separatist movement (Men Going Their Own Way – MGTOWs), their unifying belief is in the need to fight back against the domination of feminine values and a misandrist culture perpetuated by feminists (Marwick & Caplan, 2018: 546).

While fathers' rights, male suicide and men's health issues are regarded as vital, worthy issues which legitimise parts of the manosphere, its 'customarily extreme right wing ... hate-filled, resentment-fuelled cultures of quite chilling levels of misogyny' (Nagle, 2017: 86), along with its focus on male victimhood, align it closely with the Alt-Right (Anti-Defamation League, 2018: 6).

A number of events have brought the manosphere and the Alt-Right to the mainstream media's attention. In 2013, the 4chan-driven misogynistic reaction to women's influence in video gaming, known as *Gamergate* (Neiwert, 2017: 233), moved both factions into mainstream consciousness when prominent female gamers and reviewers received online abuse and death threats. Then in 2014, Elliot Rodger, who self-identified as belonging to the incel movement, killed six people and injured 14 others in a revenge attack in Isla Vista, California (Marwick & Caplan, 2018: 46). Rodger's main motive for the killing was based on seeking punishment against women for their disinterest in him.

The Project

Although both the Alt-Right and the manosphere ostensibly focus on two different concerns (the former on race and the latter on men's rights), they overlap in the anti-feminist rhetoric they espouse. Both reframe rape and sexual assault in ways that further their ideologies (Gotell & Dutton, 2016); however, little linguistic analysis has been carried out as to how this manifests within their online content. As the manosphere has been described as the gateway into the Alt-Right (Romano, 2016), an examination of the narrative strategies in rape and sexual assault discourse may help determine a linguistic as well as ideological connection between these factions. Similarly, understanding the identities inhabited and ascribed in both the Alt-Right and manosphere discourses on rape and sexual assault could establish how counter-narrative strategies can be used to challenge these accounts.

Data collection

The data for my research are derived from websites and blogs from both the Alt-Right and the manosphere which contain references to rape and sexual assault between 2016 and 2017. Given the abundance of potential sources of discourse online, pinpointing and selecting texts can itself be challenging. For my research, it was necessary to identify websites which shared an ideological affinity – those that espoused far-right ideologies and those that promoted misogynistic views. To locate sources that explicitly identified as Alt-Right and manosphere, and to determine which of these shared any ideological affinity, it was necessary to carry out a network analysis, enabling coding for self-identification and content.

Using two Alt-Right aggregator sites (http://theshitlordhub.blogspot.com and http://nxx14.blogspot.com) as my starting point, I constructed the network analysis for my project by using the sites they recommended as promoting Alt-Right ideologies. A total of 707 sites were recorded and were tagged for content and self-identifying features. These *nodes* were then numbered and revisited and the links (or *edges*) between the sites were recorded (a total of 4492 edges). The data were uploaded into *Gephi*, a network visualisation tool, to create the far-right network offering an insight into where I could focus my discourse selection. From this visual representation, I was able to choose the Alt-Right sites which showed the closest online affinity to manosphere sites and narrowed down my selection to the five with the most traffic (using a website traffic checker).

A total of 100 articles were collected from my chosen data sources (giving 83,661 tokens), allowing for the manual XML mark-up of the corpus for analysis (Hardie, 2014). Using Sketch Engine, the collective identities in the discourses and attitudes towards them were categorised and analysed using frameworks adopted from Koller (2012) and van Dijk (1984). Through this corpus-assisted critical discourse analysis, my research looks at the extent to which the Alt-Right and the manosphere share representations of women; how they collectively represent sexual violence; and whether the constructed narratives on rape and sexual assault indicate overlapping ideological belief systems based on hostile sexism.

Ethical Challenges and Personal Risk

Gaining ethical clearance for this project involved completing a detailed risk assessment. I had been advised not to use my own computer to access the extremist sites as there was a risk that my online search activity would be flagged by national security services. Using the university's network offered a level of safeguarding against this, especially as there would be an academic 'paper trail' to support my motivations for searching far right websites. A designated workstation was set up for me from which I could view sites usually blocked on the university network. The position of the workstation was such that it ensured that my screen could not be seen by those with whom I share office space.

Through the process of gaining ethical clearance, a number of key ethical issues arose, some of which have been particularly challenging to overcome. These included: (1) the issue of the *publicness* (Spilioti, 2017) of the discourses being collected and problematising the concept of *vulnerable participants* (Granholm & Svedmark, 2018); (2) the issue of whether presenting the research equates to the promotion or dissemination of hateful, racist, ideologies, particularly if the site has been taken down; and (3) personal resilience and desensitisation to extreme hate. Despite the growing body of work now published on approaches to take to tackle these kinds of ethical challenges associated with mediated discourses (see, for example, Bolander & Locher, 2014; Markham & Buchanan, 2015; Spilioti & Tagg, 2017), there is no set policy or procedure available for researchers and tackling them is very much on a case-by-case basis (Page, 2017: 316). Official recommendations from the British Association for Applied Linguists (2016) and the Association of Internet Researchers advise the researcher to use ethical judgement, to work with integrity and to employ a 'reflective, dialogical process-oriented approach' to ethical decision making (Association of Internet Researchers, 2019: 23). With that in mind, the ways in which I navigated each of these challenges are discussed in the following sections.

The 'publicness' of the data and 'vulnerable participants'

Much has been written on the publicness of online data, particularly whether discourses taken from computer-mediated communication (CMC), for example on social media platforms like Twitter and Facebook, are considered in the public or private domain (see, for example, Bolander & Locher, 2014; Mackenzie, 2017; Spilioti, 2017). As Bolander and Locher point out with regard to CMC, understandings of whether the communication is public or private have changed, with the focus no longer solely on how it is accessed but also now on its content (Bolander & Locher, 2014: 17, see also Giaxoglou, 2017). In Markham and Buchanan's discussion on the status of blogs, they have found the public/private division similarly complex: 'Blogs are often considered public, published texts. On the other hand, users have described their blogs as a part of their identity, not to be treated as simply publicly accessible data' (Markham & Buchanan, 2012: 13 footnote). Conversely, they found that anonymising data collected from blogs may infringe on the author's desire to have their opinions attributed (Markham & Buchanan, 2012: 10).

From a legalistic perspective, the presence of intellectual property marks on the blogs in this project meant that attribution was necessary. Any reference to data taken from them has been clearly attributed in the form of the URL, the name of the blog or an individual author. As Pihlaja (2017) points out, however, there are a number of grey areas in using copyrighted material collected from CMC, particularly from sites considered sensitive (in his study this included material from adult video webpages) and the issue of attribution is not always straightforward. The concept of *fair use*, which allows for 'relatively insubstantial parts of copyrighted materials to be used for purposes such as research, education, review, etc.' (Weisser, 2016: 33) also applies here but the question remains as to what constitutes *relatively insubstantial parts*.

With the complexities of the online public/private distinction in mind, Bolander and Locher put forward six ethical principles for reconciling the publicness of CMC and the ethical principles guiding its use, three of which are relevant here: the vulnerability of the language producers' needs to be taken into account; care needs to be taken to ensure no harm is caused; and ethical issues need to be revisited and considered at every stage of the research process (Bolander & Locher, 2014: 17–18). A key source used in my project to address these three concerns was that of Rüdiger and Dayter (2017), whose research on the PUA community mirrors my own. Their examination on the ethics of researching 'unlikeable subjects' highlights the difficulties of applying a strict public/private dichotomy to CMC discourses from communities such as PUAs. They argue that the community itself seeks media coverage (2017: 257) to promote their work. Although they acknowledge that ethical responsibilities towards the community still exist (Rüdiger & Dayter, 2017), this willingness to be part of the public sphere somewhat mitigates the need for the participants to be treated as vulnerable.

Rüdiger and Dayter posit a lack of vulnerability in the men in their study based on the white, male, aggressive identity they project online – an identity which is reflected in the authors of the texts I am using in my study. However, Spilioti and Tagg point out that, regardless of the researcher's personal view of the language producer, it is problematic to try to distinguish between communities which deserve data protection and those that do not (Spilioti & Tagg, 2017: 166). If vulnerability is interpreted to mean susceptibility to harm (and 'harm' is to be defined contextually; Markham & Buchanan, 2015: 607), then it is unlikely the extremist authors will experience this mentally or physically. However, they may well be legally vulnerable outside of the online communities within which they exist and where they are protected by free speech laws. This became an issue for the PUA Daryush Valizadeh, known as Roosh V, who was banned from entering the UK in 2016 after there were protests against him being able to advocate his views on rape in 'meet ups' for men across UK cities. Exposing these authors in contexts outside those in which they were originally writing online, for example, in an academic paper of conference, could, arguably, make them vulnerable. Following the principle that ethical decision-making should take place at every step of the process, this is certainly something that needs to be considered when the results of this project, and those like it, are disseminated.

Disseminating extreme ideologies

A particularly difficult challenge to overcome with regard to this project on extremist discourses relates to the question of whether I am disseminating the hateful rhetoric present in my datasets. Could simply acknowledging and reproducing the extreme views put forward in the discourses I collected be considered a type of promotion of the authors' racist and misogynistic values? As highlighted below in the discussion on representing the authors' voices, balancing researcher bias against objectivity and normalising extremist views is not an easy task. Related to this is the risk of revictimising the women used as examples in the online discourses. As McEnery and Hardie highlight, 'Less obvious than the privacy of the speakers in a corpus, but nonetheless important, is the privacy of the people talked about in the corpus' (McEnery & Hardie, 2012: 62). The risk of exploiting the women further, in a wider, offline context, is a particular worry. Their names frequently appear in my corpus search results and I have to be careful to anonymise them at every stage of the writing up process.

Another point concerning the dissemination of extreme material relates to whether the site from which it came has been shut down. Since collecting my data, three out of the five websites have been put on hiatus by the owners themselves. In the scant details given on the sites, this decision seems to have come from difficulties with the platform provider and cuts in advertising revenue owing to the offensive content. Spilioti (2017) and Pihlaja (2017) question the ethics of using material collected from sites which are no longer available and the importance of adjusting the way this material is then disseminated. The posts collected for my project are still available as individual posts through a search of the post title and author, despite the blog no longer being updated. However, if and when it is no longer possible to access the original source, I will have to make it clear that the content has been removed from public view. Bearing this in mind along with whether it should make any difference as to who removes digital content (i.e. whether it would make a difference if the platform provider, security services or search engine prevented access to the original form of the data) is something that I will need to consider in the future as it is highly likely that my data sources will be made unavailable.

Researcher desensitisation and resilience

Arguably, the most pressing ethical issue regarding projects on extremism is the toll it can take on the researcher themselves. While it is true that distance is created between the researcher and those in the far right if conducting an online study of extremism, as opposed to ethnographic, 'close up' research in the field (Pearson, 2019; Pilkington, 2016), it is, nonetheless, unsettling to be confronted with the material posted online. The process of creating my network analysis and identifying the target area of online blogs from which I could collect my data was particularly harrowing. In order to log and classify the 707 sites, I had to enter a world where there were very few limits on what could be expressed and discussed. A list of the more extreme material I encountered through this process included: graphic photos of people who had died by suicide; photos of murder victims; sexually explicit images (for example, point-of-view pornographic material); shaming pages, used to humiliate the (often ex-)girlfriends of those posting the content and which usually included graphic images of them in sexual positions; photos from Jewish concentration camps and a range of Nazi imagery and memorabilia; and seemingly innocent photos of young children but in poses or positions which enabled easy photoshopping and manipulation for paedophiles. The images accompanying these types of posts are impossible to unsee. The final data sources for the corpora selected through the sampling frame are significantly less explicit and extreme but contain language derogating women, use sexual assault in humour and discuss the extermination of minorities. It is easy to acknowledge that more distressing research is being carried out elsewhere by applied linguists, perhaps those looking at child grooming online or those analysing legal documents from trials involving particularly violent crimes. However, being exposed to the dark views offered from within the extremist's world certainly tests emotional resilience. Some of the issues that have been raised by academics researching extremism online range from experiencing vicarious trauma to feelings of guilt at being able to deal with harrowing material from a safe 'ivory tower' and reduce such violence to data (Allam, 2019). For me personally, I found it difficult to dismiss the feeling of wanting to defend the women who were being so aggressively targeted and having their reputations ripped apart in order to advance extreme misogynistic viewpoints.

Granholm and Svedmark, in their paper on researching vulnerable populations online, highlight the challenges involved in dealing with distressing online material and how emotional engagement is unavoidable (Granholm & Svedmark, 2018: 508). They question the level of institutional safeguarding made available to researchers involved in these types of projects and reiterate that, ultimately, it is the responsibility of the researcher to ensure that their emotional wellbeing is protected (Granholm & Svedmark, 2018: 507). The risk assessment filed for this research project on far-right extremism included an express obligation to consider attending the university's counselling services, with quarterly updates on how I was coping with the data collection. The risk of being radicalised was also discussed (as outlined in the Prevent Scheme; H.M. Government, 2015), with supervisors needing to be aware of any attitudinal or behavioural changes they might see. Allam's (2019) article interviewing academics looking at extreme misogynistic texts details a range of personal coping mechanisms which include viewing pictures and videos in black and white, being open with colleagues about the effect the research is having and incorporating daily escapism – in the case of one researcher, by 'defeating evil' in video games. Rüdiger and Dayter's coping mechanism was to set up a separate file to keep their most disturbing data in one place (2017: 263). For me, exercise and playing games with young family members gave me the escapism I needed.

Further aspects of researcher vulnerability and risk were included in the risk assessment. These included taking care to ensure that any future reference to the research is presented objectively and to limit reference to the research on social media sites. The very real risk of trolling, online threats and backlash from far-right supporters and those who feel exposed by academic scrutiny of their ideologies means that care has to be taken at every stage of the research process.

Perhaps less obvious at the time the project started was the risk of what Winter (2018) terms *amplifying the extreme* and the feelings of guilt for not focusing on more integral misogynistic and racist rhetoric. As Winter points out, there are a number of issues related to focusing on the far right and other extremist organisations:

> These include the risk of elevating and amplifying the 'extreme' and the threat that it poses, and distracting from or ignoring mainstream, state, institutional, structural and everyday racisms that can fuel the far-right or be rendered more acceptable, legitimate or invisible by being juxtaposed with them. (Winter, 2018)

This acknowledgement points to the plethora of readily accessible material showing systemic racist and sexist discourses that needs to be studied in order to bring about institutional, societal and social change. Extremist views are just that, 'extreme', but, dealing with them intensely over a period of time makes it easy to lose perspective on how exceptional they are. Reconciling the benefits of a project designed to expose them is not easy when considering how harmful less extreme, but more disguised, views can be.

The Challenge of Being the Outsider

Having considered the ethical issues and risks associated with this research project, I turn now to the challenge of attempting to analyse discourses from communities to which I am not affiliated. This relates to how I situate myself in terms of my research interactions, or my personal positioning (Van Langenhove & Harré, 1994: 364). The linguistic data for this project originates from websites and blogs written by authors who identify as being part of 'an aggregate of diverse communities brought together by a common language' (Marwick & Caplan, 2018: 553). As Angouri (2016: 324) points out, the 'conceptualization of what constitutes an online community and how it operates is constantly evolving for lay users and scholars alike'. However, what *is* clear is that I am not part of any community which identifies as far right or as part of the manosphere and, therefore, the common language used to transcend the diversity of factions is not one in which I am fluent. Indeed, my personal positioning as a female, liberal-leaning academic puts me in stark contrast to the assumed readership of the online material.

In her research on marginalised groups, Bhopal (2010) emphasises the need to reflect on how we position ourselves in relation to the participants in our studies, 'As researchers we have to be aware of the realities and difficulties of being an insider or outsider which enables us to question our own position in the research process' (Bhopal, 2010: 194). This *insider* and *outsider* positioning correlates to the epistemological perspectives I am taking as a researcher (Lett, 1990: 131), namely whose knowledge and interpretation of the language taken from this community am I using. This maps onto the *emic* and *etic* analytical approaches to analysis. Emic constructs have been described as 'descriptions, and analyses expressed in terms of the conceptual schemes and categories regarded as meaningful and appropriate by the native members of the culture whose beliefs and behaviours are being studied' (Lett, 1990: 130). Etic constructs, on the other hand, are those expressed as meaningful and appropriate by 'by the community of scientific observers' (Lett, 1990: 131). Examples of emic approaches being (expressly) taken in linguistic studies include the critical discourse analyses of newspapers' attitudes towards racism and xenophobia (Taylor, 2014), and the documenting of life history narratives by students self-identifying as lesbian, gay, bisexual and/or queer (LGBTQ+) (Olive, 2014). See also Sauntson's discussion on LGBTQ+ researchers engaging in work on sexuality and language in educational sites in Chapter 5.

Although there is some disagreement as to the mutual relationship between emic and etic approaches (Salzmann, 1998: 84), and the terms themselves have been described as outdated (Yin, 2010: 11), reflecting on the two approaches offers a chance to monitor the position I am taking in my research. In her ethnographic study of the English Defence League (EDL), a populist, radical right and anti-Islamist movement (Pilkington, 2016: 4), Pearson observes that 'views of those in "extreme" but "marginalized" groups (some might argue, self-marginalised) are frequently judged against a white middle-class liberalism and regarded as exceptional, rather than a manifestation of wider social discourse' (Pearson, 2019: 1253). In earlier work on the EDL, Pilkington (2016) highlights how these associations can be pathologised through the application of theoretical frameworks or how research on secondary, online material produced by their members distances the researcher from those being researched (Pilkington, 2016: 13), risking the homogenisation of their views (Pearson, 2019: 1253). A major challenge of this study is to rebalance this by attempting to apply as much of an emic perspective as possible to the analysis and look at the language produced online 'through the eyes of members of the culture being studied' (Willis, 2007: 100).

How far it is possible, or important, to take an emic approach in the analysis of online extremism is debateable. From a linguistic perspective, issues include having to classify or define neologisms, slang words and acronyms which are unique to that online environment. These are often taken from pornography (*gloryhole faces*) or far right literature (*DOTR* – an acronym for Day of the Rope, taken from the racist, anti-Semitic novel *The Turner Diaries* by William Luther Pierce). Even familiar terms (such as *slut*) show a fluidity of nuanced meaning which, as an outsider, is difficult to decipher. For example, in one blog post from the blogger *Chateau*

Heartiste (2017)[1] the term *slut* is used as both a degradation and a badge of honour: '*Slut, or pretensions to sluttery?*' Another extract from the post exemplifies the linguistic blending frequently found in the data, which takes a lot to unpack:

> The shitlib cities are filled with CUNDTs like herself: totally converged into the technofemcuntyassqueen man-hating spiteborg, committed to spending their prime nubility years hunting elusive alpha males in the urban junglelove. ('Meet the CUNDT: Converged, Urban, Narcissistic, Delusional, Tubbo' – Chateau Heartiste, 8 August 2017)

Online dictionaries and 'translators' from the factions themselves can be used to gain an insight into the semantic and pragmatic uses of particular terms. Urban Dictionary (UD)[2], an online, crowdsourced dictionary of 'slanguage', was my initial 'go to' source for unfamiliar words. However, according to Ging *et al.*, its appropriation by those in the manosphere and the subsequent editing of terms, 'shape meaning not only by generating or tagging neologisms but also by redefining and classifying existing terms into folksonomies of misogynistic and anti-feminist rhetoric' (Ging *et al.*, 2020: 852). While this undesired development of UD may allow for a more emic analysis of lexical features taken from the manosphere, studies on UD show that it has a 'high presence of opinion-focused entries, as opposed to meaning-focused entries' with the more offensive terms receiving less support and lower scores via the site's approval rating feature (Nguyen *et al.*, 2018: 1). Looking at UD entries such as the term *soyboy*, a slang term used to disparage men who are deemed pathetic, unmasculine and displaying non-alpha male traits, it can be seen that the top definition (most popular) was uploaded in June 2017. Subsequent entries, showing a more up-to-date opinion on the term, have fewer positive votes. Ascertaining how the term is used within the communities that use this insult, therefore, is problematic. The PUA Lingo[3] site provides a more comprehensive dictionary of terms used by PUAs in the manosphere. The site claims that it has the largest collection of terms, jargon and definitions for PUAs on the web, although some of the definitions date back more than 10 years so the extent to which the collection represents contemporary usage is questionable. To circumvent some of these issues, researchers on extremism have tried to get insiders' perspectives on the far right by recruiting 'formers' – reformed extremists (see, for example, Perry & Scrivens, 2016), although this type of resource would not be available to many in the field of applied linguistics.

The use of online dictionaries to interpret unique online language can help mitigate some of the interpretative difficulties brought about by differences in age, gender or value systems, all of which contribute a more etic perspective (Yin, 2010: 12). However, as an emic perspective relies on seeing through the first-hand experience of the participants or contributors, where can a corpus-based critical discourse analysis be considered on the emic/etic spectrum? In fact, using the legal terms *rape* and *sexual assault* for my search criteria during the data collection already places it towards the etic end of that scale. It is highly likely that other terms for those crimes are used by the far right and manosphere members, establishing a relatively etic approach to my study from the outset.

Having touched on the difficulties of taking an emic approach to the interpretation of language used by the far right and manosphere, the question remains as to whether it is important to do so. Although employing an objective/subjective distinction to positionality has been argued to be reductionist in the insider/outsider debate (Nero, 2015: 348), it has been suggested that the objectivity afforded to those on the outside of their research contexts allows for more challenging research questions to be posed (Nero, 2015). Yin argues that it is enough for a researcher to acknowledge their own (etic) interpretations of data (Yin, 2010: 13), a point that is reiterated by Rüdiger and Dayter (2017). They believe that 'openly admitting bias, and accepting that all social research ultimately involves perspectivisation, allows one to avoid the main ethical pitfall of research on unlikeable subjects: framing one's disparaging account as the one and only scientific truth' (Rüdiger & Dayter, 2017: 254). They go on to say that researchers should not feel any guilt at personally evaluating their data and that analysis is enriched through human responses to it (p. 264). The necessity for the researcher to include some distance between themselves and their data, which inevitably makes for a more etic analysis, is also something to bear in mind. The challenges of balancing the need to represent the opinions and voices of the participants in the dataset (and not taking a pathologised, judgemental view as advocated by Pilkington (2016) and Pearson (2019), above) with the researcher's need to acknowledge bias and personal stance is not easy to achieve. Personally, the more time I spend on this project, the more I find I am siding with Rüdiger and Dayter's point of view.

Is it Worth it? Concluding Remarks

So, is it worth taking the risk and tackling the types of ethical, personal and epistemological challenges outlined above? The obvious answer is that it depends hugely on the researcher, their motivations and their capacity for resilience. From a linguistic perspective, the inventive metaphors, neologisms and overt attempts at persuasive discourse provide a fascinating, albeit disturbing, source for analysis, especially for linguists interested in critical discourse analysis, identities, power and rhetoric in discourse, and narrative structures. An overarching principle that comes through the literature on ethics underscores the need for assessing the rights, possible harms and negative effects of the research against its social benefits (see, for example, Markham & Buchanan, 2015: 607). With recourse to appropriate support and a growing network of academics and applied linguists researching extremist material, the negative effects and potential for harm can be mitigated and the social benefit of such research can be maximised.

Finally, it is true that perhaps more insidious, socially accepted misogynistic and xenophobic attitudes need to be addressed as a priority. However, the tangible rise in far-right rhetoric in mainstream media and the expansion of right-wing populist parties across Europe also warrant linguistic study. The shooting of nine churchgoers in Charleston, South Carolina in June 2015 by Dylann Roof, who was influenced by racist misinformation online about crime in the area (Khan *et al.*, 2019), indicates a greater need to investigate fake news and hateful, radicalising discourses. Racist, anti-Semitic, anti-Islam and misogyny-based hate speech can all be exposed by studying extremist material online. Any attempt to uncover and inoculate against extremist rhetoric through counter-extremism measures makes studying these types of discourses worthwhile.

Notes

(1) www.heartiste.org
(2) www.urbandictionary.com
(3) www.pualingo.com

References

Allam, H. (2019) 'It gets to you': Extremism researchers confront the unseen toll of their work. NPR (online). See https://www.npr.org/2019/09/20/762430305/it-gets-to-you-extremism-researchers-confront-the-unseen-toll-of-their-work?t=1574971932751 (accessed 10 August 2020).

Angouri, J. (2016) Online communities and communities of practice. In A. Georgakopoulou and T. Spilioti (eds) *The Routledge Handbook of Language and Digital Communication* (pp. 323–338). Abingdon: Routledge.

Anti-Defamation-League (2018) *When Women are the Enemy: The Intersection of Misogyny and white Supremacy*. See https://www.adl.org/ resources/reports/when-women-are-the-enemy-the-intersection-ofmisogyny-and-white-supremacy#introduction (accessed 10 August 2020).

Association of Internet Researchers (2019) *Internet Research: Ethical Guidelines 3.0.* See https://aoir.org/reports/ethics3.pdf

Berger, J.M. (2018) *Extremism*. Cambridge, MA: The MIT Press

Bhopal, K. (2010) Gender, identity and experience: Researching marginalized groups. *Women's Studies International Forum* 33 (3), 188–195.

Bolander, B. and Locher, M.A. (2014) Doing sociolinguistic research on computer-mediated data: A review of four methodological issues. *Discourse, Context and Media* 3, 14–26.

British Association of Applied Linguists (2016) *Recommendations on Good Practice in Applied Linguistics*. See http://www.baal.org.uk/public_docs.html

Burley, S. (2017) *Fascism Today: What Is It and How to End It*. Chico, CA: AK Press.

Conway, M., Scrivens, R. and Macnair, L. (2019) *Right-wing Extremists' Persistent Online Presence: History and Contemporary Trends*. International Centre for Counter-Terrorism Policy Brief (October 2019). DOI: 10.19165/2019.3.12

DiSalvo, D. (2012) *Engines of Change: Party Factions in American Politics, 1868–2010*. Oxford Scholarship Online. doi:10.1093/acprof:oso/9780199891702.003.0001

Giaxoglou, K. (2017) Reflections on internet research ethics from language-focused research on web-based mourning: Revisiting the public/private distinction as a language ideology of differentiation. *Applied Linguistics Review* 8 (2–3), 229–250.

Ging, D. (2019) Alphas, betas, and incels: Theorizing the masculinities of the manosphere. *Men and Masculinities* 22 (4), 638–657.

Ging, D., Lynn, T. and Rosati, P. (2020) Neologising Misogyny: Urban Dictionary's Folksonomies of Sexual Abuse. *New Media & Society* 22 (5), 838-856.

Gotell, L. and Dutton, E. (2016) Sexual violence in the 'Manosphere': Antifeminist men's rights discourses on rape. *International Journal for Crime, Justice and Social Democracy* 5 (2), 65–80.

Granholm, C. and Svedmark, E. (2018) Research that hurts: Ethical considerations when studying vulnerable populations online. In R. Iphofen and M. Tolich (eds) *The SAGE Handbook of Qualitative Research Ethics* (pp. 501–509). London: Sage.

Hale, W.C. (2012) Extremism on the World Wide Web: A research review. *Criminal Justice Studies* 25 (4), 343–356.

Hardie, A. (2014) Modest XML for corpora: Not a standard, but a suggestion. *ICAME Journal* 38 (1), 73–103.

Hawley, G. (2017) *Making Sense of the Alt-Right*. New York: Columbia University Press.

H.M. Government (2015) *Counter-extremism Strategy*. Policy Paper (19 October 2015). See https://www.gov.uk/government/publications/counter-extremism-strategy

Khan, S.A., Alkawaz, M.H. and Zangana, H.M. (2019) The use and abuse of social media for spreading fake news. *2019 IEEE International Conference on Automatic Control and Intelligence Systems (I2CACIS 2019)*, 29 June, pp. 145–148.

Koller, V. (2012) How to analyse collective identity in discourse – Textual and contextual parameters. *Critical Approaches to Discourse Analysis Across Disciplines* 5 (2), 19–38.

Lett, J. (1990) Emics and etics: Notes on the epistemology of anthropology. In T.N. Headland, K.L. Pike and M. Harris (eds) *Emics and Etics: The Insider/Outsider Debate* (pp. 127–142). London: Sage.

Mackenzie, J. (2017) Identifying informational norms in Mumsnet talk: A reflexive-linguistic approach to internet research ethics. *Applied Linguistics Review* 8 (2–3), 293–314.

Markham, A.N. and Buchanan, E.A. (2012) *Ethical Decision-making and Internet Research: Recommendations from the AoIR Ethics Working Committee* (version 2.0). See https://aoir.org/reports/ethics2.pdf

Markham, A.N. and Buchanan, E.A. (2015) Internet research: Ethical concerns. In J.D. Wright (ed.) *International Encyclopedia of the Social & Behavioral Sciences* (2nd edn, pp. 606–613). Amsterdam: Elsevier.

Marwick, A.E. and Caplan, R. (2018) Drinking male tears: Language, the manosphere, and networked harassment. *Feminist Media Studies* 18 (4), 543–559.

McEnery, T. and Hardie, A. (2012) *Corpus Linguistics*. Cambridge: Cambridge University Press.

Mudde, C. (2000) *The Ideology of the Extreme Right*. Manchester: Manchester University Press.

Mudde, C. (2019) *The Far Right Today*. Cambridge: Polity Press.

Nagle, A. (2017) *Kill All Normies: Online Culture Wars from 4chan and Tumblr to Trump and the Alt-Right*. Alresford: Zero Books.

Neiwert, D. (2017) *Alt-America: The Rise of the Radical Right in the Age of Trump*. London: Verso.

Nero, S. (2015) Language, identity, and insider/outsider positionality in Caribbean Creole English research. *Applied Linguistics Review* 6 (3), 341–368.

Nguyen, D., McGillivray, B. and Yasseri, T. (2018) Emo, love and God: Making sense of the Urban Dictionary, a crowd-sourced online dictionary. *Royal Society Open Science* 5, 172320. http://dx.doi.org/10.1098/rsos.172320

Olive, J.L. (2014) Reflecting on the tensions between emic and etic perspectives in life history research: Lessons learned. *FQS Forum: Qualitative Social Research* 15 (2), article 6.
Page, R. (2017) Ethics revisited: Rights, responsibilities and relationships in online research. *Applied Linguistics Review* 8 (2–3), 315–320.
Pearson, E. (2019) Extremism and toxic masculinity: The man question re-posed. *International Affairs* 95 (6), 1251–1270.
Perry, B. and Scrivens, R. (2016) Uneasy alliances: A look at the right-wing extremist movement in Canada. *Studies in Conflict and Terrorism* 39 (9), 819–841.
Pilkington, H. (2016) *Loud and Proud: Passion and Politics in the English Defence League*. Manchester: Manchester University Press.
Phillips, W. (2015) *This Is Why We Can't Have Nice Things: Mapping the Relationship between Online Trolling and Mainstream Culture*. Cambridge, MA: MIT Press.
Pihlaja, S. (2017) More than fifty shades of grey: Copyright on social network sites. *Applied Linguistics Review* 8 (2–3), 213–2287.
Romano, A. (2016) How the alt-right's sexism lures men into white supremacy. *Vox*, 14 December. See: http://www.vox.com/culture/ 2016/12/14/13576192/alt-right-sexism-recruitment
Rüdiger, S. and Dayter, D. (2017) The ethics of researching unlikeable subjects. *Applied Linguistics Review* 8 (2–3), 251–269.
Salzmann, Z. (1998) *Language, Culture & Society: An Introduction to Linguistic Anthropology* (2nd edn). Oxford: Westview Press.
Spilioti, T. (2017) Media convergence and publicness: Towards a modular and iterative approach to online research ethics. *Applied Linguistics Review* 8 (2–3), 191–212.
Spilioti, T. and Tagg, C. (2017) The ethics of online research methods in applied linguistics: Challenges, opportunities, and directions in ethical decision-making. *Applied Linguistics Review* 8 (2–3), 163–167.
Taylor, C. (2014) Investigating the representation of migrants in the UK and Italian press: A cross-linguistic corpus assisted discourse analysis. *International Journal of Corpus Linguistics* 19 (3), 368–400.
van Dijk, T.A. (1984) *Prejudice and Discourse*. Amsterdam: John Benjamins.
Van Langenhove, L. and Harré, R. (1994) Cultural stereotypes and positioning theory. *Journal for the Theory of Social Behaviour* 24 (4), 360–372.
Weisser, M. (2016) *Practical Corpus Linguistics: An Introduction to Corpus-Based Language Analysis*. Chichester: Wiley.
Wendling, M. (2018) *Alt-Right: From 4chan to the White House*. London: Pluto Press.
Willis, J.W. (2007) *Foundations of Qualitative Research: Interpretative and Critical Approaches*. Thousand Oaks, CA: Sage.
Winter, A. (2018) Researching the far right in a 'post-racial' context. *Monitor Racism Blog*, April. See http://monitoracism.eu/researching-the-far-right-and-racism/
Yin, R.K. (2010) *Qualitative Research from Start to Finish*. New York: Guildford Press.

10 Critical Incidents in a Teacher–Researcher and Student–Participant Relationship: What Risks Can We Take?

Sal Consoli

Introduction

Doing classroom-based research such as Action Research (Burns, 2019), Exploratory Practice (Allwright & Hanks, 2009) and Reflective Practice (Mann & Walsh, 2017) means doing research about and with people, and such research is 'messy' (Mckinley, 2019). This is because people's lives are complex and investigating people entails dealing with their 'life capital' (Consoli, 2021). People's life stories and behaviours are rich, unique and unpredictable and, therefore, result in research messiness (Rigg, 1991). Crucially, this type of research leads to the researcher's life and identity (or identities) becoming interwoven with the lives of their participants, thereby pointing to the need to revisit the researcher's 'role, relationship and ethical responsibilities' (Kubanyiova, 2008). These last three concepts are at the heart of this chapter. Drawing upon a project which combined the methodological traditions of Exploratory Practice and Narrative Inquiry, I will share critical incidents of my story as a teacher researching my own students during a pre-sessional course in the UK, and after the end of this programme in a more traditional researcher capacity. My overarching research aim was to understand the students' motivation(s) to study at a UK university. Coming from what they defined as 'a formal and serious' educational context in China, these students found themselves being taught by a 'friendly' teacher in the UK. This may have positively influenced their motivation; however, through ethical, reflexive and reflective considerations, I discuss several tensions, challenges and compromises which raise the question of what risks a teacher(-researcher), investigating their own students, can take in order to obtain 'good' research data.

The First Phase of the Study: The Pre-sessional

The first part of the study consisted of my experience as an English for Academic Purposes teacher on a UK university pre-sessional programme. A pre-sessional is a course designed to equip international students with basic academic language and study skills which will facilitate successful completion of a degree at an English-speaking university. Within this specific pre-sessional, I was in charge of a module concerning the development of reading and writing skills for postgraduate studies. Therefore, my primary role entailed responsibilities typical of a pre-sessional teacher who must ensure that their students complete the course successfully and progress to the target master's degree programme. However, I was also interested to investigate these students' motivation(s) to study and live in the UK.

In order to fulfil these research aims during the pre-sessional, I adopted Exploratory Practice (EP) – a form of practitioner research which lends itself well for a busy teacher on an intensive high-stakes course such as this. EP offers teachers the opportunity to investigate their own practices by drawing on the notion of puzzle(ment) which instigates a search for understanding (Allwright & Hanks, 2009). The main advantage of using EP is that the teacher(-researcher) does not need to devise additional investigative instruments to fulfil their research aims, thereby avoiding extra work. Rather, EP promotes the use of potentially exploitable pedagogic activities (PEPAs) which are nothing less than the very lesson activities that teachers would design/use for their teaching purposes but, possibly, with some small tweaks to suit the research objectives. Therefore, EP is an approach that may mitigate risks such as workload management for teachers as well as the impact research may have on students' performance (Galloway, 2016).

As an illustration of what I did in this context, I now share the instructions for a sample PEPA I used to research my students' motivation(s). At the start of a pre-sessional, I generally ask my students to write a short text about themselves, and normally give them very broad guidelines to write freely (e.g. about their educational background and interests). However, this time, in the spirit of EP, I formulated the following instructions to guide them in writing about their motivation or somehow touch upon it:

Write a paragraph for each question:

(A) What are your reasons for choosing to study at [name of the university]? Describe your personal motivation for coming here and what you hope to achieve.

(B) Why are you doing the pre-sessional?

(C) What are your expectations of the pre-sessional?

(D) What are your expectations of the Text-based Studies module with me?

For a fuller illustration of the EP experience on this pre-sessional, see Consoli (2020). I will now focus on my role and responsibilities in this phase of the study.

My Initial Role and Responsibilities as a Pre-sessional Teacher–(Researcher)

I should begin this section with a micro-ethical consideration (Kubanyiova, 2008), which was crucial in shaping my conduct during the pre-sessional. My main duty as a teacher was to develop these students' study skills and their academic writing. This also involved a strong focus on understanding and developing academic integrity (e.g. avoiding plagiarism or collusion). Given the rich curriculum for this module as well as my responsibility to offer regular formative feedback on their writing, I was aware that both my students and I had a very busy schedule during each week of this 5 week course (week 6 was devoted to summative assessment and feedback).

I must also highlight here my longstanding pedagogic desire that everyone in the classroom should have a good time or be happy. This, in turn, leads to my disposition to create an educational environment where everyone feels safe to make mistakes, express their voices and ultimately learn. The first step towards generating this safe and motivational learning space is to create good rapport with the students. Through some PEPAs produced in weeks 1 and 2, it became apparent that the students' understanding of my role and teaching persona aligned with my desire of creating such a pleasant learning environment, and they noticed my efforts to achieve this goal. As a result, they described me as 'humorous', 'patient' and 'nice'.

One could reasonably argue that these students wrote what they thought I would be happy to read in their PEPAs or that they expressed their thoughts to please me (social desirability bias; Riazi, 2016: 299). I cannot discard these concerns because, arguably, any teacher researching their students may have to live with such student bias. However, it is worth noting that the students 'justified' their statements with specific reasons, for instance, my use of humour made May's experience of the pre-sessional 'delightful' and Velika referred to my 'patience to answer their questions'. While this friendly rapport and atmosphere in the classroom seemed to encourage a healthy learning experience, it does not mean that unexpected challenges and surprises are uncommon. I now describe two 'ethically important moments' (Guillemin & Gillam, 2004: 262) or critical incidents concerning my teacher–student relationship with one student, George (pseudonym), whose behaviour was shaped, to some extent, by this friendly teaching demeanour and atmosphere.

Fostering Rapport

The first episode relates to a PEPA where George expressed his admiration for my teaching persona by referring to an icebreaker joke which I used on the first day of the course. I had told the students I could speak four languages (which is true), but with the twist that I had learnt these by being with four girlfriends (one per language) at the same time. This joke aimed to generate an opportunity for humour at the beginning of the course. This kind of humour, in my view, would lay the foundation for good rapport and a pleasant classroom atmosphere. However, when I read the following in George's reflective writing, which I collected as research data (PEPA), I questioned the appropriateness of my joke:

> I met a nice teacher in my pre-sessional course and learnt a lot from him in these days. Sal, our tutor for reading and writing, is a smart man from London. What interests me most was that he said he had had 4 different girlfriends from 4 different regions, speaking 4 different languages. (George, PEPA-1)

This joke was framed in such a way for me to say that having multiple relationships at the same time was a struggle and therefore stimulate laughter in the classroom. The joke seemed to be well received by these students and certainly contributed to creating a pleasant classroom ambience enriched with humour. However, when I read the above extract in George's first PEPA, I realized that this joke had had a lasting impact which I had not expected and led me to challenge its appropriateness. Despite my good intentions I began questioning whether this kind of humour might actually entail considerable risks within an international and culturally rich context such as the UK higher education sector. While there was no consequence on this occasion, I believe that my teacher–(researcher) ability to identify this potential risk is significant and this now leads me to discuss the notion of humour further.

Is Humour a Risk?

I should clarify that on this pre-sessional I taught Chinese students who had completed an undergraduate degree in mainland China and were now aiming to begin a master's in the UK. During the pre-sessional, these students foregrounded the value of humour as part of my teaching, and despite some learning challenges, my use of humour reduced their learning anxiety and kept them motivated to study. Megan, for instance, highlighted that my use of jokes helped when she was unable to answer a question I asked, which, in turn, made her feel less stressed about her inability to respond.

Humour has been characterized as the intentional use of behaviours that stimulate laughter and delight (Booth-Butterfield & Booth-Butterfield, 1991: 215), which positively contributes to the mental health of the individual as well as the collective emotional climate of a social group. The benefits of humour have reportedly been numerous with reduction of student anxiety being a recurrent one (Aylor & Opplinger, 2003; Wanzer & Frymier, 1999). However, careful consideration is required in relation to the appropriateness of humour and how certain cultural influences may interact with humour. For example, humour may help lessen students' anxiety within individualist societies, but Zhang (2005) suggests that, for Chinese students, seen as collectivists, humour may have countereffects. Nonetheless, my pre-sessional students clearly showed that teachers' use of humour may indeed have positive effects on Chinese students as well.

This debate requires a consideration about culture and how this concept may be operationalized within an international context like this UK pre-sessional. In light of my Chinese students who actually enjoyed the use of humour, I do not take an essentialist view of culture. Therefore, while I recognize the influence of 'large culture', I place stronger emphasis on the notion of 'small culture' (Holliday, 1999), a space where individuals form their own cultural stance(s) with their own unique cultural traits and in relation to the (multi)cultural context(s) and other actors where they find themselves and the other social actors cohabiting such context(s). As such, my debate here, as a teacher–researcher, concerns the attention teachers may need to pay when forging a 'good' rapport with their students and handle humour sensitively without taking the risk (as I did) of clashing with students' cultural personalities. This would, possibly, require some groundwork tasks whereby the teacher gains a clearer understanding of the students' characters and personalities, thus establishing what kind of humour may be possible. Ultimately, from a researcher perspective, it is worth noting that a favourable relationship that takes care of these cultural sensitivities in forming a good teacher–student rapport will open up opportunities for data generation. This would be in contrast with a teacher–student relationship presenting 'cultural blocks' (Holliday & Amadasi, 2019), which may actually disrupt the relationship altogether. I now return to the teacher–researcher's ability (and disposition) to create a safe and friendly learning environment as part of forging such 'good rapport' with their students (participants).

Is Friendliness a Risk?

The notion of friendliness within the teacher–student relationship is another one which deserves careful attention in the context of my study, especially because it led to a second critical incident which I wish to illustrate. In my teacher–researcher journal I have called this, the 'WhatsApp' incident. WhatsApp is probably one of the most popular messaging applications in the world and I am one of those people who use it. However, one night (close to midnight) during the time of the pre-sessional, I received a WhatsApp message from George who had found my mobile phone number on the university website and thought that we could be 'friends' on WhatsApp and communicate better through this channel. While I appreciated the gesture, my professional teacher-self felt that this was not appropriate despite my desire to foster a friendly rapport with the students. Therefore, the following day, I approached George after class and explained that I did not think it was possible for me to be 'friends' on WhatsApp during the pre-sessional course. He seemed to struggle to understand why as they often use WeChat in China (a similar application to WhatsApp). I explained that after the end of pre-sessional maybe this could be a possibility.

This episode shows that my desire to create a friendly and safe learning environment was somehow misconstrued by some students who began seeing me as a 'friend'. The concept of friendship stems from my attempt to adopt a caring teaching persona which was compounded by my aim to create a bond or connection with the students. The notions of caring and connectedness between teachers and students have been largely researched at primary and secondary education levels, but less within higher education contexts (Hagenauer & Volet, 2014). The small debate about this adult–adult relationship at university has brought up the argument that caring for students is important (Fitzmaurice, 2008), and that a safe environment should be created for students and teachers to interact (Ayres, 2015); but others have stressed that students should not be coddled (Lahteenoja & Pirttila-Backman, 2005). Therefore, while the benefits of becoming involved in students' learning are evident, e.g. increased motivation (Komarraju et al., 2010), there is also a need for this student–teacher relationship at university to be 'balanced'. For instance, Holmes et al. (1999) have highlighted that a friendship dimension is inappropriate whereas Sibii (2010: 532) has argued for the university teacher to be 'friendly but not a friend'.

The 'WhatsApp' episode during the pre-sessional indicated that a friendly connection between teacher and students may involve the risk of blurring professional boundaries which may then compromise the student–teacher relationship. I cannot deny that in this challenging experience I was exclusively contemplating my professional ethics as a teacher; after all, I had wished to continue my interactions with George post-pre-sessional in order to complete my research. As such, while I was adamant about my teacher–student boundaries, I was also concerned about the possibility of compromising a relationship with this student, which in the future, may lead to 'good' data. However, this begs the question what is good data?

Good Data: What Risks Can we Take?

What constitutes 'good' data in the context of practitioner research like mine, and what risks should one take to obtain such good data? To address these questions, I refer to Hanks's (2017) discussion of 'good enough research'. By drawing on Yates's (2004) ambitious and, potentially for some, unattainable definition of research, Hanks proffers the notion of 'good enough research' whereby she acknowledges the superb value of the research work promoted by Yates, whilst appreciating that much research exists which is worthwhile despite not meeting all of Yates's criteria. 'Good enough [research is able] to contribute to understandings in the field, good enough to build upon, good enough to inspire others' (Hanks, 2017: 34). As such, good enough research is possible and valuable despite the potential epistemological and methodological limitations encountered by most (if not all) researchers, whether teacher–researchers or 'traditional' researchers.

Following from this debate, I propose the notion of 'good enough data' which can offer some insights into the phenomenon under investigation through whatever means and methods conceivable by the researcher. Good enough data can contribute nuanced understanding(s) to the field despite the possible contradictions, complexities and limitations which one may experience throughout the research process. In the first phase of my study, in my capacity as pre-sessional teacher, I made the ethical decision to prioritize my students' pedagogic needs over my research and thus followed my professional ethics. One could argue that doing so may have compromised a potential source of 'superb data'. For instance, if I had decided to 'become friends' with George on WhatsApp I may have been able to seek and obtain very rich data about his experiences on the pre-sessional; however, this would have been, in my view, ethically complex and led to the challenge of managing certain professional boundaries. I therefore chose to avoid the risk of compromising a teacher–student relationship for the sake of 'superb data', and instead obtained less rich, yet good enough data which supported my research aims whilst remaining loyal to my professional code of practice. The discussion of 'good enough data' in practitioner research applies to more traditional forms of applied linguistics research – more about this in the second phase of the study below.

Owing to space constraints, I cannot share further details about my pre-sessional experience. Nonetheless, the above-mentioned critical incidents seem sufficient to recognize the complexity of teacher–student relationships and the risks which such relationships may involve when a teacher invests in a friendly approach which might, however, lead to questions of professionalism and appropriateness. These are risks which all caring teachers are certainly aware of; however, in the context of a teacher conducting research involving their students, we must account for these complexities more carefully in order to shape our conduct as ethical educators as well as ethical teacher–researchers. As such, an approach towards 'good enough data' seems to support practitioners wishing to conduct inquiries into their practice(s).

Ethical Questions About Practitioner Research

Any research project that involves people requires ethical attention prior to the beginning of the research work and throughout (e.g. Mann, 2016).

More crucially, when research brings the researcher and participants together within a longitudinal dimension, macro- and micro-ethical considerations are required to ascertain the sustainability of this relationship (Kubanyiova, 2008; Consoli & Aoyama, 2020). For the research experience here reported, the overarching ethical principle that guided my teacher–researcher behaviour was putting the students' educational and pastoral needs before my research aims. Nonetheless, one can see that EP, as a form of practitioner research, lends itself well to fulfilling ethical responsibilities such as monitoring student academic and pastoral wellbeing. In other words, if, as educational researchers, we adopt an approach that ecologically accounts for the student's (or other participant's) life story and capital (Consoli, 2021), which constantly influence their present and future experiences, we are well positioned to produce ethically sound research. I believe that it is important for other practitioners or teacher–researchers doing similar research in their practice context(s) to consider the following questions. These questions follow a Practitioner Research approach (Hanks, 2017), where practitioner refers to both teachers and students.

- Who are the practitioners of your context? Are they students or/and other colleagues? Are they fully aware of their roles and how these may support, impair, facilitate your research?
- Are the practitioners involved in your research fully aware of your research intentions and timescale? Are they willing to participate or has the research inadvertently been imposed on them?
- Are all practitioners fully aware of what is expected of them?
- Have principles of respect, confidentiality and anonymity been fully discussed with all practitioners involved?
- Do you frequently check that all practitioners involved are happy to continue to be engaged in the research?
- Are all practitioners (teachers, students and whoever else is involved) given enough space and opportunities to fully express their voices and views as they wish?
- What happens to the findings (or understandings) at the end of the research? Who owns these? Is everyone happy with how they have been represented in any report, conference paper or poster?
- Is everyone fully aware of the benefits of the research? If there is a lead practitioner, has this person ensured that everyone is happy with how work has been concluded?

I now move to a discussion of my relationship with these students after the end of the pre-sessional programme, in the new phase of the study.

New Phase of the Study: New Roles, New Identities

After the pre-sessional, the students all progressed to their master's programme, and therefore I was no longer their teacher. However, in order to obtain a longitudinal understanding of their motivation to study and live in the UK, I was minded to follow them throughout their master's year. As such, I was willing to position myself as a researcher, rather than the 'friendly' pre-sessional teacher, and obtain data through several rounds of interviews. However, this was not possible without ethical difficulty. While it would have been useful to capitalize on the good rapport formed throughout the teacher–student relationship, one should not aim to exploit their participants just because they may agree to help out of good will.

Therefore, I wished for the students and me to turn our student–teacher relationship into a researcher–participant one. In order to foster my 'new' identity as the 'researcher' in the more traditional sense of the term, i.e. as an outsider of their experience, I asked the students if they would be willing to meet for a few rounds of interviews. However, I was aware that they could have 'far more important things to do and think about' than joining a research project (Holliday, 2015: 56), which, I think, is a valid argument, especially for international students completing a demanding postgraduate course with various deadlines and heavy workload.

During the pre-sessional it was easy to observe this ethical consideration because, thanks to the EP principle of integrating pedagogy and research through PEPAs, the students did not do anything 'extra' to fulfil my research objectives. However, this became more challenging when my student–participants became fully engaged with a demanding master's after the pre-sessional. In this light, I aimed to show appreciation and generate some kind of 'benefits' by offering a compensation of £10 for each interview, and up to 30 minutes of tutorial-like interactions at the end of each interview or other convenient time for them.

These tutorial-like interactions were intended to offer the students an opportunity to share their academic concerns, doubts or questions with someone in whom they may have academic trust and had experience of working in different UK higher education settings. However, I made it clear both in writing and verbally that I did not wish to provide universal advice that might conflict with the guidance offered by their new academic department. Rather, my support was meant as an opportunity for them to articulate their thoughts with a sympathetic and empathic listener who could help them make sense of their own thinking or offer views on academic matters (e.g. how to prepare a dissertation proposal).

The Student–Participants' Perspectives

Unsurprisingly, my desire to establish a new identity in this new phase of the study, when I was no longer a teacher, proved challenging. I kept 'seeing' them as students and in our interview interactions I could not separate my experience as their teacher from my new capacity as researcher. More interestingly, the six (out of 15) students who eventually allowed me to follow their journeys on the master's saw me as a 'friend' or still as their 'teacher'. Below are two illustrations from some early interviews:

> now that I can talk to you because you're like my friend I like to think of what I do in the MSc and learn from you because you are still my teacher. (May – second interview)

> You are my teacher so I am happy to talk to you and I am interested in your work because it can help other people. I think there should be more teachers like you to improve teaching at University. (Megan – first interview)

These students show that my intention to be seen as a friendly teacher, rather than a friend, was not matched by the perceptions of some of them, and they clearly continued to view me as a teacher or friend after the pre-sessional. One may argue that the shift to considering me a friend may be natural after a successful pre-sessional experience where we forged good rapport. Whilst, at times, I was still unsure about my professional boundaries and whether their positioning me as a 'friend' was a risk for my professional wellbeing, I found that being a 'teacher', even after the pre-sessional, was equally challenging. For example, Xiaoxin consistently refused my research money because I was her teacher and I struggled to convince Amber that this money was to recognize her time and thank her for her availability.

Outsider–Insider Identities in a Longitudinal Relationship

If we frame these students in their UK journey as communities of 'small culture(s)', I would argue that I was an outsider–insider to these small cultures: insider in the sense that I had insights into the immediate educational background of the students as well as a solid understanding of their characters and personalities; outsider in the sense that I was 'external' to their new unfolding experiences during the master's. In a cross-cultural debate, Suwankhong and Liamputtong (2015) maintain that cultural insiders are in a stronger position than outsiders because of their resonance with the research population and their clearer insights about the group under investigation. In this respect, the students and I shared the experience of forming our small culture of learning and teaching during the pre-sessional and, as such, they exhibited a favourable disposition towards sharing their opinions about all matters related to teaching and learning at university in the UK. However, the privilege of being so 'close' to the students' previous small culture on the pre-sessional did not come without data collection challenges. For instance, when I interviewed them about aspects of their life and experiences on the pre-sessional they often assumed or appeared to retain information which they thought could be taken for granted. This is similar to Gawlewicz's (2016) research experience where she felt disconnected from her participants because, being from the same cultural heritage as her participants, they seemed to keep insightful information from her by saying: 'We both know what I mean' (2016: 35).

Overall, I considered having a 'unique' position because I was the teacher (or friend) who knew about life in the UK and particularly at university, and these students seemed to enjoy meeting with me and asking questions or sharing their UK stories with me. Nonetheless, this sometimes led to my sympathetic self becoming entangled with dilemmas I had not anticipated. I soon developed a sympathetic attitude during my interviews and, arguably, in my relationship with these student–participants, which resulted in them opening up about personal matters which I struggled to respond to. For example, David once began disclosing a very personal motivation which concerned his desire of shaping a new identity in the UK, a new identity which would include the presence of more friends in his life despite his shy character. This was something that David had not disclosed during the pre-sessional whilst completing PEPAs which elicited data about his motivation. Perhaps this was because David felt comfortable talking to me and trusted me, but I cannot deny feeling emotional whilst I discovered these aspects about his motivation. From a research perspective this was an enriching experience, as I gained a greater quantity of, and more nuanced, data than I had through the pre-sessional PEPAs (Consoli, 2018), but I felt that my code of practice as an interviewer was challenged because I had developed such a caring attitude towards these people.

Normally, issues of empathy like this are debated in relation to the danger of 'creating a warm bath effect that shifts towards the kind of understanding and empathy that is characteristic of therapy or counselling' (Mann, 2016: 164). However, if we go beyond the concern for 'limited data', we realize that we have, to some extent, an ethical responsibility towards our participants. This is clearly debatable and arguably depends on the specific background and circumstances of the researcher and participants. Srivastava (2006) maintains that the multiple identities and positionalities that we adopt and perform in the research contexts we find ourselves are 'constantly in flux' and, crucially, these are connected to our understanding of who we are, and what she defines 'real life identities outside the field' (Srivastava, 2006: 211). Therefore, in my complex positionality as a researcher who also embodied the lived experiences and identity of a caring, friendly teacher, it was impossible to ignore some of the controversial data or disclosures which some student–participants made. Perhaps, unwittingly, I was still performing my pastoral role from the pre-sessional experience, which is why, at times, I conferred with more experienced researchers and colleagues when more complex dilemmas were brought to my attention during interviews. On these occasions, I attended to the participant's wellbeing (academic or somewhat personal) even if this meant limiting the potential for 'superb' data. This behaviour is in line with Ushioda's (2020: 140) call for an ethical research agenda whereby the researcher or teacher–researcher negotiates a balance between 'investigating' and 'supporting' their participants.

One Critical Episode: New Year's Party

After a few months from the beginning of the master's programme, I decided to organize a mini social gathering for the six participants I was following throughout the academic year. This was an opportunity to meet them outside the confines of interviews and show them that I cared about them and their wellbeing in the UK in a way that went beyond my need to generate research data. I thought this would also be an opportunity for them to meet with each other because, while they were together on the pre-sessional, they were in different master's groups and, as such, no longer had the time to socialize. Also, I was aware of the heavy master's schedule and workload, and therefore wished to create an opportunity for them to take a little time off their academic work and enjoy a pleasant social experience. Organising this gathering was not easy as it involved coordinating six different people as well as my own availability.

After several attempts, I organized one, but most people cancelled on the day except David. I decided to take him for dinner to honour his commitment. Nonetheless, I must confess I felt somewhat uncomfortable because it felt like these circumstances brought down all barriers, bringing us into a closed proximity at a social event where I had envisaged other people. David disclosed some difficult details about a sad experience he had had on the master's, and while I aimed to be supportive, I also tried not to perform the 'therapist' role mentioned above. I offered advice maintaining some distance in the matter, and I presume that this attitude to maintain certain boundaries was driven by the social context, a restaurant as opposed to a classroom where I would usually conduct interviews. This clearly shows how the physical context may have major effects on people and their behaviour (Mann, 2016). However, David also capitalized on the meal time to ask for advice on job opportunities and internships in the UK, which was a pleasant exchange.

A week or so later, I managed to organize a gathering with all of the students; this time I ordered plenty of food and hired a room at the university. The illustrations of data I share below are excerpts of my researcher journal which I wrote at the end of the evening after all the students had left:

> It was a very pleasant event. Alita arrived first and brought me a present. May arrived and gave me a hug. I noticed a level of ease and comfort amongst all. (…)

> We started the meal by talking of what we did during the Xmas break. (…) we told a lot of funny jokes and exchanged thoughts like they would invite me to their weddings one day.

These impressions confirm the positionality which the students had ascribed to me picturing me as their 'friend'. However, in this group context, unlike the one-to-one meal with David, I felt rather comfortable and joined in the exchanges easily, but later in the evening, this sense of comfort was challenged.

During dinner, I perceived that the barriers or filters between what they think and what they say came down more noticeably. They talked about my age and jokingly speculated about it. They then brought up 'my girlfriend'; they tried to enquire more about this area of my 'private' life and I didn't feel comfortable sharing such information

My perception of this part of the evening clearly indicates a sense of discomfort as if the students were pushing the boundaries of our social relationship, which to them may have appeared natural given the social event and my friendly disposition. However, I did not allow for these boundaries to disappear completely as I did not wish to run the risk of meshing this social, yet somewhat research-related, relationship with my private life. Having said this, I am not arguing that a fully fledged friendship is not possible between a researcher and their participants, especially when they become involved in a longitudinal experience such as this.

Conclusion: Ethical Reflection and Reflexivity

I would argue that a study involving a complex and dynamic relationship with research participants, especially teachers researching their students, merits constant ethical reflection on one's actions and reflexivity about one's self or selves. I began this project with the expectation that I would be able to follow a dichotomous approach to my relationship with these people whereby at the beginning I would be a teacher researching his own students. At this stage I employed Exploratory Practice to ensure that the students' learning objectives would not be compromised by my research interests. However, I soon realized that I took the risk of fostering a strong and friendly rapport which challenged my positionality as a teacher because the students began seeing me as a friend and acting accordingly, thereby pushing some professional boundaries of this relationship. In the second phase of the study, I expected to turn my relationship with these students purely into a researcher–participants relationship. This was perhaps naive of me because it was indeed challenging to separate our life capital (Consoli, 2021) as teacher and students and the good rapport forged previously.

Given the complexities that emerged from my effort to manage a professional research relationship alongside my caring and friendly disposition, I argue that our multiple identities are not to be seen as 'dichotomous; rather, they [draw] on each other to facilitate exchange, alter power differentials, and access data' (Srivastava, 2006: 211). This means being ethical and constantly acknowledging one's self in the research process, where 'the self is not some kind of virus which contaminates the research. On the contrary, the self is the research tool, and thus intimately connected to the methods we deploy' (Cousin, 2010: 10). Importantly, one needs to accept that identities and related behaviours 'are frequently situational, depending on the prevailing social, political, and cultural values of a given social context' (Kusow, 2003: 592). I, for example, cannot deny developing a genuine friendship with some of my participants after the end of our research interactions. However, whilst researching, one must inspect their sense of self with ethical reflection and reflexivity, thereby performing good conduct even if this means sacrificing opportunities for 'superb data' and being left with less but, at least, safeguarding our human integrity and individual boundaries.

References

Allwright, D. and Hanks, J. (2009) *The Developing Language Learner: An Introduction to Exploratory Practice*. Basingstoke: Palgrave Macmillan.
Aylor, B. and Oppliger, P. (2003) Out-of-class communication and student perceptions of instructor humor orientation and socio-communicative style. *Communication Education* 52 (2), 122-134.
Ayres, R. (2015) Lecturing, working with groups and providing individual support. In H. Fry, S. Ketteridge and S. Marshall (eds) *A Handbook for Teaching and Learning in Higher Education: Enhancing Academic Practice* (4th edn). Abingdon: Routledge.
Booth-Butterfield, S. and Booth-Butterfield, M. (1991) Individual differences in the communication of humorous messages. *Southern Journal of Communication* 56 (3), 205–218.
Burns, A. (2019) Action research: Developments, characteristics, and future directions. In J. Schwieter and A. Benati (eds) *The Cambridge Handbook of Language Learning* (pp. 166–185). Cambridge: Cambridge University Press.
Consoli, S. (March, 2018) Understanding motivation through exploratory practice: Early Musings Paper presented at the FOLLM research seminar, King's College London.
Consoli, S. (2021) Understanding motivation through ecological research: The case of exploratory practice. In R.J. Sampson and R.S. Pinner (eds) *Complexity Perspectives on Researching Language Learner and Teacher Psychology* (pp. 120–135). Bristol: Multilingual Matters.
Consoli, S. and Aoyama, T. (2020) Longitudinal L2 motivation inquiry: A response to Lamb's (2016) 'when motivation research motivates: Issues in long-term empirical investigations'. *Innovation in Language Learning and Teaching* 14 (2), 178–187.
Cousin, G. (2010) Positioning positionality. The reflexive turn. In M. Savin-Baden and C.H. Major (eds) *New Approaches to Qualitative Research: Wisdom and Uncertainty* (pp. 9–18). New York: Routledge.
Fitzmaurice, M. (2008) Voices from within: Teaching in higher education as a moral practice. *Teaching in Higher Education* 13 (3), 341–352.
Galloway, N. (2016) Researching your own students: Negotiating the dual practitioner–researcher role. In J. McKinley and H. Rose (eds) *Doing Research in Applied Linguistics. Realities, Dilemmas, and Solutions*. New York, NY: Routledge.
Gawlewicz, A. (2016) Language and translation strategies in researching migrant experience of difference from the position of migrant researcher. *Qualitative Research* 16 (1), 27–42.
Guillemin, M. and Gillam, L. (2004) Ethics, reflexivity, and "ethically important moments" in research. *Qualitative Inquiry* 10 (2), 261–280.

Hagenauer, G. and Volet, S.E. (2014) Teacher–student relationship at university: An important yet under-researched field. *Oxford Review of Education* 40 (3), 370–388.

Hanks, J. (2017) *Exploratory Practice in Language Teaching: Puzzling About Principles and Practices*. London: Palgrave Macmillan.

Holliday, A. (1999) Small cultures. *Applied Linguistics* 20 (2), 237–264.

Holliday, A. (2015) Qualitative research and analysis. In B. Paltridge and A. Phakiti (eds) *Research Methods in Applied Linguistics: A Practical Resource* (pp. 49– 62). London: Bloomsbury.

Holliday, A. and Amadasi, S. (2019) *Making Sense of the Intercultural: Finding Decentred Threads*. London: Routledge.

Holmes, D.L., Rupert, P.A., Ross, S.A. and Shapera, W.E. (1999) Student perceptions of dual relationships between faculty and students. *Ethics & Behavior* 9 (2), 79–106.

Komarraju, M., Musulkin, S. and Bhattacharya, G. (2010) Role of student–faculty interactions in developing college students' academic self-concept, motivation, and achievement. *Journal of College Student Development* 51 (3), 332–342.

Kubanyiova, M. (2008) Rethinking research ethics in contemporary applied linguistics: The tension between macroethical and microethical perspectives in situated research. *Modern Language Journal* 92 (4), 503–518.

Kusow, A.M. (2003) Beyond indigenous authenticity: Reflections on the insider/outsider debate in immigration research. *Symbolic Interaction* 26 (4), 591–599.

Lähteenoja, S. and Pirttilä-Backman, A.M. (2005) Cultivation or coddling? University teachers' views on student integration. *Studies in Higher Education* 30 (6), 641–661.

Liamputtong, P. (2008) *Doing Cross-cultural Research: Ethical and Methodological Perspectives*. Dordrecht: Springer.

Mann, S. (2016) *The Research Interview: Reflective Practice and Reflexivity in Research Processes*. London: Palgrave Macmillan.

Mann, S. and Walsh, S. (2017) *Reflective Practice in English Language Teaching: Research-based Principles and Practices*. Abingdon: Routledge.

Mckinley, J. (2019) Evolving the TESOL teaching research nexus. *TESOL Quarterly* 53 (3), 875-884.

Riazi, A.M. (2016) *The Routledge Encyclopedia of Research Methods in Applied Linguistics*. London: Routledge.

Rigg, P. (1991) Whole language in TESOL. *TESOL Quarterly* 25 (3), 521–542.

Sibii, R. (2010) Conceptualizing teacher immediacy through the 'companion' metaphor. *Teaching in Higher Education* 15, 531–542.

Srivastava, P. (2006) Reconciling multiple researcher positionalities and languages in international research. *Research in Comparative and International Education* 1 (3), 210–222.

Suwankhong, D. and Liamputtong, P. (2015) Cultural insiders and research fieldwork: Case examples from cross-cultural research with Thai people. *International Journal of Qualitative Methods* 14 (5), 1–7.

Ushioda, E. (2020) *Language Learning Motivation: An Ethical Agenda for Research*. Oxford: Oxford University Press.

Wanzer, M.B. and Frymier, A.B. (1999) The relationship between student perceptions of instructor humor and students' reports of learning. *Communication Education* 48, 48–62.

Yates, L. (2004) *What Does Good Education Research Look Like?* Maidenhead: Oxford University Press.

Zhang, Q. (2005) Immediacy, humor, power distance, and classroom communication apprehension in Chinese college classrooms. *Communication Quarterly* 53 (1), 109–124.

11 Taking Risks in Literacy Research – Using an Interpreter in Multilingual Research Interviews

Annika Norlund Shaswar

Introduction

This chapter focuses on methodological, ethical and epistemological challenges and risks involved in performing multilingual and cross-cultural research interviews where an interpreter is involved. The data explored here consist of excerpts from a research interview where an interpreter was brought in as a mediator because the interviewee and the researcher did not speak the same language. The interview was performed in the context of an ethnographic study, researching the digital and multilingual literacy practices of adult second language (L2) learners taking part in the language programme 'Swedish for immigrants'. The L2 learners participating in the study lacked or had limited formal schooling.

Performing multilingual and cross-cultural interviews is for several reasons a risky project and if the interviewee is a recently arrived immigrant with limited schooling the challenges are increased. There are methodological and ethical as well as epistemological concerns that need to be taken into consideration in order to ensure that the interviewee understands the purpose of the interview and what their participation in it means, and to ensure that the construction of data is performed in accordance with the overarching purpose of the project. When an interpreter is involved there is a chance of coming to terms with these concerns, but at the same time the process of face-to-face social interaction that the interview consists of is complicated by the fact that an additional participant is included. The interpreter can therefore be understood as a potential resource as well as a potential risk to the quality of the data produced in the multilingual cross-cultural interview.

Consequently, the aim of this chapter is to explore the methodological, ethical and epistemological challenges and risks involved in conducting a qualitative research interview with the help of an interpreter when the interviewee is a newly arrived migrant with limited former education.

Research Basis of the Digital Literacy Practices Study

The interview analysed in this chapter was conducted within a study named *Digital literacy practices* (DigiPrac), which had as overarching aim the exploration of the connections between adult second-language learners' digital literacy practices in their everyday lives and in the educational context of Swedish for immigrants (SFI). SFI offers education in Swedish as an L2 for those adult immigrants who live in Sweden and who lack basic knowledge of the Swedish language. Included in SFI is basic literacy education for those students who are not yet functionally literate in any language (SNAE, 2018). The SFI students who participated in the DigiPrac study were taking part in such basic literacy education. The study focused on the participants' linguistic repertoires (cf. García & Li Wei, 2013; Paulsrud *et al.*, 2017). Literacy was understood as a social practice and relations between language, power and democracy were focused. The research fields of Literacy Studies (Baynham & Prinsloo, 2009) and Critical Literacy (Janks, 2010) constituted parts of the theoretical framework. Ethnographic methodology was used for the data production in the DigiPrac study. Participants were two SFI teachers teaching at two SFI schools and their students. In one group there were 18 students and in the other there were 13 students. Classroom observations and qualitative semi-structural interviews were performed.

Data Explored in this Chapter

The interview discussed in this chapter was audio-recorded and field notes were taken after it was conducted. Participating in the interview were the female researcher (Annika), a male interpreter (referred to as Reza) and a female interviewee (referred to as Alia). The interview focused mainly on Alia's digital literacy practices before her migration.

Before the interview, the researcher had visited the interviewee's SFI group three times to inform the students about the study. The group was linguistically heterogeneous and as the project budget was limited, interpreters were only brought in for the most represented L1s in the group, namely Somali and Arabic. Alia, who speaks Dari, Persian and some Swedish, was given information in Swedish. In the course of the interview, it was clear to the researcher that Alia had not fully understood the purpose of the interview. This will be reflected on below in the Results section.

Before booking an interpreter, the researcher asked the interviewee if she preferred a male or female interpreter and she answered that the gender did not matter. In order to book the interpreter, the researcher contacted a translation and interpreting agency and requested an authorized interpreter who was experienced in conducting interpretation in qualitative research interviews. However, the agency was not able to offer an authorized interpreter in Dari or Persian. Still, according to the information on the agency's website, all of their interpreters have at least either received training from an interpreting agency or have completed a national interpreting education or equivalent. The researcher informed the agency that the interview was going to be audio-recorded so that the interpreter would be aware of this before the interview.

The interviewee's L1 is Dari and since she had been living in Iran for several years, she is also fluent in Persian. In addition, she understands and speaks some Swedish. When the researcher in the interview asked questions in Swedish, the interviewee sometimes answered before the interpreter had translated them. On some occasions during the interview, the interviewee answered the researcher's questions in Swedish, but most often she interacted in Persian. The interpreter interacted in Swedish and Persian, and the researcher interacted in Swedish, her L1. However, although the researcher does not speak Persian, she can understand some words because she is fluent in Sorani, a Kurdish language that is related to Persian.

The researcher had booked the interpreter for one hour. Before the interview commenced, the researcher gave the interpreter an information letter that included information about the purpose and methods of the study and the interview guide that the researcher was going to use, so that he could read them and prepare. However, the interviewee arrived a little early, only a few minutes after the interpreter, which meant that there was very little time for preparation. The interpreter devoted some minutes to the reading of the information letter and hastily glancing through the interview guide. He said that he was used to these types of interviews. The researcher informed him that she did not intend to follow the interview guide strictly but might change the order of questions and add further questions depending on how the interview developed. When transcribing and analysing the interview the researcher later concluded that the information she had given him before the interviews had not been sufficient. These reflections will be developed in the discussion section.

The interview with Alia was conducted in an empty classroom in her SFI school. The participants sat at a round table, with the researcher facing the interviewee and the interpreter sitting to their side. The researcher preferred this seating arrangement because she believed that it would improve her contact with the interviewee during the interview.

The interview was 50 minutes long and the interpreting process was mainly consecutive. Interpreted segments were approximately between a few seconds and half a minute long.

Methods of Data Analysis – Goffman's Participation Framework

The initial step of analysis consisted of transcribing those parts of the interaction which were performed in Swedish. Subsequently, excerpts were selected where the interaction seemed somehow problematic, for example in that it resulted in misunderstandings or other types of miscommunications. These excerpts were sent to a translation agency so that spoken interaction in Persian was transcribed in Persian and translated into Swedish.

Aspects of the interaction characteristic of spoken discourse in general, or spoken L2 Swedish, are of importance for the analysis, and are therefore represented in the transcripts, in the original language of Swedish as well as in the English translation. General characteristics of spoken interaction are for example repetitions within the same utterance or restarts. Since the interpreter is an L2 speaker of Swedish, there are some traits typical of an L2 speaker' language in his spoken interaction. Such characteristics are for example non-idiomatic choice of words and deviations from word order.

The analysis of the excerpts is informed by a dialogic perspective on language, which implies that content and organization of the interaction are controlled in parallel with the progress of the interaction (Wadensjö, 2004).

Goffman's (1981) participation framework and his (1981: 128) concept *footing* have been applied in the analysis of the excerpts, in order to understand the risks that are connected to the construction of meaning in the interviews. *Footing* refers to the varying stances or alignments of participants in situated social interactions (1981: 127). When a speaker or listener changes footing, they go from one mode of social interaction to another, changing between showing themselves as more or less responsible for the content of the ongoing interaction and how it progresses (Wadensjö, 2004: 113). Seen from this perspective, participation status is seen both as an analytical tool used by the researcher and a resource accessible to the listeners and speakers participating in the social interaction (Wadensjö, 2015: 301).

According to Goffman's model, there are three different roles that a speaker can take. Acting as an *animator* means taking little responsibility for the interaction, acting as 'the talking machine, a body engaged in acoustic activity, or, if you will, an individual active in the role of utterance production' (Goffman, 1981: 144). A speaker who takes the role of an animator reports the utterances of somebody else (Goffman, 1981: 151). A second possibility is acting as an *author*, which implies being to a greater extent responsible for the ongoing interaction. An author, according to Goffman (1981: 144) is 'someone who has selected the sentiments that are being expressed and the words in which they are encoded'. A speaker can also take the role of a *principal*, that is 'someone whose position is established by the words that are spoken, someone whose beliefs have been told, someone who is committed to what the words say'. In all, these three concepts carry information about *the production format* of the interaction (Goffman, 1981: 145).

In accordance with Goffman's understanding of the production format, an interpreter who participates in a multilingual research interview can employ varying, continually changing ways of orienting in relation to the interviewee and the researcher and to those utterances that are produced as they interact. As the footing of the interpreter changes, the degree of their responsibility for the content as well as the progression of the ongoing interaction also changes (Wadensjö, 2004: 113).

An additional concept used in the analysis is *face*, which is defined by Goffman (1955: 213) in the following way: 'The term face may be defined as the positive social value a person effectively claims for himself by the line others assume he has taken during a particular contact'.

Literature Review – Risks Connected to Using an Interpreter in Research Interviews

This literature review focuses on questions related to risks connected to using an interpreter in research interviews, and particularly risks connected to the roles and responsibilities of the researcher in those interviews.

Risks connected to multilingual and cross-cultural research interviews involving an interpreter

Performance of cross-cultural interviews in general, and interviewing with an interpreter specifically, is common in multilingual research studies in many different fields. However, until 20 years ago there was a lack of reflection on the methodological, ethical and epistemological vulnerabilities and risks that interviewing with an interpreter caused for the production and analysis of data (Shah, 2004: 550; Temple, 2002: 844; Temple & Edwards, 2002: 2). An abundant literature gave advice on more technical aspects of finding and using an interpreter or other third party in multilingual interviews, but only very few texts (Edwards, 1998; Temple, 1997, 1999; Temple & Edwards, 2002) offered reflection on how the use of interpreters might affect the processes of producing and interpreting research data. The lack of attention to the use of interpreters diverged from the growing interest in the researcher's own impact on the research process and data. It also differed from the field of translation studies, where the translator's influence on the research process was explored. Presently, however, this has changed and the role of interpreters in multilingual research has been given attention by a limited but increasing number of researchers in several areas like anthropology (Borchgrevink, 2003), education research (Andrews, 2013), geography (Caretta, 2015), health research (Björk Brämberg & Dahlberg, 2013; Sleptsova *et al.*, 2017), social psychiatry (Ingvarsdotter *et al.*, 2010) and sociology (Bradby, 2002).

Different research paradigms have different interests and therefore focus on different questions in relation to methodological, ethical and epistemological concerns in multilingual and cross-cultural research. One way of understanding if and how different types of risks attract attention in different research fields is looking at them in terms of how they are placed along the continuum where one end point is sometimes called *positivism*. Researchers whose perspective is close to this end point tend to regard the role of interpreters as the neutral transmission of information between researcher and interviewee. From this perspective, the risk involved in using interpreters is that they might 'add or subtract from what the primary parties communicate to each other' (Freed, 1988: 316). In accordance with this view, it is possible to define the product of translation as correct or incorrect, as there exists one correct version. If the interpreter translates verbatim what the interviewee and researcher say, the risk of incorrect translation is avoided. At the other end point of the continuum is the field called *social construction*. Aligned to this field are those researchers who represent the 'reflexive turn' in social research (e.g. Atkinson, 1990; Hammersley & Atkinson, 2007; Holstein & Gubrium, 1995; van Maanen, 2011; Stanley & Wise, 1983, 1993) and who challenge the understanding that the research process is objective and value-free (Temple & Edwards, 2002: 5). From this perspective, interpreters as well as researchers are actively taking part in the production of knowledge (Temple, 2002: 845). Wadensjö (2011: 14) has described the interaction between researcher, interpreter and interviewee as 'a communicative pas-de-trois'. The three participants together construct new knowledge in a triadic process, all three of them actively taking part (Andrews, 2013: 319; Wadensjö, 2004). From this notion of the interpreter as an active participant in construction and creation of understanding, it is necessary that the interpreter understands the utterances that are going to be translated, and is well aware of the linguistic, social and cultural context where the utterances belong (Maclean, 2007). Otherwise there is a risk that privileged understandings are perpetuated in the research process.

A concern connected to methodological and epistemological questions in multilingual and multicultural research interviews is the risk of power asymmetry between the participants. This question has attracted attention for example by Caretta (2015: 490), who refers to the relation between researcher and interviewee as 'power-loaded'. The researcher controls the processes of producing, analysing and publishing the product of research (Maclean, 2007: 786). However, on the other hand, involving an interpreter in a research interview means that the researcher risks losing some of their control over the interaction in the interview (Wadensjö, 2004), including the possibility of making sure that the interviewee is treated respectfully.

Risks connected to the roles and responsibilities of the interpreter

In connection to the varying views on the methodological, ethical and epistemological aspects mentioned above, there are varying notions of the responsibilities of interpreters in research interviews. On the one hand there are researchers who aim to fully control the process of interaction in the interview and who want the interpreter to stay neutral and take the role of a 'passive interface' (Ingvarsdotter *et al.*, 2010: 35) between researcher and interviewee, translating verbatim. On the other hand, there are researchers who want the interpreter to take a leading role in the interaction of the interviews. Such a role can for example mean that in the interview the interpreter and interviewee interact directly, with the researcher taking a passive role (Andrews, 2013). In many cases, researchers do not align with either of these two extremes but place themselves somewhere along the continuum between them.

The interpreter as translator of language and culture

In a multilingual and cross-cultural research interview, the interpreter can be understood as a mediator (Andrews, 2013) who performs linguistic as well as cultural translation. These two aspects of translation are intermingled. An example of this is performing rephrasing of the researcher's questions to the interviewee starting out from an understanding of the interviewee's cultural background. This position as a mediator is aligned with active participation in negotiation and mediation of meaning (Temple, 2002).

In discussions of how to select a suitable interpreter for a multilingual and cross-cultural research study, it is frequently suggested that the interpreter and interviewee should have a common cultural background (e.g. Björk Brämberg & Dahlberg, 2013: 242). Such a piece of advice presupposes that a person's view on life can be extrapolated from their linguistic or cultural background, and from a critical view on cultural aspects, such a view needs to be questioned (Temple, 2002: 847).

The interpreter as responsible for discourse management and translation

Wadensjö (2004, 2015: 116) has suggested that dialogue interpreters in multilingual interactions have two responsibilities: (1) to manage discourse, or in other words to take responsibility of the management of the organisation of interaction; and (2) to translate the interaction. The discourse management is described by Wadensjö (2015: 116) as helping the two parties in the interaction with the coordination of their turn-taking. The coordinating moves that the interpreter performs in order to manage discourse can be *implicit* or *explicit* (Wadensjö, 2015: 117). Explicit coordinating moves can be of two kinds: text oriented or interaction oriented. These explicit moves aim to coordinate the utterances of the interacting parties and are made up of varying types of petitions, whereby the interpreter for example asks for time to translate or for clarification or makes meta-comments for example on linguistic matters. Implicit coordinating moves consist for example of the interpreter's turn-taking, i.e. for most of the time taking every second turn. Those moves affect how the interaction progresses and how its content is constructed by the interpreter's decisions on what to include or exclude in the translations (Wadensjö, 2015: 116). The management of discourse and the translation are mutually interdependent.

The interpreter as co-researcher

Researchers who identify with the 'reflexive turn' have contended that interpreters need to take a role of co-researchers (Andrews, 2013: 317; Bradby, 2002: 852; Temple & Edwards, 2002: 6). Given that the interpreters affect the construction of data and production of meaning in research, it is argued that their role in the research process needs to be visible. Interpreters' social location and their views on the matters researched in interviews should be made visible (Temple & Edwards, 2002: 6). In addition to making sure that the interpreter fully understands the epistemological and theoretical basis of the interview, the interpreter should be given an opportunity to reflect on the research themes (Andrews, 2013; Temple & Edwards, 2002; Norlund Shaswar, 2021). In that way the researcher can map out the interpreter's view on those themes.

An additional theme that has been underlined in relation to cross-cultural interviews is the risk of the participants experiencing anxiety. A researcher and interviewee who have different cultural backgrounds are unsure of how the interview situation will develop and thus might experience 'unpredictability, helplessness, a threat to self-esteem and a general feeling of "walking on ice" – all of which are stress producing and hamper understanding' (Shah, 2004: 564). The interviewee, who has the least information about the research process, will most likely experience a higher degree of anxiety than the researcher or interpreter. If the interviewee is in a marginalized and vulnerable position, it is probable that they will withhold information (Shah, 2004: 566). Adult immigrants with limited educational background are an example of persons in such a vulnerable position. In many social contexts, limited schooling and lack of functional literacy are regarded as signs of disease, poverty, lack of intelligence and knowledge (Wedin, 2004: 9). To my knowledge, reflections on methodological, ethical and epistemological risks and vulnerabilities involved in performing research interviews with this group of interviewees are scarce in qualitative research in general and also in applied linguistics. Attaining an understanding of a person's fundamental view on life is very difficult, but also very important, as it will have an impact on the interpreter's way of interacting with the interviewee. When interviewing vulnerable interviewees, it is of fundamental importance that the interpreter will show them respect. How can this be done in a smaller research study where literacy is researched from a social practice perspective? The analysis of data and discussion of results in this chapter will address these questions.

Results – Risks Connected to the Negotiation of Roles and Responsibilities in the Interview

In the exploration of risks connected to the roles and responsibilities of the interpreter, excerpts from the transcribed interview are ordered in accordance with the two roles of dialogue interpreters outlined by Wadensjö (2004, 2005). In the next section the role of translating the interaction is focused and in the following section attention is directed towards the role of managing the organization of interaction. However, in the account of the analysis it will be clear that the two roles are interconnected in the interpreter's participation in the interaction. For the analysis, Goffman's notion of *footing* and his participation framework have primarily been used.

Translating the interaction

In this section focus is directed towards situations where the interpreter's acts of translating the interaction either cause or prevent methodological, ethical or epistemological risks. In Excerpt 1 there is a misunderstanding that is constructed by the three interacting participants. Just before the interaction that is represented in this interview excerpt takes place, Annika has asked Alia what it was like when she went to school in Afghanistan as a child and then the following interaction about school experiences follows.

Excerpt 1

In original languages	Translation
1 An: Okej. Det kanske var lite bättre med	An: *Ok. Perhaps school was a little bit better when*
2 skolan när du var barn än vad det är nu?	*you were a child than it is now?*

#		
3	شاید وقتی میگه شما کوچک بودی خُرد بودی، بچه R	R: When you say when you were small, a small
4	بودی شاید مکتب اونموقع بهتر بوده تا الان، خوب تر	child, perhaps school was better then than now,
5	بوده	been better
6	نی، الانم مکتب خوب هسته، هر وقت مکتب خوب Al	Al No now as well school is good, school is always
7	است.	good.
8	R: Nä men alltså skolan är bra här just nu	R: *No but well school is good here right now as well.*
9	också. Skolan är alltid bra.	*School is always good.*
10	الان بگید در پنجاه‌سالگی که در مکتب می‌آیم :Al	Al: **Now that I go to school in my fifties I am very**
11	خیلی خوش دارم، خیلی دوست دارم مکتبه، اینجا که	**satisfied, I like it when I go here,**
12	میایوم خیلی خوش هستوم.	**like it a lot**
13	R: Fast jag är femtio år jag gillar vara i	R: *Although I am fifty years old I like being in school,*
14	skolan, faktiskt.	*actually.*
15	An: Hade du bra lärare?	An: *Did you have good teachers?*
16	Al: Mycket bra.	Al: *Very good.*
17	R: معلم خوب بود؟	R: **Was the teacher good?**
18	Alخیلی	Al: **Very**
19	T: Okej.	R: *Ok.*
20	A: Jaha. Ja. Ehm så du lärde dig bra i	An: *I see. Yes. E so you learned well in*
21	skolan?	*school?*
22	R در مکتب، مدرسه خوب یاد گرفتی؟	R: **You learned well in MAKTAB, school?**
23	Al: بگو خیلی یاد گرفتوم، اگر یاد نمیگرفتوم روزاول	Al: **Say that I have learnt a lot, if I hadn't learned,**
24	که آمده بودوم هیچی نمی‌فهمیدوم، حتی سلام هم بلد	**the first day when I came to school I couldn't even**
25	نبودوم.	**say hello.**
26	الان که همه، در نظر خود خوب میتانم همه مشکلات	**But now I believe that I can manage to solve my**
27	خود را...	**problems.**

Note: Italics is used for English translation of interactions in Swedish and bold is used for English translation of interactions in Persian.

When Annika (lines 1–2) asks 'Perhaps it was a little bit better with school when you were a child than it is now?' her question concerns the school in Afghanistan. Alia in lines 6–7 answers 'No, now as well school is good, school is always good'. Her answer does not show whether she thinks of school in a specific place or in general, but in his translation into Swedish in lines 8–9 the interpreter adds the phrase 'here right now', and thus directs focus to the SFI school where Alia is presently studying Swedish. Here Reza together with Alia are construing an answer to Annika's question that is directed towards SFI school. In her next utterance, in lines 10–12, Alia also clearly directs attention towards SFI school today when she says 'Now that I go to school in my fifties I am very satisfied, I like it when I go here, like it a lot'. Since Alia understands some Swedish, it is probable that she has heard and paid attention when Reza has added (line 8) 'here right now'. This has probably influenced her and made her focus on her studies in SFI school in her utterance in lines 10–12.

However, Annika goes on asking about school in Afghanistan, which can be seen by the use of the past tense in her questions on lines 15 and 20–21. In line 20, Annika asks 'E so you learned well in school?' In his translation of the Swedish 'skola' (school) in line 22, Reza first uses the word مدرسه، (school) and then uses the word مکتب (school) and pronounces the latter word with extra stress. In this act of translation Reza seems to use the word مکتب in order to point out to Alia that Annika is not asking about school in general but is interested in her experiences of going to school in Afghanistan.

In the interaction that takes place in this excerpt it can be concluded that Reza's acts of translation partly cause the misunderstanding between Alia and Annika, but he is also in his acts actively taking part in drawing their attention to this misunderstanding.

In Excerpt 2 the theme of the interaction is what the interviewee did after leaving school in Afghanistan.

Excerpt 2

	In original languages	Translation
1	An: Vad gjorde du när had när du var färdig	An: *What did you do when ha when you had*
2	med skolan, efter fem år i skolan, vad	*finished school, after five years in school, what did*
3	gjorde du sen?	*you do after that?*
4	R بعد از پنج سال که مکتب تمام کردی بعد چکار کردی؟	R: **After five years when you finished school,**
5	شوهر کردی؟	**what did you do after that? Did you get married?**
6	Jag sade gifte du dig)skrattar	*I said did you get married.* (laughs)
7	اوه... طالب اومد دیگه شوهر کردم هه هه هه، میدونی	Al: **Oh, the talibans came and I got married,**
8	Al:خودت!	**(laughs). You know that best yourself.**
9	R: De brukar gifta sig alltså vad heter den	R: *They usually get married at what's it called, the*
10	tidiga ålder	*early age.*
11	Al نی، بزرگ شدم دیگه نمیمونم، آره	Al: **When you grow up you don't remain.**
12	R: چه شد؟ طالب اومد؟	R: **What happened? Did the talibans come?**
13	All آره نی، بزرگ شدم دیگه نمیمونم	Al: **No, I grew up and couldn't ...**
14	R Nej اون پنج سال تمام کردی دیگه مکتب نرفتی؟	R: *No.* **When you had finished five years you no**
15	خُب، چرا نرفتی؟	**longer went to school, okay? Why didn't you go?**
16	Al از خاطر اینکه طالبان اومد نمی مانن بزرگا را...	Al: **Because the talibans came and they don't**
17		**allow adults walk**
18	R: Okej. A ja nu kom talibanerna så vi fick	R: *Okay. A, yes now the talibans came so we*
19	inte gå i skolan.	*weren't allowed to go to school.*

Note: Italics is used for English translation of interactions in Swedish and bold is used for English translation of interactions in Persian.

Annika asks Alia what she did when she had left school (lines 1–3), and Reza in his translation of this question (lines 4–6), adds the question of whether she got married (line 5). He then in lines 5–6 makes an explicit coordinating move when he informs the researcher that he has added this question, and then he laughs. In lines 9–10, he adds a comment to the researcher that seems intended to explain to her why he has added this question: 'They usually get married at what's it called, the early age'. This utterance gives an indication of the interpreter's understanding of what 'de' (they) are like. This third-person pronoun can here be understood to refer to Afghan women generally. Reza seems to have an opinion on what persons with Alia's gender, ethnic and educational background generally do after finishing school, and based on this understanding he suggests an answer to her before she has answered herself. Alia seems to understand Reza's comment to Annika in Swedish (linea 9–10), because in her answer (lines 7–8) she laughs and says 'Oh, the talibans came and I got married, (laughs). You know that best yourself'. Her laughter can be understood here as a strategy used in order to avoid losing face (Goffman, 1955).

The part of the interaction represented in Excerpt 3 concerns Alia's experiences of reading and writing in her work at a factory in Afghanistan where she produced dolls made of textiles.

Excerpt 3

	In original languages	In translation
1	An: Okej. Eh behövde du läsa eller skriva	An: *Okay. Ehm did you need to read and write*
2	någonting när du sydde? För att anteckna till	*something when you were sewing? To take notes*
3	exempel om nån skulle köpa nåt eller för att	*for example if someone was going to buy*
4	läsa någon instruktion eller någonting?	*something or in order to read an instruction or something?*
5	R: وقتی بهر حال میخواستی بدوزی، میگه چیزی رو هم	R: She says when you wanted to sew something,
6	میخواندی، دستورالعمل میخواندی یا اینکه...	directions for use ...
7	Al قرآن، أره قرآن میخواندم....	Al: **Yes, the quran, the quran**
8	T: (نه قرآن)(skrattar) Hon läste koranen.R	R: Not the quran. (laughs) *She read the quran.*
9	Al قرآن میخواندی دیگر چی نمیتونستی...	Al: **Read the quran, not something else**
10	R نه میدونم، یعنی تو کارخونه که بودی یک ورقه بهت	R: Yes, I know, so when you were at the factory,
11	میدادن میگفتن از روی این بذور	did they gave you a paper and say that you were supposed to sew in accordance to the paper?
12	Al: نه...	Al: **No**
13	R:: (نه دیگه تو وارد بودی دیگه) Nej man lärde sig	R: No, not like that, you were skilled at the work.
14	alltså utantill	*No, you learned you know by heart*
15	R: (نشان میداد خودوم می دوختم؟)	Al **They showed and you yourself**
16	R: De visade oss	R: *They showed us.*

Note: Italics is used for English translation of interactions in Swedish and bold is used for English translation of interactions in Persian.

To Annika's question (lines 1–4) of whether Alia used to read or write when she was sewing, Alia answers (line 7) that she was reading the quran. As a reaction to her answer, Reza (line 8) corrects her, saying 'Not the quran', and then laughs. His correction and laughter are problematic because these acts can be, in Goffman's (1955) terms, threatening the interviewee's face. By correcting her he indicates that she has given an incorrect answer, and his laughter can be understood as a reaction to her answering the question in a way that is laughable. When he translates the interviewee's answer (line 8) he says 'She read the quran' using the third-person pronoun 'hon' (she) to refer to the interviewee. In this choice of pronoun, he distances from the interviewee and talks as an author or a principal, rather than as an animator who mediates the interviewee's utterance to the teacher.

Managing the organisation of the interaction

In this section the focus is primarily directed to the interpreter's role of organising the interaction in the interview. In Excerpt 4 the theme of the interaction is the interviewee's literacy skills in Swedish and in Dari. In lines 1–3 Annika asks Alia to compare her skills of reading and writing in the two languages.

Excerpt 4

	In original languages	Translation
1	An: Mhm. Okej. Ehm skriver om du ska	An: *Mhm. Ok. Ehm write, if you are going to*
2	jämföra svenska och dari, vilket kan du läsa	*compare Swedish and Dari, which can you read*
3	och skriva bättre på?	*and write better?*
4	R: إه اگر که مثلاً سویدی و دری مقایسه کنی، کدامش	I: **If you for example Swedish and Dari, which can**
5	Skriva eller läsa sa du? بهتر میتوانی بخوانی	**you read, write, or read** *Read or write you said?*
6	An: Både och.	Al: Both.

7	R:کدام زبان، زبان سوئدی بهتر می توانی خواندن یا	R: Can you read and write in the Swedish language or Dari?
8	نوشتن یا زبان دری؟	
9	Al د بویه، مو بد چیز هستوم که فراموش میکنوم	Al: The thing is that I forget.
10	فراموشم میایه	
11	R: Okej	R: Okay.
12	Al اگر اینه ماله دری را زیاد گپ نزنوم یا که چی نکنوم،	Al: If I don't speak Dari, I forget, I can talk but writing is not so that.
13	هم گپهایش رو یاد داروم، نوشتشه زیاد چیز نیستوم	
14	R: Okej, ja.	R: Okay, yes.
15	Al حا لا که در اینجا در سوئیدن هستوم، فشارو که میارم	Al: Now that I am in Sweden and stress writing.
16	سر نوشتن،	
17	R: Okej, ja.	R: Okay, yes.
18	Al حالا اینجا نوشته از اینجه رو میتونوم، او رقمی هستوم	Al: Now I can write, so I am you can say.
19	بگو.	
20	R: A men jaja, det är så här att om jag inte	R: Yeah but oh well, it is this way that if I don't practice and write, then I can forget you know.
21	alltså träna och inte skriva då jag kan	
22	glömma alltså.	
23	An: Mhm.	An: Okay
24	R: Men eftersom nu jag är här i Sverige så	R: But since I am now in Sweden I have to.
25	jag är tvungen.	
26	A: M	A: Yeah.
27	R: Alltså så skriva	R: So writing.
28	A: Ja	A: Yes.
29	R: Faktiskt nånting. Men du fick inte svar på	R: Actually something. But you didn't get an answer to your question. You wanted you mean some kind of comparison actually. Don't you?
30	din fråga. Du ville alltså du menar du nån	
31	jämförelse faktiskt. Eller hur?	
32	A: M.	A: Yeah
33	T بین اه... سوال اینطوری بود، پرسان کرد زبان سوئندی	R: M. The question was like this, she asked do you know Swedish or Dari better?
34	بهتر میتوانی یا زبان دری؟	
35	دری دری	Al: Dari Dari!
36	R: Dari	R: Dari.

Note: Italics is used for English translation of interactions in Swedish and bold is used for English translation of interactions in Persian.

In lines 29–30 Reza's comment can be understood as an explicit coordinating move made in order to point out to Annika that Alia did not answer the questioned posed by Annika in lines 1–4. Annika in line 32 agrees. Reza's explicit coordinating move here seems to be made in order to ensure that Annika's question is answered correctly by Alia. From that perspective he supports the researcher in attaining her research goal. However, there is a risk that the interviewee's face is threatened by this act from the interpreter.

A different kind of explicit coordinating move is made by Reza in Excerpt 5.

Excerpt 5

	In original languages*	Translation
1	R: och de är dyra den som jag har man kan	R: and they are expensive, the one that I have, you can't so much with do with but iPad is good actually because you can send text messages, you can send you know what is it called, you can email actually. You don't get the answer that you are looking for. Do you understand, because [she says something else].
2	inte så mycket med göra med men iPad är	
3	bra faktiskt eftersom man kan skicka sms,	
4	man kan skicka alltså vad heter man kan	
5	mejla faktiskt. Du får inte det svar som du	
6	alltså är ute efter. Förstår du, eftersom hon	
7	[hon säger nånting annat]	
8	An: [Jo men jag får] Men hos Facebook hon	An: [Yes but I get] But with Facebook she said something about Facebook.
9	sade nånting om Facebook	
10	R: Nej	R: No.
11	An: Jo. Hon sa nåt om Facebook	An: Yes. She said something about Facebook.

*Brackets are used for overlapping talk.

Before the interaction represented in the excerpt takes place, Annika has asked Alia what she thinks of mobile telephones. In lines 1–5, Reza translates her answer, and then changes footing (line 5) when he goes from mediating Alia's utterance into addressing Annika in the second-person pronoun 'du' (you), thereby expressing his own opinion. In lines 5–7 he consequently refers to Alia in third person. 'You don't get the answer that you are looking for. Do you understand, because she says something else'. He is of the opinion that Annika is looking for a specific answer and that Alia is not giving her this answer.

Here, in similarity with Excerpt 4, the interpreter seems to be aligned with the researcher's project, aiming for her to attain the answers that she, according to his understanding, is looking for. The problem is that his comments can be face threatening to Alia, because it suggests that she does not answer the researcher's question. Annika contests Reza's view in lines 8–9, 'Yes but I get', and thus takes back some of the control over the organization of interaction.

In Excerpt 6, Reza raizes the question of whether Alia really understands the purpose of the interview and her role in it.

Excerpt 6

	In original languages	Translation
1	R: Jag undrar om hon verkligen förstår vad	R: *I wonder if she really understands what you*
2	du menar med allt det här. (می فهمی منظور	*mean by all this.* **Do you understand what she**
3	این چیه؟ ایشون محققه...)	**means, she is a researcher and wants to.**
4	Al: Nä	Al: *No.*
5	R: Det är det som hon inte förstår, faktiskt.	R: *That is what she doesn't understand, actually.*
6	An: Vill du f	An: *Do you want to a*
7	R: Jag frågar om du förstå hela den här, nej	R: *I ask if you understand all this, no she says, not*
8	säger hon, inte förstår alltså eftersom	*understand you know because*
9	An: Vill du fråga mig nånting?	An: *Is there anything that you want to ask me?*
10	T میخوای از من سوالی پرسان کنی؟	R: **Do you want to ask me something?**
11	Al آره...	Al: **Yes, certainly.**
12	R: A	R: *Yeah.*
13	Al:آره میخوام	Al: **Yes I do!**
14	R: A. Ja, det vill jag.	R: *Yeah. Yes I do.*
15	A: Vad	An: *What*
16	Al بگو از خاطر از این مو از تو سوال میکنوم که	Al: **I want to ask about why you do it, do you**
17	چطور تو اینکار را رو میکنی، یعنی مثال میخوای تو	**want to be a teacher, do you want to get work**
18	معلم شوی، تجربه کار شنی...	**experience?**
19	R: Okej a. Eh varför du frågar såna grejer.	R: *Okay, yeah. Ehm, why do yo ask that kind of*
20	Vill du bli lärare, vill du bli forskare?	*things? Do you want to become a teacher, do you want to become a researcher?*

Note: Italics is used for English translation of interactions in Swedish and bold is used for English translation of interactions in Persian.

As mentioned above, Alia had been given information about the research, but in this part of the interview Reza with his explicit coordinating move in line 1 makes clear to Annika that Alia has not understood the purpose of the interview and the research project. He talks in the first person, as a principal, taking responsibility for the interaction. Consequently, he is here not only translating what Alia says but also making a statement of his own, starting out from his conclusion that Alia has not understood why Annika wants to have this conversation with her.

Reza's act is of great value to the research process, because he points out a risk of ethical as well as epistemological importance for the construction of data in the interview. An interviewee who understands the purpose of the interview that she is taking part in will probably be able to answer the questions better. In addition, it is an ethical challenge and risk to make an interview with a person who does not understand the purpose of the interview. The interpreter could here also be seen as supporting the interviewee who is in a subordinate position in the interview, in pointing out to the researcher that she has not understood the purpose of her participation in the interview.

Discussion – the Risks of Interviewing with an Interpreter

The research data explored in this chapter illustrates the risks involved in interviewing an adult migrant with limited educational background, including how her face (Goffman, 1955) is threatened, especially by the interpreter's explicit coordinating moves, for example when he comments that she has not answered the researcher's question. In addition, the interpreter expresses a stereotype understanding of the interviewee based on her ethnicity, for example when he comments on 'their' marrying habits. Such understandings in the interpreter risk perpetuating dominant understandings (Maclean, 2007) of interviewees who are in a vulnerable position. This is not only a risk to the interviewee's self-esteem, but also stands in the way of her possibilities of narrating her experiences and the researcher's possibilities of understanding her digital literacy practices in the study.

The present interviewee used the face-saving strategy of laughing. This strategy can be understood as an expression of a feeling of insecurity and vulnerability, and an interviewee who experiences such feelings will not be prepared to open up and narrate experiences (Shah, 2004). This is a problem in a study where the social and cultural context is understood as fundamental for the possibilities of understandings the phenomena that are researched.

A cause of some of the misunderstandings and miscommunications in the interview originated from a discrepancy between the researcher's and the interpreter's understanding of how a research interview should be performed. While the researcher's perspective was aligned with the 'reflexive turn' (e.g. Atkinson, 1990), the interpreter seemed to understand the interview from a positivist perspective.

From the perspective on interaction contended in this chapter, involving an interpreter in a research interview implies a complex 'communicative pas-de-trois' (Wadensjö, 2004) where interviewee, interpreter and researcher together construct new knowledge. The interpreter is affected by and dependent on the communicative acts of the other participants and is not alone responsible for the translation and organization of interaction, for the interviewee's possibility of expressing their voice or for the new knowledge that is constructed. It also needs to be underlined that in the interview explored in this chapter, the interviewee takes acts that mitigate misunderstandings between researcher and interviewee.

Conclusion

As has been made visible in this chapter, there are many risks and vulnerabilities involved in performing an interview with an adult migrant with limited educational background and adding an interpreter as an additional participant in the interaction can increase the challenges. However, there are ways of coming to terms with and mitigating some of the explored risks, vulnerabilities and challenges. The researcher needs to reflect on ethical aspects of the researcher's role in relation to the interviewee (cf. Consoli, Chapter 10). In addition the researcher needs to be aware of those aspects of power, such as gender, ethnicity and educational background, that might affect the interviewee and the data production negatively and reflect on them together with the interpreter. The researcher also needs to inform the interpreter of the theoretical and epistemological starting points of the study (cf Severo & Makoni, Chapter 2) so that the interpreter is aware of how the researcher wants the interview to be performed. The roles and responsibilities of researcher and interpreter also need to be made clear to the interpreter. If researcher and interpreter spend enough time together discussing these matters before the interview, the chances increase of the interpreter being able to take the role of a co-researcher in the research interview so that s/he can alleviate, rather than add to, the risks involved.

References

Andrews, J. (2013) 'It's a very difficult question isn't it': Researcher, interpreter and research participant negotiating meanings in an education research interview. *International Journal of Applied Linguistics* 23 (3), 316–328.

Atkinson, P. (1990) *The Ethnographic Imagination: Textual Constructions of Reality*. London: Routledge.

Baynham, M. and Prinsloo, M. (2009) Introduction. The future of literacy studies. In M. Baynham and M. Prinsloo (eds) *The Future of Literacy Studies* (pp. 1–20). Houndmills: Palgrave Macmillan.

Björk Brämberg, E. and Dahlberg, K. (2013) Interpreters in cross-cultural interviews: A Three-way coconstruction of data. *Qualitative Health Research* 23 (2), 241–247.

Borchgrevink, A. (2003) Silencing language: Of anthropologists and interpreters. *Ethnography* 4, 95–121.

Bradby, H. (2002) Translating culture and language: A research note on multilingual settings. *Sociology of Health & Illness* 24 (6), 842–854.

Caretta, M.A. (2015) Situated knowledge in cross-cultural, cross-language research: A collaborative reflexive analysis of researcher, assistant and participant subjectivities. *Qualitative Research* 15 (4), 489–505.

Edwards, R. (1998) A critical examination of the use of interpreters in the qualitative research process. *Journal of Ethnic and Migration Studies* 24 (1), 197–208.
Freed, A.O. (1988) Interviewing through an interpreter. *Social Work* 33 (4), 315–319.
García, O. and Li Wei (2013) *Translanguaging: Language, Bilingualism and Education*. London: Palgrave Pivot.
Goffman, E. (1955) On face-work: An analysis of ritual elements in social interaction. *Psychiatry* 18 (3), 213–231.
Goffman, E. (1981) *Forms of Talk*. Oxford: Basil Blackwell.
Hammersley, M. and Atkinson, P. (2007) *Ethnography: Principles in Practice* (3rd edn). New York: Routledge.
Holstein, J.A. and Gubrium, J.F. (1995) *The Active Interview*. Qualitative Research Methods Series 37. London: Sage.
Ingvarsdotter, K., Johnsdotter, S. and Östman, M. (2010) Lost in interpretation: The use of interpreters in research on mental ill health. *International Journal of Social Psychiatry* 58 (1), 34–40.
Janks, H. (2010) *Literacy and Power*. New York: Routledge.
Maclean, K. (2007) Translation in cross-cultural research: An example from Bolivia. *Development in Practice* 17 (6), 784–790.
Norlund Shaswar, A. (2021) 'I should really interpret word by word for you': Researcher, interpreter and interviewee negotiating roles, responsibilities and meanings in two multilingual literacy research interviews. In E.O. Breuer, E. Lindgren, A. Stavans and E. Van Steendam (eds) *Multilingual Literacy* (pp. 63–93). Bristol: Multilingual Matters.
Paulsrud, B., Rosén, J., Straszer, B. and Wedin, Å. (eds) (2017) *New Perspectives on Translanguaging and Education*. Bristol: Multilingual Matters.
Shah, S. (2004) The researcher/interviewer in intercultural context: A social intruder. *British Educational Research Journal* 30 (4), 549–575.
Sleptsova, M., Weber, H., Schöpf, A.C., Nubling, M., Morina, N., Hofer, G. and Langewitz, W. (2017) Using interpreters in medical consultations: What is said and what is translated—A descriptive analysis using RIAS, *Patient Education and Counseling* 100, 1667–1671.
SNAE (2018) *Syllabus for Municipal Adult Education in Swedish Tuition for Immigrants (SFI)*. See: https://www.skolverket.se/download/18.4fc05a3f164131a7418ce9/1535097772538/Kursplan%20sfi%20engelska.pdf
Stanley, L. and Wise, S. (1983) *Breaking Out: Feminist Consciousness and Feminist Research*. London: Routledge & Kegan Paul.
Stanley, L. and Wise, S. (1993) *Breaking Out Again: Feminist Ontology and Epistemology*. London: Routledge.
Street, B. (1993) Introduction. The new literacy studies. In B. Street (ed.) *Cross-cultural Approaches to Literacy* (pp. 1–21). Cambridge: Cambridge University Press.
Temple, B. (1997) Issues in translation and cross-cultural research. *Sociology* 31 (3), 607–618.
Temple, B. (2002) Crossed wires: Interpreters, translators and bilingual workers in cross-language research. *Qualitative Health Research* 12 (6), 844–854.
Temple, B. (1999) Diaspora, diaspora space and Polish women. *Women's Studies International Forum* 22 (1), 17–24.
Temple, B. and Edwards (2002) Interpreters/translators and cross-language research: Reflexivity and border crossings. *International Journal of Qualitative Methods* 1 (2), 1–22.
van Maanen, J. (2011) *Tales of the Fields: On Writing Ethnography* (2nd edn). Chicago, IL: Chicago University Press.
Wadensjö, C. (2004) Dialogue interpreting: A monologising practice in a dialogically organized world. *Target* 16 (1), 105–124.

Wadensjö, C. (2011) Interpreting in theory and practice: Reflections about an alleged gap. In E. Tizelius and A. Hild (eds) *Methods and Strategies of Process Research: Integrative Approaches in Translation Studies*. Amsterdam: John Benjamins.

Wadensjö, C. (2015) Discourse management. In F. Pöchhacker (ed.) *Routledge Encyclopedia of Interpreting Studies*. London: Routledge.

Wedin, Å. (2004) *Literacy Practices in and out of School in Karagwe: The Case of Primary School Literacy Education in Rural Tanzania*. Stockholm: Stockholm University.

Part 4
Education

12 A Challenge for Applied Linguistics: Developing a Novel Curriculum in the Field of Language and Integration

Liana Konstantinidou and Ursula Stadler

Introduction

In the last two decades, communication skills in the 'new' language, i.e. in the language(s) of the receiving country, have been at the core of political and media discourse about migration and migrants' integration. The linguistic enablement of newcomers has turned into a major political mission considering that language is the key to successful societal and labour market integration (Mateos, 2009): state-funded language programmes have been designed and have become mandatory for migrants and training programmes for language teachers have been developed and promoted. At the same time, language skills have become a major requirement for obtaining the right to enter a country and gain residency and ultimately citizenship in a growing number of countries (ALTE & Council of Europe, 2019; McNamara & Shohamy, 2008; Krumm, 2005).

After years of political reluctance to tackle the issue of migrants' integration, this sudden urgency of political action as well as the linking of language command with restrictive migration policies as well as assimilative tendencies (Krumm & Plutzar, 2016) is hardly understandable without taking into account the economic crisis and what is often referred to as the refugee crisis that European countries have experienced in recent years (Sierocka, 2018). The economic crisis raised issues such as local labour market protection, illegal immigration and unemployment, social expenses and vulnerable groups that occupied a dominant and often emotional position in the discourse especially of right-wing populist and right-wing extremist parties in Europe (Konstantinidou, 2017), in which 'socially accepted (...) xenophobic attitudes' (Barber, Chapter 9) were a common denominator. During the refugee crisis, this discourse was further intensified by Europe failing to react appropriately and member states clashing over how to share responsibility for processing and offering protection to refugees (Beirens, 2018). In this context, the implementation of measures for language integration seems to be one of the responses of the European migration policy, which struggles to cope with transnational challenges and at the same time protect national sovereignty.

Against this background, the positioning of applied linguistics as an interdisciplinary and transdisciplinary field of research and practice dealing with practical problems of language and communication (AILA, 2020) has come into focus. While it is generally recognised that language skills are important for participating in the 'new' society, there is a lack of research evidence about a direct connection between language and social integration (ALTE & Council of Europe 2019) and applied linguistics has so far not succeeded in giving clear and research-based answers to this socially relevant problem.

In this paper, we will describe the challenges of launching a novel curriculum in applied linguistics in German-speaking Switzerland. Firstly, we will embed the curriculum in the overall discourse on language and integration in Switzerland. Then, we will explain why we think that applied linguistics should take responsibility in this discourse. The development of the curriculum as well as the challenges faced in this process will be described, discussed and reflected on.

The Language Discourse in the Context of Migration and Integration in Switzerland

According to the Federal Statistical Office, 2,175,400 people of foreign nationality were resident in Switzerland in 2019, which corresponds to 25% of the total population. The majority of the foreign residents are European (83%) and come from an EU/EFTA member state (66%). The most represented nationalities are Italians, Germans, Portuguese, French, Kosovars and Spanish (Federal Statistical Office, 2020).

Despite its clearly European background, the foreign population in Switzerland includes quite heterogeneous migrant profiles as far as immigration reasons, legal and socio-economic status, education background, religion orientations and linguistic competences are concerned (Federal Statistical Office, 2020a, 2020b), and can thus be classified as a superdiverse community in the sense of Vertovec (2007), with diverse needs and consequently diverse linguistic needs. This diversity seems not to be sufficiently considered in the social and political discourse about language and integration.

In contrast to expectations from a multilingual country where national identity is not connected with one single language (Konstantinidou, 2014), the discourse on language and integration in Switzerland does not differ from the discourse in other European countries as described above. Skills in the local language are required for residency and citizenship and immigrants need to at least register for a language course before entering the country (AIG, Federal Act on Foreign Nationals and Integration; BüV, Regulation on Swiss Citizenship). The term *local language* refers to the language spoken in the respective language regions of Switzerland: German, French, Italian or Romansh. Specifically, in German-speaking Switzerland, local language refers to the standard variety of German, also called 'Written Language', and not to the spoken Swiss-German dialects.

In general, the social and political discourse on migrants' integration in Switzerland is based on the formula of 'promoting and demanding' (= *fördern und fordern/ promouvoir et exiger/promuovere e esigere*). 'Promoting' includes all targeted measures taken by the state authorities to promote the integration of foreigners, such as measures for access to health care, to the labour market, to education. 'Demanding' focuses on the self-responsibility of migrants (State Secretariat of Migration, 2015; Mateos, 2009).

Applying this formula to the concept of linguistic integration, in 2007, the Swiss Federal Council initiated the development of a national framework for the linguistic enablement of adult migrants. Its main aims were to ensure the quality and efficacy of language courses and to develop valid tools for the evaluation and certification of the linguistic skills of adult migrants (Schleiss & Hagenow-Caprez, 2017).

As a result of this political decision, an outline curriculum was published in 2009 (Lenz *et al*., 2009) and a number of national projects were initiated in the field of linguistic integration that were subsequently united under the *fide* programme (Lenz, 2013). *fide* is the acronym used to refer to the overall system for linguistic integration in Switzerland and stands for *français, italiano, deutsch*. It offers teaching materials and guidelines for teachers, reference examples of migrants' linguistic performance, a qualification profile for teachers as well as a training and qualification system, placement and language assessment tools, a quality assurance system and a coordinating national office (Schleiss & Hagenow-Caprez, 2017).

The development of the *fide* system occurred in parallel to the revision of the AIG, the adoption of the BüV and regulations on the integration of foreigners (VIntA). In art. 4 of the AIG, foreign nationals are required to familiarise themselves with the social conditions and way of life in Switzerland and in particular to learn a national language. At the same time, integration is recognised as a joint task of the confederation, cantons and municipalities (art. 53): they are required to create favourable regulatory conditions for equal opportunities and for the participation of the foreign population in public life and make use of the potential of the foreign population, taking into account diversity and encouraging individual responsibility. Among other things, the confederation, cantons and municipalities need to encourage the development of language skills. The cooperation of the confederation, the cantons and the municipalities in the field of integration is regulated in the VIntA, which also includes aspects of financing of the integration measures.

National, cantonal and local authorities invest around 50 million Swiss Francs per year for the linguistic enablement of adult immigrants. In 2011, this allowed for the funding of approximately 4240 language courses with an estimated total of 100,000 participants (Flubacher & de Cillia, 2017). Furthermore, language courses are offered and financed by regional employment offices. The financing of these courses amounts to about 40 million per year. At the same time, national and cantonal projects aiming at social integration and employability through language education receive complementary funding. For example, for a project targetting the fast integration of young refugees into the professional education system, the confederation invests another 54 million Swiss Francs (State Secretariat for Migration, 2018).

While these investments show the political will to create favourable conditions for integration (promote/fördern/promouvoir/promuovere), the integration criteria spelled out in the law illustrate the expectations of the host country (demand/fordern/exiger/exigere). When assessing integration, Swiss authorities take the following criteria into account: (a) respect for public safety, security and order; (b) respect for the values of the Federal Constitution; (c) language skills; and (d) social participation (work or education). The minimum language skills for residence and family reunification are specified in the regulation on admission, residence and employment ('VZAE'); the minimum language skills for citizenship are defined in the BüV. Cantons and municipalities may adapt the minimum language requirements upwards. For example, the canton of Thurgau specified the language requirements for citizenship at level B1 in written communication and B2 in oral communication instead of the levels stipulated in the regulation: A2 in written communication and B1 in oral communication.

In this context of political conviction that language skills are necessarily related to integration, the discipline of applied linguistics is called upon to take a stand. On the one hand, research is urgently needed to critically evaluate the link between language skills and social integration; on the other hand, applied linguistics has to ensure the quality of language learning and testing. Both tasks are associated with challenges, among others the difficulty of defining and measuring the construct of integration or the occupation itself, which is in the process of professionalisation and not yet institutionally anchored.

The Responsibility of Applied Linguistics

Applied linguistics aims at having an impact on today's society and therefore assumes social responsibility. In its policy, the School of

Applied Linguistics of the Zurich University of Applied Sciences defines its strategic objectives as identifying, describing, analysing and solving socially relevant problems in which language-based communication plays a central role (Strategy School of Applied Linguistics). One of the most important social challenges of the past few decades concerns migration and, related to this, second language acquisition of migrants as a precondition for social and professional participation and thus, it is no surprise that applied linguistics has turned its attention to tackling this challenge.

In the research field of language and migrants' integration, as in most research areas of applied linguistics, a trandisciplinary approach is essential. Transdisciplinarity is understood not simply as 'transcending the concept of discipline within academia', but rather as a 'deep collaboration across and beyond academic and non-academic disciplines and fields' (Perrin & Kramsch, 2018). Effective professional practice in the field of language and integration presupposes a thorough understanding of the highly diversified needs of language learners (e.g. areas of language use – professional or every day communication) as well as language skills for participation in activist citizenship (Hepworth, Chapter 13), of psychological and motivational aspects depending on individual learning biographies and cultures, and of individual factors (e.g. family situation, motives of migration). It also requires an understanding of the local language situation (e.g. diglossia in German-speaking Switzerland) as well as knowledge of the legal and political frame (e.g. migration laws). This wide range of required competences makes transdisciplinarity a prerequisite: applied linguists need to transform knowledge from other disciplines (e.g. health care) into linguistic communicative action; they also need to transform practical knowledge into practice-informed linguistic knowledge. We understand this capability as reflective practice, as defined by Hatton and Smith (1995: 46): 'The professional practitioner is able consciously to think about an action as it is taking place, making sense of what is happening and shaping successive practical steps using multiple viewpoints as appropriate'.

In order to meet the increasing need for skilled experts in the field of linguistic integration of adult migrants, the School of Applied Linguistics has decided to launch a novel bachelor study programme, 'Language and Integration'. This programme focuses on the issues described above and aims at enabling students to become reflective practitioners; it contributes to tackling socially relevant, language-based challenges while being anchored in the discipline of applied linguistics, which itself, as shown above, invites openness to transdisciplinary approaches and inputs.

In the following section, we will describe how we approached the task of integrating applied linguistic research knowledge, knowledge from other disciplines and practical knowledge when developing the curriculum of the Bachelor programme.

Curriculum Development

On a concrete level, the team in charge of developing the curriculum had to meet the challenge of identifying the necessary skills and competences required for enabling future graduates to act as reflective practitioners. The team included both scholars and practitioners in the field of second language acquisition but, in the light of what was discussed above, it was clear that this task could not be performed on the basis of mere practical or research-based knowledge. Therefore, the project group's approach additionally aimed at the involvement of a wide variety of stakeholders in order to identify not only as many of the issues as possible that needed to be addressed in the development of the curriculum but also effective methods to meet them. The procedure included qualitative and quantitative methods and the following steps and stakeholders were defined:

A. Analysis of migrants' needs
B. Expectations of prospective students
C. Market Analysis:
    1. Required skills and competences of professionals
    2. Expectations of potential employers
    3. Market needs analyses
D. Validation of curriculum by scholars and stakeholders

Table 12.1 illustrates steps A–D, the methodological approach and the database.

In the following, we will briefly summarise the main results of our survey in the context of the curriculum development. A detailed presentation of the results would be beyond the scope of this chapter, which aims at identifying essential challenges when launching a novel curriculum in the field of language and integration.

A. Interviews with migrants

The interviews with 11 migrants included questions on first impressions of Switzerland, linguistic challenges especially when dealing with diglossia (Swiss German), experiences and requirements regarding language teaching in Switzerland, and professional and personal aims when living in Switzerland.

The main points raised by the interviewees regardless of background, age or sex can be summarised as follows:

- the importance of didactic qualifications of language teachers;
- the relevance of intercultural competence of language teachers;
- the significance of contents oriented to everyday life; and
- the necessity of promoting receptive competences in Swiss German dialects.

Table 12.1 Methods in the process of the curriculum development

Aim	Method	Data
A Analysis of migrants' needs	Interviews	**Number of participants:** 11 **Age:** 24–48 **Sex:** 5 F, 6 M **Length of stay in Switzerland:** 1–13 years **Country of origin:** Eritrea, Seychelles, Cameroon, Taiwan, Philippines, Afghanistan, UK, Hungary, Iran **Educational background:** from elementary school to PhD
B Expectations of prospective students	Interviews	Students from different middle schools (professional middle school, high school), university students **Number of participants:** 29 (total number) – 26 middle school students and 3 university students **Sex:** 20 F, 9 M **Age:** 17–23 (middle school students), 21–26 (university students)
C1 Required skills and competences of professionals	Quantitative analysis of job advertisements	96 job advertisements (91 online, 5 print) in the fields of language schools (45%), institutions of migration/integration (47%), job placement agencies (8%), years 2015–2017
C2 Expectations of potential employers	Interviews	**Number of participants:** 12 **Work fields:** language schools (4), institutions of integration (4), publishing houses (2), academic institutions (2)
C3 Market needs analyses	Questionnaire	**Number of participants:** 105 **Work fields:** institutions of migration/integration, educational institutions, social institutions, health service, private business and commerce, publishing houses
D Validation of curriculum by scholars and stakeholders	Focus group discussions	**Group 1:** Scholars and academics of universities in Switzerland and Germany (field of research, linguistics and education) Number of participants: 6 **Group 2:** Practitioners from different work fields, 12 (language schools, publishing houses, government institutions, placement agencies, NGOs, health institutions) Number of participants: 12

Considering these results, a challenge in the curriculum development is to reflect the diglossic situation in Switzerland. The understanding of the Swiss German dialects in specific contexts is a prerequisite for social and labour market participation. Furthermore, natural language acquisition in many domains of Switzerland's everyday life includes the learning of the local dialect, which itself has an impact on the acquisition of the standard variety of German used in Switzerland. Another challenge, and one on a different level, is given by the fact that the questions to migrants outlined above are per se defined by an 'insider and outsider positioning' (Barber, Chapter 9) and hence imply the necessity to critically scrutinise our own positions and perconceptions as developers of a curriculum when analysing the answers.

B. Interviews with prospective students

The interviews with prospective students were conducted either individually or in groups. The questions covered expectations of the curriculum (content, subjects), motives for possible choice of the new degree programme, career opportunities and prospective salary.

The results of this stakeholder analysis varied widely depending on interviewees and their individual interests; however, no differences between age groups and current educational programme (grammar school vs professional school or university) could be observed. Only the gender aspect seemed to be relevant when expressing interest in the new degree programme, with female participants claiming a greater interest.

The expected contents of the curriculum mentioned by prospective students cover areas like German grammar and grammar of Non-European languages, psychology, learning psychology, intercultural competences, andragogy and language didactics.

The interviews also showed that the new degree programme appeals to students with an interest in languages, different cultures and working with people. The possibility of working both in teaching and in administrative functions is considered attractive. Reasons against choosing the new degree programme were also mentioned: lack of interest in teaching, preference of working with children rather than adults, limited career opportunities and no interest in languages and humanities. As far as the prospective salary is concerned, interviewees expected to earn a living, but beyond that it was of little interest to them. Interest in and passion for the subject of the studies were considered more important by nearly all of the interviewees.

Considering these findings, a challenge in the curriculum development is to anticipate career opportunities in a field that is currently in the process of professionalisation: professionalisation naturally leads to new working areas beyond the field of language teaching. The competences required for these new working areas have to be reflected in the curriculum in order to enable students to extend their career opportunities.

C1. Analysis of job advertisements

The analysis of the job advertisements clearly shows the professionalisation promoted by the Swiss authorities: a large spectrum of skills and competences is asked for by recruiters for jobs in the field of linguistic, social and professional integration. The most frequent requirement refers to specific skills for working with adult migrants of low educational background: qualifications in the field of literacy training are a desired asset, closely followed by experience and skills in language support for job coaching and job recruitment. The analysis further shows a clear demand for specialised teaching staff in domain-specific contexts: German for banking, German for health care, German for construction workers and German as a second language for mothers of small children.

On a less immediately linguistic level, intercultural competence, knowledge of teaching methods and andragogy as well as familiarity with legal aspects and institutional regulations (social institutions, institutions of vocational training) are important assets when working with adult migrants – all of them being mentioned as important qualifications in the job advertisements examined.

Summing up, we can state that professionals in the field of linguistic, social and professional integration need a highly diversified profile consisting of competences in applied linguistics, language didactics and andragogy, intercultural competences and familiarity with legal and institutional aspects.

In the light of these findings, it seems clear that interdisciplinarity is of crucial importance for the development of the BA curriculum.

C2. Expectations of potential employers

The questions answered by interviewees who were considered to be potential employers referred to required skills, employability and acceptance of the new degree on the job market.

All of the interviewees envisage employment options for graduates of the planned degree programme, provided that graduates obtain a thorough knowledge of teaching methodology, considered to be by far the most essential asset. Other areas considered important by employers included project management, curriculum development and evaluation, language coaching, literacy training, legal aspects, intercultural communication, staff management, budgeting and financial management.

In the eyes of the employers interviewed, the recognition of the new BA degree on the work market is crucial to ensure employability. Additionally, and partly as a consequence of the above, employers stress the necessity to equip students during their university years with practical work experience, preferably in different areas of language and integration, but especially in the field of teaching.

Considering these results, there is a risk in developing a curriculum for reflective practitioners without giving the practice part enough weight: practical work experience, especially in the field of teaching, has to be a central part of the curriculum and is crucial for its success.

C3. Market needs analyses

About two-thirds of the organisations and institutions that were interviewed employ staff in the field of language and integration, half of whom work as language teachers. Experts in functions other than teaching are mainly employed in institutions of migration/integration, health and social services.

There is a clear interest in employing graduates of the new degree programme: 65% of the institutions interviewed express interest; 70% of the institutions state a growing need for highly qualified staff in the field of language and integration (language teachers and staff specialised to work with migrants of low levels of education being particularly high in demand). This need is particularly expressed by institutions of health services. The growing need for qualified staff might explain why nearly half of the interviewees claim difficulties in recruiting suitable candidates. The estimated number of job vacancies for specialists in the field of language and migration in the German-speaking part of Switzerland consists of 66 full-time positions a year; however, it is essential for graduates to have a profile beyond that of mere language teaching in order to be able to fill the vacant positions. Employers express concern about finding suitably qualified staff given the low salaries earned in the field of language and integration, especially by language teachers.

Summing up, the main challenge to meet here – and one that goes beyond the aspect of curriculum development – is the contradiction between, on the one hand, the growing need for experts for different and complex tasks in the field of language and migration, and on the other hand, the low remuneration associated with positions in this area owing to a lack of social recognition.

D. Validation of curriculum by scholars and stakeholders

In order to validate the curriculum, a workshop was organised with the participation of two working groups, the first one consisting of scholars and academics of universities in Switzerland and Germany, the second one consisting of practitioners. The workshop included focus group discussions, followed by presentations of results and a plenary discussion. Additionally, a written assessment of the curriculum was submitted by the participants of group one.

The most important issue raised by the practice stakeholders concerned the necessity of including legal and economic aspects in the curriculum, with a focus on migration law and social insurance law. Great importance should further be attached to subjects such as project management and educational management/business economics, in order to increase employment opportunities for graduates in the field of language and integration.

Another issue referred to the necessity of closely linking theory and practice: qualified professionals with both practical and theoretical competences being in high demand. When considering employing graduates of the new degree programme, stakeholders would particularly welcome applications by candidates with a vocational training background (e.g. professional training in health care, commercial apprenticeship), since they are deemed to be able to directly relate language promotion to specific work fields.

Finally, the issue of a double necessity of digital didactics was raised: on the one hand, it would enable students to undertake distance learning, thus allowing them part-time work and as a consequence more practical work experience. On the other hand, having experienced e-didactics in the degree programme for themselves would allow students to innovatively include digital learning methods and promote digital literacy in their own professional teaching practice, a skill much required in the field of language and integration.

Although the necessity to stretch work opportunities of graduates beyond teaching positions was also considered important by the group of academics and scholars, their curriculum assessment did not focus on giving more weight to contextual knowledge. Rather, a more clearly directed streamlining of the curriculum was asked for, with research methods and didactics being the areas considered to deserve more weight and depth. As far as research is concerned, the necessity for students to focus on socially relevant linguistic research questions was emphasised: pragmatics and sociolinguistics were here considered particularly relevant.

More, and more detailed, feedback was given on the size of the modules (in terms of ECTS [European Credit Transfer System] points), the organisation of teaching practice or the didactics of intercultural competences, to which a high degree of relevance was attached. On a different level, the question of 'recognition of prior learning' for more mature students with previous work experience was discussed.

Further, terminological issues were raised, particularly regarding the title of the degree programme and the connotations of the term 'integration'. The scholars discussed that the term of integration is connected with the idea of incorporation into an existing system. The fact that the existing system can change through the interaction and diversity of individuals and groups (in this case migrants) is mostly and deliberately ignored; probably also because any system change might question existing power relations. Other terms like inclusion, enablement and participation would be more appropriate for the understanding of integration in the context of the study programme.

Considering these results, the main challenge to be tackled is the right balance of the curriculum: while practitioners plead for broad knowledge including non-linguistic and non-didactic areas like economics, project management or law, scholars argue for a streamlining of the curriculum, stressing the significance of scientific quality and depth and the enablement of students to deal with socially relevant research questions.

Discussion

The results show the high and diverse expectations of the stakeholders both regarding the desirable qualifications seen as essential for experts in the area of language and integration and regarding the curriculum that should lead to these qualifications. At the same time, these expectations are part of an academic, social and political discourse on the connection between language skills and migration/integration policies (see above), in which the discipline of applied linguistics is called to play a key role.

The challenges outlined above reach beyond language learning and teaching (e.g. language acquisition in diglossic contexts). They include the practical aspects of a profession in the process of professionalisation (e.g. career opportunities, remuneration). The challenges are also connected with the insight that applied linguistics alone cannot provide the solution to this socially relevant problem and that a collaborative effort is needed both with (language) practitioners and with other disciplines.

On the curricular level, we respond to the challenges raised by stakeholders by including four strongly interrelated learning areas: linguistics, language didactics, practical work and contextual knowledge. While linguistics and language didactics ensure the acquisition and reflection of applied linguistic knowledge, the learning area practical work guarantees the implementation of this knowledge in the professional field. Short internships take place during the regular semesters and a longer one is scheduled in the fourth semester, to be completed either in Switzerland or abroad. In contextual knowledge, students acquire competences from neighbouring disciplines (e.g. migration law and history, education management, coaching), which are essential for professional action in the field of language and integration. These competences make it possible for graduates to undertake tasks beyond the field of language teaching, thereby increasing their career opportunities. The four learning areas are closely interconnected, as applied linguistic knowledge is valuable in its implementation and the implementation itself is context related: projects, lectures and examinations involving multiple learning areas ensure this interrelation.

Finally, the greatest responsibility of applied linguistics does not exclusively lie in recognising where the discipline is indispensable, but also lies in raising the question about the limits of its impact. The task of applied linguistics in discourse of language and integration certainly consists in the examination of the correlation between linguistic skills and integration, in the scientific evaluation of language-related measures, in the development of reliable diagnostic tools and tests and their impact.

However, the broader question of how integration is socially understood and scientifically defined has to be raised by a broader scientific community and by all social actors concerned: what are indeed the indicators of successful integration? Are they measurable? How can we go beyond narrow definitions of integration to a more substantial understanding focusing on active and critical discourse participation? These are open questions in a field in need of further and transdisciplinary research, where applied linguistics can perform a leading role in reshaping the concept of integration. Offering a new and transdisciplinary study programme for experts in the field of language and integration is one step in this direction. Language skills alone do not guarantee integration, but integration necessarily embraces linguistic participation as defined in the novel curriculum: linguistic participation relates to a broad understanding of processes taking place in multilingual societies. They include multimodal and plurilingual resources of all citizens, ranging from their ideas on democratic participation to general and institutional assumptions of social and professional responsibility.

References

ALTE and Council of Europe (2019) *Linguistic Integration of Adult Migrants: Requirements and Learning Opportunities for Migrants*. Strasbourg: Council of Europe.

AILA (2020) What is AILA? See: https://aila.info/

Bereins, H. (2018) *Cracked Foundation, Uncertain Future. Structural Weaknesses in the Common European Asylum System*. Brussels: Migration Policy Institute Europe.

Federal Statistical Office (2020a) Foreign population. See: https://www.bfs.admin.ch/bfs/en/home/statistics/population/migration-integration/foreign.html

Federal Statistical Office (2020b) Integration indicators: Language. See: https://www.bfs.admin.ch/bfs/en/home/statistics/population/migration-integration/integration-indicators/all-indicators/language.html

Flubacher, M.-C. and De Cillia, R. in Cooperation with Daase, A., Debiasi, V., Demmig, S., Kloyber, C., Konstantinidou, L., Rizzo, R.-M., Schleiss, M. and Schmölzer Eibinger, S. (2017) DaZ im Kontext sozialer Integration in den deutschsprachigen Ländern: Berufliche Aus- und Weiterbildung im Fokus. Fribourg: IDT. See https://www.idt-2017.ch/images/03_fachprogramm/02_sig/Bericht__SIG-AG_1_2_IDT2017_def.pdf

Hatton, N. and Smith, D. (1995) Reflection in teacher education: Towards definition and implementation. *Teaching and Teacher Education* 11 (1), 33–49.

Konstantinidou, L. (2014) Some responses to Tariq Modood's Kohlberg Memorial Lecture at the 2013 AME conference, Montreal, from different regions around the world. See http://amenetwork.org/oped/?p=130

Konstantinidou, L. (2017) *Interkulturelle Erziehung: eine Erziehung zur universalistischen Moral.Die Berücksichtigung der moralischen Dimension von Integrations- und Migrationsfragenund deren Wirkung auf die Einstellungen gegenüber Migrantinnen und Migranten*. Freiburg Schweiz: RERO DOC.

Krumm, H.-J. (2005) Integration durch Sprache? Welche Chancen bieten Deutschkurse? *Rundbrief AKDaF Schweiz* 19 (52), 3 – 11.

Krumm, H.-J. and Plutzar, V. (2008) Tailoring language provision and requirements to the needs and capacities of adult migrants. In Thematic Studies prepared for the Seminar *The Linguistic Integration of Adult Migrants*, 26–27 June 2008, Strasbourg.

Lenz, P. (2013) 'Fördern und Fordern'. Das Rahmencurriculum als Instrument zur bedürfnisgerechten Sprachförderung und als (möglicher) Bezugsrahmen für Sprachnachweize. *Babylonia* 1, 24–27.

Lenz, P., Andrey, S. and Lind-Bangerter, B. (2009) *Rahmencurriculum für die sprachliche Förderung von Migrantinnen und Migranten*. Bern: BFM.

Mateos, I. (2009) 'Sprache als Schlüssel zur Integration' – eine Metapher und ihre Folgen. In E. Piñeiro, I. Bopp and G. Kreis (eds) *Fördern und Fordern im Fokus: Leerstellen des schweizerischen Integrationsdiskurses*. Zürich. Seismo Verlag.

McNamara, T. and Shohamy, E. (2008) Language tests and human rights. *International Journal of Applied Linguistics* 18 (1), 89–95.

Perrin, D. and Kramsch, C. (2018) Transdisciplinarity in applied linguistics: Introduction to the special issue. *AILA Review* 31 (1), 1–13.

Schleiss, M. and Hagenow-Caprez, M. (2017) fide – On the way to a coherent framework. In J.-C. Beacco, H.-J. Krumm and D. Little (eds) *The Linguistic Integration of Adult Immigrants – Some Lessons from Research*. Leck: De Gruyter.

Sierocka, H. (2018) Linguistic integration of adult migrants in the era of the migration crisis. In E. Kuzelewska, A. Weatherburn and D. KlozaIrregular (eds) *Irregular Migration as a Challenge for Democracy* (pp. 257–275). Cambridge: Intersentia.

State Secretariat of Migration (2015) Schweizerische Integrationspolitik. See https://www.sem.admin.ch/sem/de/home/themen/integration/politik.html

State Secretariat of Migration (2018) Zahlen und Fakten zut Integrationsagenda. See https://www.sem.admin.ch/dam/data/sem/integration/agenda/faktenblatt-integrationsagenda-zahlen-d.pdf

Vertovec, S. (2007) Super-diversity and its implications. *Ethnic and Racial Studies* 30 (6), 1024–1054.

13 Teaching Controversial Issues in the Language Education of Adult Migrants to the UK: A Risk Worth Taking

Michael Hepworth

Introduction

Discussing controversial issues can be of real value in language teaching and learning and language teacher education and therefore it very definitely is a risk worth taking. This is because debating controversial issues can help promote democratic citizenship (for ESOL, English to Speakers of Other Languages, teachers as well as learners) as well as developing language learning skills. This argument is urgent because, while the value of controversy in language learning is increasingly attested to in the research literature (e.g. Cooke & Roberts, 2007; Hepworth, 2015), some teachers (Hepworth, 2015) and most materials writers (Gray, 2002) choose to avoid the challenge.

In making this argument, I begin by establishing the context and theoretical background for my approach and go on to discuss the opportunities afforded by and the risks of making space for controversial issues in the language and language teacher education classroom. I illustrate and support my argument with data from Adult ESOL classrooms and voices from student and teacher interviews. In the interests of reflexivity, and in order to position myself within this research, it is necessary to state that the classroom-based data was sourced through exploratory practice, a form of practitioner-research (Hanks, 2017) in which I took up the role of teacher–researcher in my own classroom.

The Nature and Value of Controversy

In order to illuminate something of the nature and value of controversy I offer the following vignette from the language education classroom. I do not offer any substantive analysis here, as I have written more extensively about it elsewhere (Hepworth, 2019). In brief, I was a non-participant observer in an advanced-level general English class, in which the students had just found out about the new policy to introduce fees for their (previously free) language classes. It is the beginning of the class. In response to student demands for clarification, the teacher is forced to state the new policy:

> **Teacher:** if you are on a low income you pay half price (...) but from next year it's not going to be available
>
> **Student:** good news

The student interrupts the teacher and the response is ironic, indeed, mocking. Controversial issues 'arouse strong feelings' (Fiehn, 2005: 11). They emerge spontaneously and unexpectedly and the irony and interruption position the teacher awkwardly, making them vulnerable in front of the students, and me, the observer, feel uncomfortable on their behalf. Perhaps unexpectedly, this can also generate playfulness or creativity, visible here through irony, which also does politeness work by blunting the edge of the disagreement.

The vignette also tells us something about the value of controversy in terms of language learning and critical thinking. The irony is a sophisticated politeness strategy. The subsequent discussion generated productive language interaction, extended turns of talk and critical thinking around the right to free language provision. In some cases, this led to students and teachers getting involved in an Action for ESOL campaign to defend the right to language provision.

This issue was controversial in line with the general characterisation below:

> problems or disputes which divide society and for which significant groups within society offer conflicting explanations and solutions based on alternative values. (Stradling *et al.*, 1984: 2)

Such issues are complex and cannot simply be settled by an appeal to evidence; instead they rest on belief and value judgement, in this case whether or not migrants should have the right to free language classes. The government, college authorities and the students often had sharply differing views here. After all, a given issue is not intrinsically controversial but only becomes so from particular perspectives (Hess & Avery, 2008: 510). This is why these issues provide a fertile seedbed for developing both language and critical thinking skills. However, it is, of course, precisely these qualities that bring risk and potential vulnerability.

The Neoliberal Context for Controversy

Controversy, like everything else, is situated within a network of power relations and this implicates ideology. I understand ideology to refer to: 'the ways in which meaning (or signification) sustains relations of domination' (Thompson, 1984: 4). In economic and political terms, the currently dominant ideology of the world we live in is neoliberal. Broadly speaking, this can be defined as:

> a theory of political economic practices that proposes that human well-being can best be advanced by liberating individual entrepreneurial freedoms and skills within an institutional framework characterized by strong private property rights, free markets and free trade. (Harvey, 2005: 2)

Under neoliberalism, education in the form of pedagogy and research (see Conama, Chapter 4) is commodified and viewed as a source of profit. In order perhaps to maximise global reach and profit in the free market, controversial topics are sometimes avoided in pedagogy (Hepworth, 2015) and research (see Sauntson, Chapter 5) with teachers and researchers sometimes reporting feeling vulnerable if topics such as religion, politics and sexuality are engaged with.

The dominant ideology around pedagogy within neoliberalism is that it is: 'a set of strategies and skills to use in order to teach pre-specified subject matter' (Giroux, 2011: 3). According to this formulation, English is a commodity for sale in the marketplace. Most migrants are now expected to pay for their language classes (hence the new policy introducing fees discussed briefly earlier) and teaching and learning are viewed in terms of a 'banking' model (Freire, 1996), with the teacher or teacher educator delivering relevant knowledge and skills to the student, whether this is connected to the language itself or to the set of skills required to teach it. In this way, teaching is also viewed as uncontroversial.

The post-Brexit climate is risky for adult migrants to the UK with the issue of immigration dominating the debate. Many adult migrants move to the UK to seek employment. However, migrants are often represented in the British press as 'fleeing, sneaking or flooding' into the UK (Gabrielatos & Baker, 2008). When migrants are 'othered' (Said, 1978) in this way, and seen as outsiders, their very presence can be seen as a risk, and this makes them vulnerable. Indeed, there is evidence that discrimination based on xenophobia and nationalism is increasing (Burnett, 2016; Forster, 2016).

Activist Citizenship

Mention of the nation state brings us to citizenship. Much UK policy discourse emphasises citizenship as a matter of legal status along with the rights and, especially, responsibilities of the citizen in relation to the nation state (Peutrell, 2019). The Life in the UK test and the Citizenship materials (Department for Education and Skills, 2005) certainly focus on learning about the nation state.

In contrast, I understand citizenship as lived experience, something enacted through the: 'routines, rituals, customs, norms and habits of the everyday' (Isin, 2008: 16). In these terms, it manifests itself through 'acts of citizenship' that have the potential to be transformative i.e. challenge the status quo and create new identity rights and identity positions (Isin, 2008).

Thus activist citizenship conceptualises participation more radically and sees students or teachers as democratic actors across a range of sites, e.g. the classroom, the workplace, the local and global community (Peutrell, 2019). In the context of adult ESOL, this might encompass the struggle for affordable language learning or workplace rights or community building. However, being an activist student or teacher brings risk with it and renders them more vulnerable to college authorities. Some teachers and students joined the Action for ESOL campaign to protest the cuts in the sector. This demonstrates that TESOL (Teaching English to Speakers of Other Languages) pedagogy can connect to social justice.

Critical Pedagogy and Language Teaching and Learning

Like the activist citizenship just discussed, critical pedagogy aims to be transformative and to create a fairer world. Unlike the neoliberal stance outlined earlier, critical pedagogy views teaching and learning as contextualised practice, tightly implicated in relations of power and inequality, and grounded in issues of ethics, value and the furtherance of social justice (Freire, 1996; Giroux, 2011: 3).

The emphasis on the importance of dialogue and debate as a means of performing democratic citizenship also links into a view that dialogue and debate can be used to promote language learning. In making these connections, I draw upon Sociocultural Theory, which originates in the work of Lev Vygotsky and has been applied to second language learning by Lantolf (2000).

The main point to make is that language learning is developed in dialogue with others, i.e. through 'collaborative dialogue', which is concerned with problem-solving and knowledge-building (Swain, 2006: 102) and is internalised and through a process of what Swain refers to as languaging, i.e. 'the process of making meaning and shaping knowledge and experience through language' (Swain, 2006: 89).

Dialogue and debate can also develop critical thinking – again in teachers as well as students. This is what Freire (1996) referred to as 'conscientizacao', where different points of view are explored and evaluated, with a view to educating informed citizens and promoting social justice and democracy. Sometimes this critical thinking can emerge humorously through what Bakhtin (1968) termed the carnivalesque, which is where strategies like irony and parody are used to for satirical purposes and served to subvert, forming a 'a counter-hegemonic tradition' (Caldas & Coulthard, 2003: 90).

Adult ESOL Classrooms

Adult ESOL classrooms are often superdiverse places (Vertovec, 2006), reflecting broader patterns of global migration (Cooke & Simpson, 2008), both the economic migration of those seeking a better life and the forced migration of those fleeing persecution. The same diversity characterises the language teacher education classroom as: 'ESOL teachers collectively are almost as diverse as their students' (Cooke & Simpson, 2008: 30). They are also dynamic places and the composition of ESOL classrooms may change further, as a result of diminishing migration from the European Union.

This diversity brings risk with it when controversy emerges in the multicultural classroom. Controversial issues present the risk of offence to individuals or communities. This can be understood in terms of face or the image of yourself that you present to others (Goffman, 1955). There are threats to positive face, to a person's need to be accepted, to be liked by others, and threats to negative face, or a person's need to be free and independent (Brown & Levinson, 1987). Such threats can be mitigated by face-saving strategies. There may be conflict between notions of face, discussed above, in the learners' 'home' cultures and those they might encounter with teachers and other learners in the multicultural classroom.

However, it is precisely this superdiversity which makes adult ESOL classrooms powerful sites in which to debate controversial issues. This is because they reflect the superdiversity of the wider world more closely than other community-based pressure groups, such as faith groups or political parties. Moreover, adults, in theory at least, bring experience, maturity and adult sensibilities to controversial issues.

There is a debate around the extent to which the TESOL classroom should be seen as a 'safe haven' (Baynham, 2007) or a classical agora (Hepworth, 2019) in which open and robust civic debate should take place. In reality, there is no reason why it should not be both. If the classroom is an agora, then it is important that students and teachers are equal. Just as slaves and women were silenced and excluded from debate, we need to recognise that the classroom, too, has its hierarchies, as has the world beyond.

Adult ESOL students are vulnerable in that they often lack audibility (Block, 2007), defined in terms of the linguistic, economic and social capital needed to succeed in wider society. For example, how much riskier must it be to debate controversial issues if English is not your first language? One teacher put it thus: 'the trouble with language is that it reduces your ability to be articulate', with the concomitant risk that 'people have got all these thoughts in their head and they just can't articulate it' and 'it's good when people have complex ideas in their head and they can articulate them' (Hepworth, 2015). Furthermore, many are also vulnerable in that they work in low-paid, part-time unskilled and semi-skilled employment, often in the service sector. Those who teach them often lack audibility too, largely owing to insecure employment conditions, with many on part-time or hourly paid contracts (Cooke & Simpson, 2008).

Controversial Issues in the Language Classroom

A controversial curriculum

I have written elsewhere (Hepworth, 2015, 2019) about how controversial issues are largely avoided in government-produced Skills for Life materials (Department for Education and Skills, 2003) and the Citizenship materials (Department for Education and Skills, 2005) and how, in ethnically diverse classrooms, teachers are less likely to introduce controversial issues (Campbell, 2007) for fear of offending communities or individuals within them (Philips, 1997). This concern about offence coupled with the desire to promote cohesive classrooms is common among teachers (Baynham, 2007; Hepworth, 2015), with some reporting how debates around controversial issues had the potential to create division in the classroom, with the risk that it might 'fragment', creating a damaging 'them and us' situation.

In contrast, critical pedagogy emphasises that the curriculum should be emergent (Auerbach, 1992: 62) and not prescribed, thus empowering students. Making decisions on which issues are likely to cause offence to students is not only undemocratic; students are more likely to be offended by having decisions taken on their behalf than by the controversial issues themselves (Wallace, 1992). This is because the students are adults who can make up their own minds about what they find controversial and what they are (and are not) prepared to discuss.

To illustrate how all this might play out in the adult ESOL classroom, I now discuss the benefits, risks and vulnerabilities at play in the language and language teacher education classroom. I take issues around religion and politics as my starting points as these are amongst the most commonly cited controversial issues to avoid. In the extracts that follow the students are debating what they would do, if they could do one thing, in order to make the world a better, happier place. This was preparation for a discussion task in a Level 2 Speaking and Listening examination. However, this task also encouraged a more participatory curriculum in that, rather than imposing topics, the students could raise issues for debate, drawing upon what was important to them in their own lives (Freire, 1996). Moreover, this task positioned the students as citizens of the world, not just the nation state, and as activist citizens (Isin, 2008) who have the power to transform the world by imagining how it might be different.

Religion

In the extract that follows, the students are debating the proposal that religion should be deleted – not abolished but imagined as something that never existed:

M = A Polish student

J = A Polish student

B = A Polish student

1   M   I think religion is some kind of manipulation of people and what I mean by that is that for many years I've been training to attend to the church because it's just the way what must to be taken and er people in Poland they just before not now maybe not now when I was a kid I just had to because I'll go with the parents then everything was great to meet on Sunday see that kids are that's great but the grandmothers think they have some kind of brainwashing like the radio that is some kind of (laughter).
2   J   I think brainwashing is starting from few years.
3   M   Because I think my grandmother she don't really pray for everything better in our country she just pray for erm
4   J   The church.
5   M   for the erm prest priest.
6   J   Church.
7   M   Actually they don't really church they just think it's they think it's in the name of god but in the next moment we can found that the priest has slept with a very young boy the priest buy new car he just go to the holiday so you know I don't know where is that money going to but it's some kind of sabotage in Poland with the catholic religion maybe not now not all people but just adults of my age turn against.
8   J   I think maybe.
9   M   They say my friend he is from he was for really long time with his girlfriend and they were engaged the priest just asked whether they slept with each other and they said ok yes we have.
10   J   Too late.
11   M   So it's not allowed to be married like countries like England and Poland they asked why and he said because you not clean.
12   J   And give him a sum (laughter).
13   M   And after a while the parents arrived give it like 500 I'll do that once.
14   J   I cleaned you are clean now my son.
15   M   They went for some lessons after they paid and the priest said now you ready which was silly and insane.
16   B   Yeah I'm agree and I think I know what you mean when I been I'm not religion but it's a kind of difficulty in our country because 99% is religions so I always struggling the troubles when I met the girl and the parents and I had to let to know the parents that I so they've been treating me like a devil sometimes.
17   M   Like my grandma (laughter)
(Hepworth, 2015)

The extract contains much potentially controversial content about religion in general, and specifically, the church and the priesthood. Thus, we have religion as 'some kind of manipulation' or 'brainwashing', hardly inoffensive terms. More specifically, we have paedophile priests, exploiting and profiting from the contributions of believers in Turn 7, corrupt priests absolving believers for financial incentives in cases of sex before marriage in Turn 9 and last, but by no means least, B's declaration of atheism. This contrasts starkly with the avoidance or, at best, the rather bland focus on learning about other religions as part of a more general focus on culture (especially religious festivals) in more conventional adult ESOL materials (Department for Education and Skills, 2003).

The extract provides clear evidence of learning in the form of dialogic critical thinking as the students expose the manipulative power of religion (sustained through the family, the media, here 'the radio') and the corruption of the Catholic Church and the priesthood in Poland. Their general claims and critique are authorised by narrative evidence in the form of small stories (Georgakopoulou, 2007) or anecdotes, a powerful strategy in argumentation as disputing the claim involves disputing the veracity of the personal experience itself (Baynham, 1995). Thus, for example, we have the narrative of M's friend in Turn 9 or B's treatment at the hands of the girl's parents in Turn 16.

This critical thinking, seen in the light of Freire's (1996) concept of conscientizacao, is a necessary but not sufficient condition for changing the world. Here, the critical awareness of the manipulative power of religious ideology is valuable not simply in itself but as a step towards social transformation. To cite Marx (1845), 'The philosophers have only interpreted the world in various ways; the point is to change it'. J's interesting, though utopian, proposal is to 'delete religion' or make it as though it never happened. Perhaps more realistically, later on, M suggests separating religion and the institution of the priesthood and the church, with the implication that religion be a private matter rather than the business of the state. This sentiment is echoed by other students and amounts to a claim for a more secular role for religion. This locates the debate within a wider one about the role of religion in society.

This critical awareness connects closely with the benefits for language learning. The fluency of the contributions, attested to by the lack of significant pauses, the production of extended turns of talk, and the way in which the students complete each other's utterances (see Turns 11 and 12) all suggest that the topic has motivated lots of language and this is something which has increasingly been shown to be characteristic of debates around controversial issues (Cooke & Roberts, 2007; Hepworth, 2015). Moreover, this is 'collaborative dialogue' (Swain, 2000) in that the students are responding to, and building upon the arguments of, each other and in so doing developing new knowledge. So it is, for example, that in Turns 1 and 2, M claims that religious belief is a matter of 'brainwashing' and 'manipulation' and J builds upon this by asserting that this 'brainwashing' process begins at a very early age.

The role of playfulness in the dialogue, especially given the gravity of the topics being debated, is interesting and serves a number of purposes. The first one is critique in the form of the carnivalesque (Bakhtin, 1968) and, more specifically, through parody. Parody is, in effect, a dialogue within a dialogue, and one that is 'directed towards the referential object of speech, as in ordinary discourse, and towards another's discourse, towards someone else's speech' (Bakhtin, 1994: 105). Thus, in Turn 14, J takes on and simultaneously mocks the priest's voice and identity. The less powerful voice mocks the more powerful priestly one.

The humour and personalisation in evidence in the extract – and elsewhere – also serve to mitigate the potential threat to face presented when debating controversial topics. The second function of the playfulness is interpersonal. The laughter and personalisation, in the form of anecdote, help to develop cohesive classes through building rapport and solidarity between these students as they draw upon their life experiences in Catholic Poland to co-construct their critique of the priesthood and the church. There is the laughter of recognition here perhaps, as, for example, M recognises the prejudicial treatment B receives as something his 'grandma' would mete out. In order to save B's positive face, M offers solidarity and empathy by attesting to knowledge of similar treatment in the person of his grandma.

However, there is clearly risk and vulnerability in this dialogue. The mockery of the priesthood just discussed and visible in Turns 12–14 risks causing offence given the wrong audience, but this was a group of young economic migrants from the Czech Republic, Slovakia and Poland and no obvious offence was taken at the time, a state of affairs that might indeed provide evidence for M's claim of a 'turn against' the Catholic religion amongst the younger generation in Turn 7. Indeed, both J and B state they are without religion, something that, as B's anecdote about being treated 'like a devil sometimes', a threat to their positive face, was clearly risky outside, if not inside, the classroom in late 20th century Poland.

Indeed, the students seem conscious of the face-threatening nature of the topic. M says 'Can I say something about the Vatican?' and B replies 'Yes you can' (laughter.) Here, M's request for the right to speak is directed at me as the teacher, but it is B who grants speaking rights, thus usurping traditional classroom roles and identities. In the same move, he also subverts religious authority and there is a suggestion of a Papal dispensation in the granting of speaking rights. The laughter generated saves negative face, a matter of a person's – here M's – right to freedom of expression.

Perhaps even more controversially, the debate moves on to Islam:

M: for example the Muslim people are very happy when they die let's say the attackers and the terrorists exactly Muslim they so happy because they think they will get 90.

J: 100

B: 67 virgins something like that. (Hepworth, 2015)

This raises an interesting point about controversy and risk. This contribution emerges spontaneously as a response to previous contributions about the role of religion in justifying conflict and thus reflects the dialogic nature of talk (Bakhtin, 1981). This spontaneity, a feature of spoken utterance more generally, means that, even if not planned for pedagogically, controversy will emerge and present risk, for the teacher as well as the student.

There is a clear risk of offence to the teacher and other learners here. This is a parody of a theological debate, of what Bakhtin (1994) termed a speech genre, as the students –parodying fundamentalist believers – interrupt and correct each other on a point of information, speculating on the number of virgins who might be available to the male martyr on arrival in the after-life. This is an example of what Bakhtin (1968) termed the carnivalesque, a parodic performance that serves to satirise the powerful, or, more precisely here, a powerful ideology.

Offence is not the only risk here. There is the danger of political and religious stereotyping, of conflating terrorism motivated by fundamentalist Islam with 'Muslim people' more generally. This was particularly controversial in the context of a wider public debate about the role of Islamic fundamentalism in motivating acts of terrorism and the so-called 'War on Terror' that followed 9/11 and 7/7 and, more recently, the murderous assaults on the offices of Charlie Hebdo and the Bataclan Theatre in Paris (2015).

However, as observed earlier, controversy is always positioned and there were no Muslim students in the class, and therefore no direct threat to positive or negative face (Brown & Levinson, 1987). However, this does not of course absolve the teacher of the responsibility to challenge the student or mitigate potential offence caused to non-Muslim students in the class.

Discrimination in the workplace

I now move on to politics, another locus classicus for controversial issues. I focus on workplace discrimination because it was an issue that the students clearly wanted to talk about. More than one of them raised it explicitly and the others contributed to a rich, sustained discussion through a host of examples rooted in their own experience as economic migrants. Thus, the students generated their own curriculum (Freire, 1996). This proved more in terms of language learning and citizenship than existing government-generated Skills for Life materials (Department for Education and Skills, 2003), which often focus on rather dry functional matters such as how to use a photocopier or the (slightly more controversial) matter of how to deal with customer complaints.

In the following extract, the same students are discussing the issue of discrimination in the workplace. Building dialogically on a previous contribution identifying bullying and harassment from bosses in the workplace, one of the students begins to talk about workplace discrimination, saying 'I think it's more in common here if you are for example foreigner'. She cites as evidence an anecdote about a colleague who was forced to quit after suffering harassment at the hands of her boss. Another student continues:

M: with my opinion what B say and D there's a lot of truth and many people are obviously being discriminated just sometimes because of the place where they from or they just sometimes ignore it because they don't know exactly how to use the English so sometimes the big boss just laugh because of they didn't know what they would like to tell what they would like to (…) how they could explain it as well.
J: So they treat you like you stupid because you no understand.
M: But sometimes they just try to persuade you that you're stupid and after while some people just (…) actually start believe it and even like D said they try to make the perfect job they are as well inside the mind feeling disappointed of themselves because they struggle to just (…) really say straight away that look I am not kind of thick I'm the human and then sometimes for example if the boss is English then he's got more rights with his employee because he could just let him off his work without reason sometimes might just explain that it's because of the difficulty in language.

The lack of visible pauses within these extended utterances show this to be a fluent performance, exemplifying the following comment made by a teacher in interview: 'when you're using argument as a teaching tool it motivates a lot of language' (Hepworth, 2015). Despite some disagreement, there is a consensus around some of the forms the discrimination takes, and some of the reasons for it, with, for example, M asserting that migrants can be discriminated against because of their country of origin or because of the level of their English, or in Block's (2007) terms, their lack of audibility. This might even, it is suggested, be used as a reason to get rid of an employee. J builds on this in Turn 6 by suggesting that this leads to migrants being treated as if they are stupid. M builds further by suggesting that this might be a deliberate strategy by the bosses to inculcate feelings of inferiority.

The dialogues, here, and elsewhere, show cognitive activity, or thinking, mediated by speech, where: 'their saying becomes what I said, providing an object for reflection' (Swain, 2000: 113). They are engaging in verbalisation and languaging as they explain the concept to themselves and others (Swain, 2006). This languaging is the precursor to internalisation in Sociocultural Theory.

There were even acts of citizenship where migrants intervened on behalf of others. In the following extract M describes how they intervened to prevent sexual harassment in the workplace:

> M: I help for example to find job for one girl after few days she start crying she said that it's so hard to work and co-operate with the boss I said why where's the problem and then she said cos he's calling me that I am cute and well maybe they should make a date but after when she said no then he start to abuse her so I went to the guy and I explained look she's here for work not for pleasure and then everything I think sometimes girls come and they like machines many girls in the warehouse they just machines and they controlled by Iraqis because they make easy relationships.

Despite the fact that he hints that the intervention was successful in stopping the harassment in its tracks, this more collaborative process is not without controversy, as the reference to Iraqis attests to. His narrative coda generalises to the point of stereotyping. Shortly after this contribution another student prefaces her own contribution with:

> My boss he's Muslim as I have found out they think about white people that we have to do everything for them. (Hepworth, 2015)

The remarks went unchallenged by both students and teacher in the classroom, probably again because there were no Muslim students/Iraqis present, and would have provided a good opportunity for the further development of critical thinking in terms of the issues, both of them being rooted in stereotyping, here around sex as well as religion. Discrimination cuts both ways.

What about the role of the teacher in this debate? I ask them to focus on the task of suggesting steps that could be taken to promote social justice in the workplace. They then collaborate to suggest concrete proposals to improve workplace conditions, e.g. more 'co-operation between employees', 'more training courses' and parity of treatment and pay for employees, providing evidence of discrimination to a higher boss or even the police.

More conventionally, I elicit key vocabulary: 'does anyone know the phrase to stand up to anybody?' Immediately, one of the students provides the key phrase: 'stand up for your rights'. The debate then moves in the direction of the law and one student controversially suggests that the law is ineffective in protecting workers against discrimination:

> B: What about the law it doesn't work of course we have that kind of situation that someone has been claiming or wanting to do something with that or … has given your boss or stuff but boss can ignore that if he's clever so (…) it doesn't work of course.
>
> M: Racism and just abusing not always but law could work when our company or boss doesn't want to pay that then we fight for our rights as well we can fight for human rights because we shouldn't be abusive discriminate just we all the same so why we have to give up feel weak and just be always crushing down?

M suggests that it does work in terms of demands for equal pay and goes on to make an eloquent plea for the need to fight for human rights in the workplace. We have moved towards considering the role of the language teacher in debate. What, then, of the language teacher education classroom?

Debating Grammar: Controversies in the Language Teacher Education Classroom

I now shift focus and consider the role of controversy in the language teacher education classroom. I make the same claim, i.e. that the language teacher education classroom, just like language education classroom, should make use of controversy in order to educate teachers as what Giroux refers to as 'transformative intellectuals', i.e. teachers who:

> develop counterhegemonic pedagogies that not only empower students by giving them the knowledge and social skills they will need to be able to function in the larger society as critical agents, but also educate them for transformative action. That means educating them to take risks, to struggle for institutional change, and to fight both against oppression and for democracy outside of schools in other oppositional public spheres and the wider social arena. (Giroux, 1988: xxxiii)

The emphasis is on the need to educate teachers to 'take risks' and to develop students as 'critical agents' through the use of counter hegemonic and, most importantly, transformative, pedagogies. Note too that critical thinking is not enough; the emphasis is on critical agency in wider society. Critical pedagogy (Freire, 1996), as we have already noted, speaks of this in terms of praxis.

In order to illustrate this, I draw upon data from my own teacher education classroom. This is because, as Cooke and Simpson (2008: 18) observe, in political and media discourse, an inability to use English has often been cited as cause of a breakdown in social cohesion. Indeed, this fear that without a unified and unifying standard there will be social as well as linguistic fragmentation is longstanding (Cameron, 1995: 23). These claims have been challenged by sociolinguists (Blackledge, 2006) and the debate is something prospective adult ESOL teachers working need to be aware of in order that they might help defend migrant rights.

This is because, language itself is a controversial issue in that it is 'something which engenders strong feelings' (Cameron, 1995: vii) and engages fundamental questions of value and belief around 'the nature of persons, of power and of a desirable moral order' (Gal, 1995: 171). The trainees were working with perhaps one of the most controversial of all language topics, namely grammar, which Cameron identifies as the key term of the most powerful discourses around verbal hygiene, defined as the desire to regulate language use (Cameron, 1995). This is held to be the most controversial issue because it tapped into the 'moral panic' or 'grammar crusade' that began in schools in the late 1980s around the place of grammar in the curriculum:

> The call for a return to traditional grammar was wrapped up in a moral discourse on good and bad, right and wrong; so much so, in fact, that its moral element often obscured the linguistic and educational questions that were supposedly being addressed. (Cameron, 2012: 81)

I asked them to evaluate a number of non-standard grammatical utterances and, moreover, to try to uncover the principles that underpinned the judgements they were making. In the following extract, a discussion has begun about the utterance 'I'm liking that dress':

A: This last one could be said by an ESOL speaker.
B: It could be said by a native speaker too.
C: Yeah it could be ... this use of the present continuous is creeping in slowly it's kind of an American thing well look McDonalds I'm loving it rubbish food rubbish language that's what I always tell my students.
A: Yeah somebody asked me I was going on about how you don't use love and like and what about McDonalds I'm loving it.
C: Well yeah but there are some grammar books that say things are starting to change that people are starting to use verbs in continuous tenses rather than simple tenses so that's ...
A: That's the difference between descriptive and prescriptive approaches to grammar because you can't just say this is wrong because we don't use continuous tenses with verbs of whatever they're called.
C: So you look it up in a grammar book.
A: Yeah but then it doesn't reflect usage. (Hepworth, 2015)

In terms of critical thinking about language, there is much of value here, such as the recognition that language change is inevitable, that grammar books do not always reflect usage and the identification of prescriptive and descriptive approaches to grammar. In short, they are beginning to knowledge build and problem solve, and so are languaging (Swain, 2006). In this sense the students are also enacting good pedagogical practice in terms of what sociocultural theorists term 'concept-based instruction'.

However, there are the seeds of controversy here, most apparent in C's pejorative judgements ('rubbish food rubbish language') about language use and the conflation of these judgements with broader judgements about a fast-food culture. Indeed, A reminds C of this later when they observe that: 'when you say rubbish food rubbish English you are assigning your set of values'. This is a threat to positive face (Brown & Levinson, 1987) and makes them both potentially vulnerable and C performs a face-saving act in insisting they were 'only joking'. It also reminds us that 'popular beliefs about grammar are so difficult to shift', even among teachers in training (Cameron, 2012: 81).

As the teacher educator I realised that I missed an opportunity here in that I did not use the discussion to develop an awareness of the ways in which judgements about language use can reflect broader and deeper social and political anxieties. For example, I could have explored Cameron's questions around language prescription: who prescribes what for whom and whose purposes do they serve (Cameron, 2012)? In adult ESOL, this has very current resonance.

There are clearly ways in which this would bring risk with it. The first risk would be connected to the fact that the teacher is seen to be stepping beyond their traditional role as a language teacher and 'meddling' in politics. Moreover, the following dialogue illustrates how there are also other ways in which the professional authority and identity of the teacher might be called into question. During the discussion of non-standard usage, I said the following:

T: So how would you judge that use (…) if I said ok youse three have you finished?
S1: I'd say what is it you do for a living again? (laughs)

Here the trainee questions the authority of the trainer in response to the hypothetical question. The irony and laughter are negative face saving (Brown & Levinson, 1987) and allow the trainee the freedom to pose such a question. Indeed later, another trainee explicitly states that the trainer's use of non-standard English, coupled with a lack of awareness, would, in their words, 'question your authority in front of us in the classroom'.

S2: well you're using non-standard English and if you really really didn't understand that that then there'd be some gap in your education somewhere I would assume but and that would question your authority in front of us in the classroom.
T: And if I was from Liverpool a teacher from Liverpool?

I have suggested earlier in this chapter and elsewhere (Hepworth, 2015, 2019) that teachers can be vulnerable when controversial issues emerge. We see here the same holds for teacher educators.

Conclusion and Implications

Teaching controversial issues in order that students better understand the world they inhabit is a worthwhile aim in and of itself (Stradling *et al.*, 1984: 115). Despite the challenges, risks and vulnerabilities discussed in this chapter, the benefits of dealing with controversy outweigh them. This is because a robust democracy is surely premised upon the existence of an informed and articulate citizenry. Engaging with controversy develops both the language skills and the critical thinking ability of language adult migrant students and their teachers and so it is definitely worth taking the risk.

References

Auerbach, E. (1992) *Making Meaning; Making Change: Participatory Curriculum Development for Adult ESL Literacy*. Washington, DC: Center for Applied Linguistics.

Bakhtin, M. (1981) *The Dialogic Imagination: Four Essays* (M. Holquist, ed.). Austin, Texas: University of Texas Press.

Bakhtin, M. (1968) *Rabelais and His World*. Austin, Texas: University of Texas Press.

Bakhtin, M. (1994) Problems in Dostoyevsky's poetics. In P. Morris (ed.) *The Bakhtin Reader: Selected Writings of Bakhtin, Medvedev, and Volosinov* (pp. 110–113). London: Arnold.

Baynham, M. (1995) Narrative in argument, argument in narrative. In P. Costello and S. Mitchell (eds) *Competing and Consensual Voices: The Theory and Practice of Argument* (pp. 35–49). Clevedon: Multilingual Matters.

Baynham, M. (2007) *The ESOL Effective Practice Project: Summary Report*. NRDC.

Blackledge, A. (2006) The racialization of language in British political discourse. *Critical Discourse Studies* 3 (1), 61–79.

Block, D. (2007) *Second Language Identities*. New York: Continuum.

Brown, P. and Levinson, S. (1987) *Politeness: Some Universals*. Cambridge: Cambridge University Press.

Burnett, J. (2016) *Racial Violence and the Brexit State*. London: Institute of Race Relations.

Caldas-Coulthard, C. (2003) Cross-cultural representation of 'otherness' in media discourse. In G. Weiss and R. Wodak (eds) *Critical Discourse Analysis. Theory and Interdisciplinarity* (pp. 272–296). Basingstoke: Palgrave Macmillan.

Cameron, D. (1995) *Verbal Hygiene: The Politics of Language* (1st edn). London: Routledge.

Cameron, D. (2005) *Verbal Hygiene*. London: Routledge.

Cameron, D. (2012) *Verbal Hygiene: The Politics of Language* (2nd edn). London: Routledge.

Campbell, D.E. (2007) Sticking together: Classroom diversity and civic education. *American Politics Research* 35 (1), 57–78.

Cooke, M. and Roberts, C. (2007) *Developing Adult Teaching and Learning: Practitioner Guides. ESOL*. Leicester/London: NIACE/NRDC.

Cooke, M. and Simpson, J. (2008) *ESOL: A Critical Guide*. Oxford: Oxford University Press.

Department for Education and Skills (2003) *Learning Materials ESOL*. London: Basic Skills Agency/DfES. See http://www.dfes.gov.uk/readwriteplus/LearningMaterialsESOL (accessed 23 January 2017).

Department for Education and Skills (2005) *Citizenship Materials for ESOL Learners*. London: Basic Skills Agency/DfES. [Online]. Available from: http://esolcitizenship.org.uk

Fiehn, J. (2005) *Agree to Disagree: Citizenship and Controversial Issues*. London: Learning and Skills Development Agency.

Forster, K. (2016) Hate crimes soar by 41% after the Brexit vote, official figures reveal. The Independent. www.independent.co.uk/news/uk/crime/brexit-hate-crimes-racism-eu-referendum—vote-attacks-increase-police-figures-official-a7358866.html

Freire, P. (1996) *Pedagogy of the Oppressed*. London: Penguin.

Gabrielatos, C. and Baker, P. (2008) Fleeing, sneaking, flooding: A corpus analysis of discursive constructions of refugees and asylum seekers in the UK Press 1996–2005. *Journal of English Linguistics* 36 (1), 5–38.

Gal, S. (1995) Language, gender and power: An anthropological review. In K. Hall and M. Bucholtz (eds) *Gender Articulated: Language and the Socially Constructed Self* (pp. 169–182). London: Routledge.

Georgakopoulou, A. (2007) *Small Stories, Interaction and Identities*. Amsterdam: John Benjamins.
Giroux, H. (1988) *Teachers as Intellectuals: Toward a Critical Pedagogy of Learning*. Massachusetts: Bergin & Garvey.
Giroux, H. (2011) *On Critical Pedagogy*. London: Continuum.
Goffman, E. (1955) On face-work; An analysis of ritual elements in social interaction. Psychiatry: *Journal for the Study of Interpersonal Processes* 18, 213–231.
Gray, J. (2002) The global coursebook in ELT. In D. Block and D. Cameron (eds) *Globalisation and Language Teaching* (pp. 151–168). London: Routledge.
Hanks, J. (2017) *Exploratory Practice in Language Teaching: Puzzling about Principles and Practices*. Basingstoke: Palgrave-Macmillan.
Harvey, D. (2005) *A Brief History of Neoliberalism*. Oxford: Oxford University Press.
Hepworth, M. (2015) Spoken argumentation in the adult ESOL classroom. Unpublished PhD Thesis. University of Leeds.
Hepworth, M. (2019) Argumentation, citizenship and the adult ESOL classroom. In M. Cooke and R. Peutrell (eds) *Brokering Britain, Educating Citizens: Exploring ESOL and Citizenship* (pp. 103–119). Bristol: Multilingual Matters.
Hess, D. and Avery, P.G. (2008) Discussion of controversial issues as a form and goal of democratic education. In J. Arthur, I. Davis and C. Hahn (eds) *Education for Citizenship and Democracy*. London: SAGE
Isin, E.F. (2008) Theorizing acts of citizenship. In F.E. Isin and M. Nielsen (eds) *Acts of Citizenship* (pp. 15–43). London: Palgrave Macmillan.
Lantolf, J. (ed.) (2000) *Sociocultural Theory and Second Language Learning*. Oxford: Oxford University Press.
Marx, K. (1845) *Marxist Internet Archive. Thesis on Feuerbach XI*. [Online]. Available from: http://www.marxists.org.uk/archive/marx/works/1845/theses/theses.htm (accessed 14 May 2009).
Peutrell, R. (2019) Thinking about citizenship and ESOL. In R. Peutrell and M. Cooke (eds) *Brokering Britain, Educating Citizens: Exploring ESOL and Citizenship* (pp. 43-61). Bristol: Multilingual Matters.
Philips, J. (1997) Florida Teachers' Attitudes Toward the Study of Controversial Issues in Public High School Social Studies Classrooms. PhD Dissertation. Florida State University.
Said, E. (1978) *Orientalism*. London: Random House.
Stradling, R., Noctor, M. and Baines, B. (1984) *Teaching Controversial Issues*. London: Edward Arnold.
Swain, M. (2000) The output hypothesis and beyond: mediating acquisition through collaborative dialogue. In J.P. Lantolf (ed.) *Socio-cultural Theory and Second Language Learning*. Oxford: Oxford University Press.
Swain, M. (2006) Languaging, agency and collaboration in advanced second language proficiency. In H. Byrnes (ed.) *Advanced Language Learning; The Contribution of Halliday and Vygotsky* (pp. 95–108). Washington DC: Georgetown University Press.
Thompson, J.B. (1984) *Studies in the Theory of Ideology*. Cambridge: Cambridge University Press. 1984.
Vertovec, S. (2006) *The Emergence of Superdiversity in Britain*. Policy and Society. Paper No. 25. Oxford: University of Oxford Centre on Migration.
Wallace, C. (1992) *Reading*. Oxford: Oxford University Press.

14 Access to English in Pakistan: Differences in Instruction as a Risk to Social Integration

Sham Haidar

Introduction

Owing to colonialism and globalisation, English has become the dominant language in the world (Rassool, 2013). English plays a number of crucial roles around the world, and people dream of it as a source of social mobility (Channa et al., 2020; Haidar, 2019a; Haidar & Fang, 2019a; Haidar et al., 2019; Mohanty et al., 2010; Rahman, 2005). However, contrary to expectations, English is one of the main forces which divides society into a few elites and many ordinary people (Haidar & Fang, 2019b; Ramanathan, 2005). In Pakistan the differential schools system plays a major role in this division, as there are elite private and public schools for the children of the elite classes. The elite private schools are not accessible to the general public owing to their exorbitant tuition fees (Rahman, 2005). Some prestigious public institutions own elite public schools where the children and relatives of the employees of these institutions can easily gain admission with a low fee compared with the general public. Ordinary people can educate their children either in general private schools, charging a lower fee, or publicly-funded public schools. Several studies (e.g. Coleman, 2010; Mansoor, 2005; Rahman, 2002, 2005; Tamim, 2013, 2014) in Pakistan have concluded that students graduating from elite schools are fluent in English while general school graduates lack that fluency. However, little research has been conducted in Pakistan to observe the actual teaching and learning process that leads to differential levels of proficiency. This chapter is a part of large study which explored access to English in different school systems in Pakistan with the research question: how is access to English a risk to the social integration of students studying in different school systems in Pakistan?

Risk is defined variously in the research literature. It is usually defined as a situation in which an individual has to make a choice among different alternatives which ultimately leads to failure or success (Kogan & Wallach, 1967). It is often linked with making choices about some uncertain situations. Foreign or second language learning is also linked with risk-taking behaviour and those learners who take the risk of speaking the target language usually outperform the non-risk takers (Zafar & Meenakshi, 2012). Risk is also linked with language planning and policy in multilingual societies (Ennser-Kananen & Saarinen, Chapter 6; Hepworth, Chapter 13; Takam & Fassé, 2019). While using corpus linguistics Hamilton *et al.* (2007) found that '"risk" emphasized actions, agents or protagonists, and bad outcomes such as loss of a valuable asset'. In this chapter, risk is used in terms of social integration which results in the loss of valuable assets of the country.

The study found that the differential school system puts the society at risk of further social stratification owing to variation in access to English as the language of power (Haidar, 2019a). The pedagogical methods, the school environment, the school personnel's perspectives and practices, the school academic culture and linguistic habitus differ greatly despite having similar textbooks, medium of instruction and examination system (Haidar, 2016). There were differences in focus on English instruction which were beyond the linguistic competence of the students. These differences were separate from variation in access to the technical aspects of the English language, such as grammatical structures, vocabulary, reading, writing, speaking and listening skills, as concluded by several studies (e.g. Coleman, 2010; Mansoor, 2005; Rahman, 2002; Tamim, 2014). In the elite schools the focus was on developing the skills of comprehension, creativity, critical thinking, role-play, reading and writing beyond the prescribed textbooks (Haidar, 2019b). On the other hand, general schools focused on rote memory of the limited content of the textbooks, translating the textbook contents and learning limited grammatical rules and sentences from English to Urdu and vice versa (Haidar, 2021).

Class structure and education system in Pakistan

The class structure in Pakistan owes its origin primarily to the colonial policies pursued by the British. Broadly speaking, the Pakistani population can be divided into upper, middle and lower social classes based on property relations and commercial economy (Qadeer, 2006). The British imposed a stratified social system based on the administrative and economic needs of the Empire (Gardezi, 1991), similar to Spanish colonialism in Latin America (Murillo, Chapter 3). They created a small, privileged class whose interest was to serve the Empire in controlling the masses, including landlords, industrialists and professionals (Gardezi, 1991). Through the British schooling system senior professionals were produced, such as senior military/civil bureaucrats and administrators, lawyers, college/university teachers, medical specialists, engineers and accountants (Rahman, 2004). The middle class comprises the minor administrators, both civil and military, clerks, technicians, craftspeople, teachers and religious leaders. The lower class mostly comprises uneducated manual workers and peasants.

After independence from the British Empire in 1947, the class structure continued and the elite class not only maintained their social power but also reinforced it through differential education (Gardezi, 1991; Rahman, 2001). The elite maintains the elite model by keeping the masses uneducated or poorly educated in English, aided by the stratified education system as explained above (Rahman, 2004). The education system helps to perpetuate the existing inequalities by devaluing the local languages and restricting access to quality education and English, the language of power (Bourdieu, 1991; Bourdieu & Passeron, 1990; Tamim, 2014).

Different languages have been used for instruction in Pakistan since colonial times. The country has introduced multilingual education policies to encourage local languages, national languages and English language teaching (Canagarajah & Ashraf, 2013; Channa et al., 2020; Islam, 2013; Mahboob, 2020; Manan et al., 2020). As per policy, education in the mother tongue is encouraged in the early ages followed by education in the national languages and then the use of English in higher education (Canagarajah & Ashraf, 2013). However, in practice there are differences in the medium of instruction and in the grade level for the introduction of English in different places and types of schools (Canagarajah & Ashraf, 2013; Rahman, 2005). The language policies of the country are usually formed to safeguard the interests of the elites (see also Murillo, Chapter 3). The constitution of the country apparently supports Urdu to be used as the official language and language of education, but the dominance of English perpetuates owing to the vested interests of the elites (Rahman, 2005; Shamim, 2008). Therefore there is a gap in the rhetoric and actual language policy and Pakistan is considered an unsuccessful case in framing egalitarian language policy (Simpson, 2007). Based on the medium of instruction and other available facilities, broadly speaking, there are four types of schools: English medium elite private schools, English medium elite public schools, general private schools which are English medium in theory but use Urdu or Pashtu, and Urdu medium general public schools (Coleman, 2010; Haidar, 2016; Rahman, 2001, 2005).

The value of the different languages used for instruction in different schools varies in the linguistic market (Bourdieu, 1991) of the country. English is considered the most prestigious language, followed by Urdu and local languages (Haidar, 2019a; Rahman, 2010; Tamim, 2014). Therefore, it is crucial that all children should have equal access to the language of power, otherwise the social integration of the country will be at risk.

Theoretical Framework

As already stated, in Pakistan English has symbolic power because of its association with British colonialists and it became the language of the elites after Pakistan became independent (Rahman, 2005). Bourdieu's (1991) theory of social reproduction is relevant for understanding the role of differential education in Pakistan. Bourdieu argues that education legitimises social stratification by providing access to social capital (here the English language) to some while restricting it to others. In fact, the education institutions allow for regulation of knowledge that helps the people in power to assert social control and symbolic domination. Accordingly, the educational contents and practices are used to reproduce social hierarchy.

Bourdieu mentions elite schools (grandes écoles) that admit students from dominant classes to prepare them for leadership roles. Elite schools instill self-control that ultimately leads to control of others through both mental and physical means in the school years. Thus, the education system plays a crucial role in the reproduction of social inequality as schools not only provide technical knowledge but also socialise individuals to particular cultural traditions. It preserves, transmits and inculcates the culture of a society and thus serves the purpose of culture reproduction. In fact, a differential education system reinforces rather than redistributes cultural capital. It also legitimates certain cultural values and devalues others. Bourdieu uses 'field' and 'habitus', two interdependent terms to explain the role of cultural capital, including language, in a social hierarchy. These concepts help to explain how different linguistic habitus are considered valuable in different fields.

Language being an integral part of social life plays a crucial role in social stratification and social reproduction (Bourdieu, 1991). The language policy thus plays a crucial role in the dominance of some linguistic groups over others by legitimising their linguistic resources through making their language as the official language and language of education (Heller & Martin-Jones, 2001). Bourdieu (1991) explains:

> To speak of the language, without further specification, as linguists do, is tacitly to accept the official definition of the official language of a political unit. This language is the one which, within the territorial limits of that unit, imposes itself on the whole population as the only legitimate language ... The official language is bound up with the state, both in its genesis and its social uses ... this state language becomes the theoretical norm against which all linguistic practices are objectively measured. (1991: 45)

Thus the state language policies and educational practices are linked with the issues of power, opportunity, inequality and discrimination (Heller & Martin-Jones, 2001). In Pakistan the dominance of the English language in relation to other local languages along with differential access to it may lead to social stratification.

However, the dominance and spread of a language, especially English in the modern world, is a complicated phenomenon affected by globalisation; as such, multiple sectors of society are implicated in this dominance and spread (Dewey, 2007; Saxena & Omoniyi, 2010). Therefore, I also use Blommaert's (2010) theory of the sociolinguistics of globalisation. Sociolinguistics is concerned with the actual use of linguistic resources affected by the cultural, social, political and historical context (Blommaert, 2010). It is concerned with concrete linguistic resources instead of the abstract concept of a language as an autonomous object, since it focuses on the function of language in a society. Instead of linguistic capital (Bourdieu, 1991), Blommaert (2010) uses 'linguistic resources', which are sometimes mobile while other times not. The market value of one's linguistic repertoire is affected by access to mobile linguistic resources rather than to a static language. People who have mobile linguistic resources have more opportunities to adapt to new circumstances in terms of both geographical and social spaces.

The main point of interaction between these theories is the recognition of the power dynamics attached to the language and its varieties. These theories also consider the education system to be one of the main players determining the dominance of a language and access to it.

Methodology

The study uses a phenomenological case study design with 80 classroom observation of English instruction in natural setting and 28 qualitative interviews conducted with the study participants, which include school administrators, English teachers and students of grade 10 in four different types of schools in a town in Khyber Pakhtunkhwa, Pakistan. I used constructivist grounded theory (Charmaz, 2014) an inductive technique for data analysis to construct themes from the data through coding line by line with descriptive words and later on categorising similar codes to be developed as themes at the later stage. The data included interview transcripts and field notes of classroom observations (see also, Haidar, 2016). The quotes of participants and field notes are presented from the data while describing the themes in the findings of this chapter.

Findings

School language environment and social reproduction

Students from elite backgrounds usually receive preferential treatment in their educational institutions, which afterwards helps them in the job market (Bourdieu, 1991). The education system usually entrenches inequalities through different treatment of cultural capital of privileged and socially/economically vulnerable children. It also helps in developing the cultural capital of children, and strong linguistic resources are part of this skill set. For example, the general language environment in a school plays an important role in access to English in Pakistan as English is the most dominant language and a source of power and professional development. Gee (2006) argues that mere classroom teaching will not solve the subordinate position and linguistic problems of the speakers of other languages unless they are provided with an environment to acquire that target language naturally. Second language acquisition theory also highlights the importance of language environment in acquiring a language (Izumi, 2002; Krashen, 1985; Ortega, 2009; Swain, 2005). In Pakistan in social life, people usually speak Pashtu or Urdu for communication. School is the main source providing an opportunity to develop students' English language competence.

Most of the study participants considered an English-speaking environment crucial for learning and using English (see also Humphries *et al.*, 2015). For example, the administrator of the elite private school stated that any language, especially English, 'can only be taught (instruction) when you practice it' (Interview AD4, 05/26/15). Similarly, the administrator in the elite public school stated, 'English is supposed to be spoken at every level' (Interview AD3, 05/12/15). Most students in elite public and general schools also believed that, to learn English, they should be provided with an English-speaking environment. Reading books and learning grammatical rules only would not be enough for their language skills. For example, a student stated, 'you can learn English if you have good environment' (Interview S3S3, 05/14/15, Trans).

The elite private school provided an English-speaking environment to students. The administrator of the elite public school shared his experience as a teacher in an elite private school: 'the whole environment was an English-speaking environment' (Interview AD3, 05/12/15). The school environment helped students to develop their English language skills, as a student in elite private school stated: 'We are concerned with English …. In school we speak English with our principal, our teachers, our fellows' (Interview S4S1, 05/21/15). In this way, elite school students had opportunities to develop the linguistic skills that are highly valued in the linguistic market in Pakistan (Bourdieu, 1991).

However, the situation is different in other schools, as they do not provide an English-speaking environment for students. In general schools the medium of communication is usually Pashtu, as observed in field visits. The administrator of the general private school admitted that they had not provided an English-speaking environment in school: 'I personally agree, and I admit that I have not succeeded up to the level to make my teachers to use English as their language' (Interview AD2, 06/17/15). The teacher did not even speak English in English classes in the tenth grade. Students in general schools also complained of not having the environment to speak English in school, 'There is no environment nobody speaks English' (Interview S2S2, 06/10/15, Trans). The student believed that the English-speaking environment would have helped him to improve his English. Thus, in general school students did not have the environment to develop the market-based linguistic resources as Urdu and Pashtu are considered less important compared with English. The linguistic habitus developed at various schools has different value in the linguistic market in the country. The variation in school environment is a huge challenge for the education system as it risks social integration, further increasing the distance between the elite class and ordinary people. The linguistic capital that elite schools' students gain is highly valued but the linguistic capital of general schools' students has no value, which makes the society vulnerable to further disintegration.

Narrower and broader outlook

Apart from language abilities that different schools develop through the language environment, there are differences in developing the general outlook of students. General school students are usually 'prepared to serve in a (limited) circle. They shouldn't think out of the box, they shouldn't think something new' (Interview AD2, 06/17/15). Similarly, the administrator in a general public school stated, 'If you want to do many things but you can't do' (Interview AD1, 06/11/15, Trans). The administrators considered government policies responsible for not encouraging or developing a broader outlook in students. Rather, students mostly followed the book, and the examinations were content focused. 'There is only this book. That's why people now have high marks but do not have any general information, since they rely on the book only' (Interview S1T1, 06/13/15, Trans). Students, despite having good scores on the examinations, could not make use of their skills in real life and that risks their integration into society since expectations from them are limited.

On the other hand, students in elite schools were encouraged to acquire a broader outlook and acquire the habitus that may be used later in life. The focus was to develop their creativity and critical thinking and to learn about different aspects of life (Haidar, 2019b). As an example, while solving an exercise given in the textbook: 'Teacher explains the point that there is "why" in the question, which means that they are supposed to explain something in order to satisfy the "why". He writes "why" on the board and says that "why" needs reasons' (Field notes, 04/28/15). Thus, they not only learn to answer only one question but to use their knowledge in other similar situations.

English teaching in English medium and vernacular medium schools prepares students for different social roles (Ramanathan, 2005). While analysing textbooks, Ramanathan (2005) concluded that English medium schools train students for higher reasoning, self-expression and self-composing, whereas in vernacular schools, the focus is on the low-level technical aspects of the language. Elite schools encouraged high-level linguistic competence of the students by nurturing their creativity, critical thinking and ability to take a broader outlook (Haidar, 2019b). The elite schools' students developed the ability to use language flexibly in various circumstances, which enabled them to cope with new and unpredictable experiences. However, in general schools, English teaching revolved around the examinations, which measure low-level language competence and usually the memory of the students (Haidar & Khan, in press). They could not use their language skills beyond the limited contexts. These differences were not limited to the textbooks only, but rather they were broader, institutional and systematic (Bourdieu, 1991).

Dramatic performance of the text

While elaborating on social capital Bourdieu (1991) argues that elite class habitus is developed through opera, art galleries, concerts, symposiums and museums. In modern times, these have been replaced with personal computers, libraries, encyclopaedias, the internet, newspapers and so on (de Graaf *et al.*, 2000; Roscigno & Ainsworth-Darnell, 1999). To develop the elite habitus of the students, elite schools give them opportunities to stage English plays. In an elite public school, the administrator stated 'Julius Caesar … was dramatised by her (teacher) and the students' (Interview AD3, 05/12/15). In their interviews, the teachers and students also referred to such activities arranged in school. The teacher in an elite private school stated, 'we do the stage activities … we make the students to perform in dramas like the Shakespearean drama Macbeth' (Interview S4T2, 06/12/15). Staging a play was a common practice in the elite schools. It gave students hands-on practice in using English and also help them to adopt Western cultural values, thus making them alienated from local culture and values (Rahman, 2005) and risking social integration.

Dramatising helped students to improve their language skills for expressing themselves openly. A teacher in an elite school stated that dramatic performance positively affected students' language: 'They improved upon their dialect, their accent delivery' (Interview S3T1, 05/26/15). This not only helped those students who participated in the play, but also encouraged other students to follow them. It also developed their personality, as stated by a teacher: 'not only the English language skill, it was important in every aspect' (Interview S3T1, 05/26/15). These types of activities forced students to confront their shyness and express themselves in the crowd. Their confidence developed, and they were better equipped to face the challenges of real life.

Performing on the stage and acting increased the interest of students and provided them with opportunities to show their talent. A teacher in an elite public school described the experience of the students: 'they learn, or they are excited to do it themselves' (Interview S3T1, 05/26/15).

Teaching English in the elite schools was not confined to classrooms. Staging a drama made students work closely with the teachers and other students, which helped them to use their potential talent to improve upon their acting and language skills. From a young age, students developed the habit of Westernised lifestyle and language, which is a form of social capital (Bourdieu, 1991) for them.

Teacher training

Organisational habitus plays a crucial role in transforming dispositions and perception transfer in educational institutions (Bourdieu, 1991; Diamond & Randolph, 2004: 76; Horvat & Antonio, 1999). Teacher training and professional development play a crucial role in forming students' habitus. Teachers' quality and their training and professional development are central for effective instruction (Akyeampong & Lewin, 2002; Lewin & Stuart, 2003; Little, 2006; Westbrook et al., 2009). The elite schools provided regular training to teachers, but the general schools did not. An administrator in an elite public school described his teaching experience at an elite private school: 'Whatever I have professionally learned, that is from the city school network (name of an elite private schools' network)' (Interview AD3, 05/12/15). The administrator in the elite school described the training available to them: 'Oh! Training is like; it's the best part of (named the school system). They spent so much on training' (Interview AD4, 05/26/15, emphasis original). One teacher in the elite private school stated that the best training facilities were available for improving English instruction. Every year there was compulsory training and need-based training. 'They provide all sorts of training' (Interview S4T1, 05/29/15). The school system also hired trainers from abroad, from developed countries, for English teachers to keep them on par with modern developments.

Furthermore, the elite schools provided a lot of online material for their teachers, since online sources provide better opportunities for professional development (Duncan-Howell, 2010; Hur & Brush, 2009). The administrator in an elite public school stated, 'There is a discussion forum. Not only can the teachers download some lesson plans or other materials; but also if any teacher has done something good, it can be uploaded under his or her name' (Interview AD3, 05/12/15). Similarly, they also had access to websites for teachers, which were used by O-level teachers: 'Cambridge supported websites, teacher support websites' (Interview AD3, 05/12/15). A teacher also shared that once training was arranged for them by Oxford University on marking papers, in which teachers from Oxford participated through video conferencing. Thus, the elite schools provided many professional development opportunities for their teachers.

However, in general schools the teachers usually followed the same teaching methods that they had experienced as students. A teacher in a private school stated that the school did not provide any training: 'they do not have anything' (Interview S2T1, 06/12/15, Trans). Similarly, a teacher in general public school stated, 'It is not there in government system' (Interview S1T1, 06/13/15, Trans). Those who had served in the department for more than 20 years still followed these old methods. As a result, they did not know how to teach English as a language. Their focus was only to have students pass English papers in the matric examinations (Haidar & Khan, in press).

Some teachers in general schools felt the need for professional training, but it was not available to them. A teacher in a general public school stated, 'Training on specific skills is required' (Interview S1T1, 06/13/15, Trans). Teachers were aware of their limitations and that they had learned only one method of teaching English. They did not have the skills for arranging different activities in the class to make their teaching interesting. They were also not aware of most of the online material for English teachers, as they used the internet mostly for searching for word meanings.

Research has established that teacher preparation affects students' learning (Darling-Hammond, 2002; Gándara *et al.*, 2003; Haycock, 1998), and therefore for proper access to English, teachers should be competent and have adequate professional development opportunities (De Jong & Harper, 2005; Lucas *et al.*, 2008). The elite schools recruited highly qualified teachers while teachers in general schools were less competent. Moreover, the elite private school system provided training opportunities to teachers either in developed countries or through people trained in developed countries. The education system did not provide professional development opportunities to general school teachers. Thus, there were systematic differences in the quality of English instruction in different schools.

Schools prepare students for different roles

The study participants believed that differential access to English prepared children for different roles. Students attending elite schools were provided with all of the facilities and tools required to learn English. Their examination system encouraged students' critical thinking and creativity (Haidar, 2019b). Their English competence will help them qualify for the competitive examinations required to become a professional. Consequently, elite school graduates usually join multinational corporations, the international bureaucracy abroad, fashionable NGOs and foreign banks in Pakistan or the civil or military bureaucracy, or they become professionals, such as doctors, engineers, accountants, administrators, lawyers and college or university teachers (Rahman, 2004, 2005). The study participants when elaborating on their plans mentioned, for example, 'If I go to America as an engineer' (Interview S3S3, 05/14/15, Trans). Supporting this, a teacher in an elite school stated, 'studying at this level are supposed to be engineers and doctors' (Interview S4T1, 05/29/15). Other study participants also mentioned gaining admission to medical college or an engineering university, pursuing education and other professional jobs in advanced countries, qualifying for competitive examinations, and joining the military as an officer.

However, students in general schools were expected to assume lower positions in society. The administrator in a general school explained the preparation of his students for professional life: 'They will be their labor, clerks, or other lower positions' (Interview AD1, 06/11/15, Trans). Similarly, a teacher at the elite private school stated that students in general schools have few opportunities to be professionals, explaining, 'they are supposed to work in the offices as clerks, as accountants' (Interview S4T1, 05/29/15). Thus, differential access to English through differential schooling is a social means of dividing the people between those who become professionals and those who will serve at a lower level (Bourdieu, 1991).

Therefore, differential English instruction plays an important role in the social stratification of Pakistan. The administrator in a general public school stated that differential access to English makes a difference in students' professional life: 'English has a main role (in social stratification) and they want to keep the lower class away from English' (Interview AD1, 06/11/15, Trans). He claimed that the dominant class is responsible for government policies that keep the students in general schools away from English. Owing to limited access to English in schools, students attending general schools have to serve in lower social positions, such as small-scale businesspeople, mid-level civil/military officers, clerks, technical workers, craftspeople, writers and teachers (Gardezi, 1991).

In fact, English competence helps a person to move up the social ladder in Pakistan. The study participants believed that English was one of the tools that could help a child of the middle or lower class to improve his or her social class. The administrator from a general public school stated, 'In poor people, there are rare cases when some children learn English owing to their own interest. These students then no longer remain in the lower class, rather they move up to a higher class' (Interview AD1, 06/11/15, Trans). The administrator accepted that the school did not help all of the students to learn English as a language, but that some students learned owing to their personal motivation. Therefore, in general schools, only a few low-socioeconomic-status students become competent in English. This enables them to ascend the social hierarchy in Pakistan and to have a successful professional life.

Therefore, if poor children are provided with opportunities and maximum access to English, as in elite schools, they are more likely to perform well in their education. For example, while discussing the quick improvement of low-socioeconomic-status students in the elite school a teacher stated, 'it is not their fault ... spending two to three months with other kids in the hostel and with the teachers ... Then they are more interested'

(Interview S3T1, 06/26/15). She considered the overall education system responsible for not allowing ordinary students to have access to English and better education. According to this teacher, poor students were the highest achievers when they were provided with an opportunity to study in an elite school. The performance of low-socioeconomic-status students given better educational opportunities was very high. Rather, the limited access to English at school is the main cause of their lack of English competence.

A teacher in the elite school stated that, owing to limited access to English, Pakistan loses the talent of many ordinary children. He thought the differential schooling system must be changed; otherwise, 'we will lose our talent' (Interview S4T1, 05/29/15). The teacher blamed the differential education system for the loss of the potential possessed by low-socioeconomic-status students. Another teacher in the elite school also stated, 'many children came from the government schools and they took admission in our school. They are very intelligent people, but their grades are not very stronger compared with the students who are more efficient in English' (Interview S4T2, 05/21/15). The study participants believed that owing to limited access to English in general schools, the potential of some talented students was lost. Low-socioeconomic-status students can be a great resource, if provided with the proper opportunities.

Conclusion

The spread of English owing to colonialism and globalisation perpetuates the existing inequalities in which the poor 'remain poor, while those who were rich ... become richer' (Blommaert, 2010: 153). The traditional linguistic resources of ordinary people, Urdu and Pashtu, do not have social status, and are considered of lower quality and of less value. Thus in Pakistan a kind of symbolic violence (Bourdieu, 1991) is taking place by underestimating the local languages, the cultural resources (see Severo & Makoni, Chapter 2, for more on this). The elite school students are more competent in English than Urdu and Pashtu. Hence, the linguistic resources of the elite school students have symbolic power which privileges them over students of general schools.

Owing to differential access to English and other facilities, the schools have the potential to develop different habitus and general attitudes in the students. This has significant implications for reproduction of the students' social and linguistic capital, affecting their access to local and global resources. In fact, schools in Pakistan prepare students for life in the social class from which they have come by restricting access to the development of valued social capital for some while providing it to others. General schools provide substandard English instruction facilities, which compel students to remain in their subordinate positions in the social order because they do not possess the valued linguistic resources and social habitus (Haidar, in press). In contrast, the rich facilities at the elite schools inculcate in their students a sense of distinction by providing opportunities to develop valued linguistic habitus and social capital (Haidar, 2019b). In this way, the education system generally, and access to the English language in particular, impose a social order on students that legitimises social differences and inequalities (Blommaert, 2010; Bourdieu & Passeron, 1990; Ennser-Kananen & Saarinen, Chapter 6).

The elite schools serve the wealthy people and teach those linguistic skills and knowledge that ensure easy access for their children into the high echelons of society. The study found that the focus in English instruction in elite schools was deeply ingrained in the dominant class interest to meet the demands of the economic market. The linguistic habitus and social capital (Bourdieu, 1991) developed in school help the students to keep pace with the realities of globalisation and social and geographical mobility (Blommaert, 2010; Haidar, 2019b). It can be argued that inculcating particular linguistic resources in the students determines the foundation for modern progressive education. This is undertaken especially to maintain the hegemony of the English language and to preserve the dominance of Western culture in Pakistani society. This type of social capital has high exchange value in the job market domestically and abroad. These schools further serve the ruling class by being autonomous institutions to empower them through the use of high fees and other expenses as a 'control mechanism', making them inaccessible to the general public (Rahman, 2005). This ensures the inclusion of only the minority elite classes in these institutions. I argue that the ruling class uses the schooling system and consciously implements differential access to the English language to sustain their dominance.

Contrary to the elite schools, English instruction in general schools results in scholastic capital that obliges the students to remain in their subservient positions. Mere translation from English to Urdu and teaching limited grammatical rules do not develop their language skills (Haidar & Khan, in press). Similarly, passive rote memorisation generally does not encourage students to engage in creating knowledge, resulting in their intellectual passivity, reliance on others and ideological capitulation. The local board examinations also encourage complete reliance on memory; hence the examinations follow content-heavy patterns in which the students are graded based on the reproduction of the textbook contents (Haidar, 2016). It seems that students in general schools are prepared to perform jobs requiring low level skills, including mechanical tasks or carrying out the regulations, plans and policies made by others. These practices do not allow students to resist or protest against any kind of exploitation and affect their social mobility. This is not limited to English instruction only but the overall education system (Malik, 2012) and political economy compel ordinary people to remain in their dominated positions (Qadeer, 2006). Hence, the class structure in Pakistani society continues to be perpetuated from generation to generation.

The spread of English in the world as the main source of communication is a valuable resource for people in developing countries to have access to power and share in progress with people in developed countries. However, despite the dominance and social influence of English, overwhelmingly limited access to the English language within the educational system fundamentally propagates the marginalisation of ordinary people and further perpetuates the existing class structure in Pakistan. It is the main source of disappointment for ordinary people because its spread renders them language-less and illiterate in their own communities (see also Ennser-Kananen & Saarinen, Chapter 6; Hepworth, Chapter 13). It compels those students who fail to develop English language competence owing to limited access to it during their education to remain silent in formal environments (Haidar & Fang, 2019b). Thus, the divide between the elite and ordinary classes further increases in developing countries. This challenges the equal distribution of linguistic resources and thus variation in English instruction makes those in the ordinary classes vulnerable to failure and presents risks to social integration (see also Ennser-Kananen & Saarinen, Chapter 6).

References

Akyeampong, K. and Lewin, K.M. (2002) From student teachers to newly qualified teachers in Ghana: Insights into becoming a teacher. *International Journal of Education Development* 22 (3–4), 339–352.

Blommaert, J. (2010) *The Sociolinguistics of Globalization*. Cambridge: Cambridge University Press.

Bourdieu, P. (1991) *Language and Symbolic Power* (G. Raymond and M. Adamson Trans.). Cambridge, MA: Harvard University Press.

Bourdieu, P. and Passeron, J.C. (1990) *Reproduction in Education, Society, and Culture* (R. Nice Trans., 2nd edn). London: Sage.

Canagarajah, S. and Ashraf, H. (2013) Multilingualism and education in South Asia: Resolving policy/practice dilemmas. *Annual Review of Applied Linguistics* 33, 258–285.

Channa, L.A., Manan, S.A. and David, M.K. (2020) Global aspirations versus local resources: Planning a sustainable English teaching policy in Pakistan. *Asian Englishes* 1–19.

Charmaz, K. (2014) *Constructing Grounded Theory* (2nd edn). London: Sage.

Coleman, H. (2010) *Teaching and Learning in Pakistan: The Role of Language in Education*. Islamabad: British Council.

Darling-Hammond, L. (2002) Access to quality teaching: An analysis of inequality in California public schools. Expert report prepared for *Williams v. State of California*.

De Graaf, N.D., De Graaf, P.M. and Kraaykamp, G. (2000) Parental cultural capital and educational attainment in the Netherlands: A refinement of the cultural capital perspective. *Sociology of Education* 73 (2), 92–111. doi.org/10.2307/2673239.

De Jong, E.J. and Harper, C.A. (2005) Preparing mainstream teachers for English-language learners: Is being a good teacher good enough? *Teacher Education Quarterly* 32 (2), 101–124.

Dewey, M. (2007) English as a lingua franca and globalization: An interconnected perspective. *International Journal of Applied Linguistics* 17 (3), 332–354.

Diamond, J.B. and Randolph, A. (2004) Teachers' expectations and sense of responsibility for student learning: The importance of race, class, and organizational habitus. *Anthropology and Education Quarterly* 35 (1), 75–98.

Duncan-Howell, J. (2010) Teachers making connections: Online communities as a source of professional learning. *British Journal of Educational Technology* 41 (2), 324–340.

Gándara, P., Rumberger, R., Maxwell-Jolly, J. and Callahan, R. (2003) English learners in California schools: Unequal resources unequal outcomes. *Education Policy Analysis Archives* 11 (36), 1–54.

Gardezi, H.N. (1991) *A Reexamination of the Sociopolitical History of Pakistan: Reproduction of Class Relations and Ideology*. New York: The Edwin Millen Press.

Gee, J.P. (2006) What is literacy? In H. Luria, D. Seymour and T. Smoke (eds) *Language and Linguistics in Context: Readings and Applications for Teachers* (pp. 257–263). Mahwah, NJ: Lawrence Erlbaum.

Haidar, S. (2016) Passport to privilege: Access to English in different school systems in Pakistan. Unpublished PhD Dissertation, University of Rochester.

Haidar, S. (2019a) The role of English in developing countries: English is a passport to privilege and needed for survival in Pakistan. *English Today* 35 (3), 42–48.

Haidar, S. (2019b) Access to English in Pakistan: Inculcating prestige and leadership through instruction in elite schools. *International Journal of Bilingual Education and Bilingualism* 22 (7), 833–848.

Haidar, S. (2021) Designed for failure: English instruction as a tool for the perpetuation of students' dependent and dominated status. *International Multilingual Research Journal*. Doi.10.1080/19313152.2021.1928843

Haidar, S. and Fang, F. (2019a) English language in education and globalization: A comparative analysis of the role of English in Pakistan and China. *Asia Pacific Journal of Education* 39 (2), 165–176.

Haidar, S. and Fang, F. (2019b) Access to English in Pakistan: A source of prestige or a hindrance to success. *Asia Pacific Journal of Education* 39 (4), 485–500.

Haidar, S., Farukh, F. and Dar, S. (2019) Desire for English in youth: An exploratory study of language learners in Pakistan. *Journal of Education and Educational Development* 6 (2), 288–307.

Hamilton, C., Adolphs, S. and Nerlich, B. (2007) The meanings of 'risk': A view from corpus linguistics. *Discourse and Society* 18 (2), 163–181.

Haycock, K. (1998) Good teaching matters: How well-qualified teachers can close the gap. *Thinking K–16* 3 (2), 1–17.

Heller, M. and Martin-Jones, M. (2001) Introduction: Symbolic domination, education, and linguistic difference. *Voices of Authority: Education and Linguistic Difference* 1, 28.

Horvat, E.M. and Antonio, A.L. (1999) Hey those shoes are out of uniform: African American girls in an elite high school and the importance of habitus. *Anthropology and Education Quarterly* 30 (3), 317–342.

Humphries, S.C., Burns, A. and Tanaka, T. (2015) 'My head became blank and I couldn't speak': Classroom factors that influence English speaking. *The Asian Journal of Applied Linguistics* 2 (3), 164–175.

Hur, J.W. and Brush, T. (2009) Teacher participation in online communities: Why do teachers want to participate in self-generated online communities of K–12 teachers. *Journal of Research on Technology in Education* 41 (3), 279–303.

Islam, M. (2013) English medium instruction in the private universities in Bangladesh. *Indonesian Journal of Applied Linguistics* 3 (1), 126–137.

Izumi, S. (2002) Output, input enhancement, and the noticing hypothesis. *Studies in Second Language Acquisition* 24 (4), 541–577.

Kogan, N. and Wallach, M.A. (1967) Risk taking as a function of the situation, the person, and the group. In G. Mandler, P. Mussen and N. Kogan (eds) *New Directions in Psychology III* (pp. 111–278). Oxford: Holt, Rinehart & Winston.

Krashen, S. (1985) *The Input Hypothesis: Issues and Implications*. London: Longman.

Lewin, K.M. and Stuart, J.S. (2003) Researching teacher education: New perspectives on practice, performance and policy. Multi-site Teacher Education Research Project (MUSTER) synthesis report. Education Series Paper No. 49(a), Department for International Development, London.

Little, A. (2006) Multigrade lessons for EFA: A synthesis. In A. Little (ed.) *Education for All and Multigrade Teaching: Challenges and Opportunities* (pp. 301–348). Dordrecht: Springer.

Lucas, T., Villegas, A.M. and Freedson-Gonzalez, M. (2008) Linguistically responsive teacher education preparing classroom teachers to teach English language learners. *Journal of Teacher Education* 59 (4), 361–373.

Mahboob, A. (2020) Has English medium instruction failed in Pakistan? In *Functional Variations in English* (pp. 261–276). Cham: Springer.

Malik, A.H. (2012) A comparative study of elite-English-medium schools, public schools, and Islamic Madaris in contemporary Pakistan: The use of Pierre Bourdieu's theory to understand' inequalities in educational and occupational opportunities (Doctoral dissertation, University of Toronto).

Manan, S.A., David, M.K., Channa, L.A. and Dumanig, F.P. (2020) The monolingual bias: A critique of idealization and essentialization in ELT in Pakistan. In N. Rudolph, A.F. Selvi and B. Yazan (eds) *The Complexity of Identity and Interaction in Language Education* (pp. 25–42). Bristol: Multilingual Matters.

Mansoor, S. (2005) *Language Planning in Higher Education: A Case Study*. Karachi: Oxford University Press.

Mohanty, A.K., Panda, M. and Pal, R. (2010) Language policy in education and classroom practices in India. In K. Menken and O. García (eds) *Negotiating Language Policies in Schools: Educators as Policymakers* (pp. 211–231). New York: Routledge.

Ortega, L. (2009) *Understanding Second Language Acquisition*. London: Hodder and Stoughton.

Qadeer, M.A. (2006) *Pakistan: Social and Cultural Transformations in a Muslim Nation*. New York: Routledge.

Rahman, T. (2001) English-teaching institutions in Pakistan. *Journal of Multilingual and Multicultural Development* 22 (3), 242–261.

Rahman, T. (2002) *Language, Ideology and Power: Language-learning among the Muslims of Pakistan and North India*. Karachi: Oxford University Press.

Rahman, T. (2004) *Denizens of Alien Worlds: A Study of Education, Inequality, and Polarization in Pakistan*. Karachi: Oxford University Press.

Rahman, T. (2005) The Muslim response to English in South Asia: With special reference to inequality, intolerance, and militancy in Pakistan. *Journal of Language, Identity and Education* 4 (2), 119–135.

Rahman, T. (2010) *Language Policy, Identity and Religion: Aspects of the Civilization of the Muslims of Pakistan and North India*. Islamabad: Al-Noor.

Ramanathan, V. (2005) *The English-Vernacular Divide: Postcolonial Language Politics and Practice*. Clevedon: Multilingual Matters.

Rassool, N. (2013) The political economy of English language and development: English vs. national and local languages in developing countries. In E.J. Erling and P. Seargeant (eds) *English and Development: Policy, Pedagogy and Globalization* (pp. 45–67). Bristol: Multilingual Matters.

Roscigno, V.J. and Ainsworth-Darnell, J.W. (1999) Race, cultural capital, and educational resources: Persistent inequalities and achievement returns. *Sociology of Education* 72 (3), 158–178.

Saxena, M. and Omoniyi, T. (eds) (2010) *Contending with Globalization in World Englishes*. Bristol: Multilingual Matters.

Shamim, F. (2008) Trends, issues and challenges in English language education in Pakistan. *Asia Pacific Journal of Education* 28 (3), 235–249.

Simpson, A. (2007) Language and national identity in Asia: A thematic introduction. In A. Simpson (ed.) *Language and National Identity in Asia* (pp. 1–30). Oxford: Oxford University Press.

Swain, M. (2005) The output hypothesis: Theory and research. In E. Hinkel (ed.) *Handbook of Research in Second Language Teaching and Learning* (pp. 471–484). Mahwah, NJ: Lawrence Erlbaum Associates.

Takam, A. and Fassé, I. (2019) English and French bilingual education and language policy in Cameroon: The bottom-up approach or the policy of no policy? *Language Policy.* Online first. See https://link.springer.com/article/10.1007/s10993-019-09510-7

Tamim, T. (2013) Higher education, languages, and the persistence of inequitable structures for working-class women in Pakistan. *Gender and Education* 25 (2), 155–169.

Tamim, T. (2014) The politics of languages in education: Issues of access, social participation and inequality in the multilingual context of Pakistan. *British Educational Research Journal* 40 (2), 280–299.

Westbrook, J., Shah, N., Durrani, N., Tikly, C., Khan, W. and Dunne, M. (2009) Becoming a teacher: Transitions from training to the classroom in the NWFP, Pakistan. *International Journal of Educational Development* 29 (4), 437–444.

Zafar, S. and Meenakshi, K. (2012) Individual learner differences and second language acquisition: a review. *Journal of Language Teaching and Research* 3 (4), 439–446.

15 Afterword

Christopher J. Hall and Clare Cunningham

The chapters in this volume present a broad range of contexts and perspectives related to the theme of vulnerabilities, challenges and risks in applied linguistics. In this Afterword, we draw some conclusions and consider future prospects for the discipline.

Conclusions

Above all, the work reported in this volume reaffirms the commitment of applied linguists to mobilising their research and teaching to benefit vulnerable individuals and groups, despite the challenges and risks involved. The centrality of the vulnerable has become a core value and focus of the discipline since its foundational preoccupation with language pedagogy. This shift has been the inevitable result of our developing understanding that language is not only a communicative resource, but also a decisive factor in the social construction and perpetuation of ideological beliefs, structures and practices, favouring some and marginalising others. The reorientation of much activity in applied linguistics towards contexts involving the more vulnerable, including deaf people, Indigenous people, migrants and sexual minorities, has given the discipline a new moral and ethical dimension. Yet it has also revealed that the field's traditional epistemologies and ontologies, rooted primarily in general linguistics, are not up to some of the new tasks it has set itself. It is perhaps not surprising, then, that many of the chapters in this book also reveal vulnerability in the discipline itself – of individual researchers and participants out in the linguasphere, and also of the epistemological frameworks within which the research is conducted.

The chapters collected here dramatically highlight these vulnerabilities in the process of doing applied linguistics. Understood as the perceived or real probability of unwanted, unintended (and often harmful) outcomes and consequences, this is an issue of considerable concern for the integrity of the academic endeavour, as well as for the wellbeing of researchers, their partners outside academia and the communities they work with and within. The concern can be met, as chapter authors demonstrate, on several fronts. One way is to develop and foster an awareness of the risks and challenges involved, both real and perceived, and our positionality with respect to them. In our Introduction we conceptualised risks in terms of both the potential causes of undesirable outcomes and the probability with which such outcomes might occur. In some cases these can be anticipated and planned for, as we saw with some of the projects reported in this volume. This, accordingly, is a second strategy which applied linguists use to lower the probability that vulnerabilities remain unguarded and that people and projects are placed in jeopardy. However, risk can only be managed within limits: applied linguistics operates in complex and often opaque social and material conditions, so necessarily we must also develop and foster our tolerance and expectation of uncertainty. Thus, we observe in the contributions to this volume an open and flexible disposition to embrace unintended outcomes, turning them to our advantage so that challenges and vulnerabilities become opportunities. We saw several cases in the preceding chapters of happy accidents and silver linings.

At risk may be the people involved in the process (e.g. research participants and partners, students, researchers, teachers), but also the research itself. When we conceptualise the risks as *challenges*, this implies that they may be overcome. The projects reported in this book demonstrate that, broadly speaking, the challenges can be either conceptual or structural (but clearly these categories are not mutually exclusive). Many of these challenges are the result of socially constructed beliefs and practices, and are therefore a function of ideologically conditioned perceptions, and obviously no less real for that. Yet this means that they can be contested and deconstructed, through detailed analysis of case studies and careful attention to the ontological commitments of those involved. Several contributions highlight the need to explore and understand alternative epistemologies, especially those associated with the lived social and cultural realities of many of the vulnerable individuals and groups we work with. As applied linguists, we are particularly well equipped to understand the role of language in the construction and perpetuation of these diverse world views. However, we need to be more sensitive to the discourses in which the phenomena we explore are understood and lived by those involved. This requires heightened reflexivity and a candid assessment of our own positionality: as insiders or outsiders; interested or disinterested (but almost always privileged) parties; co-learners or experts; uncritical champions of, or constructive contributors to (or critics of) a particular theory; exercisers or contestors of symbolic power.

Our reading of the chapters in this volume suggests that if the challenges we identify or face in doing applied linguistics are structural, then two responses are favoured. If the challenge represents a risk to the intellectual integrity or academic validity of the project, then we acknowledge it and either work with or around it without reformulating our original objectives (thereby overcoming the challenge); or we reconsider and adapt (thereby submitting to the challenge). If the challenge represents a risk to our participants, students, partners, or ourselves, then we act to confront it. Where the challenges are tied to meeting our project objectives, this action will be local in scope. However, if the risk is revealed by our research (or teaching) to be more pervasive, a part of broader inequities created and/or perpetuated through access to or deployment of language resources or practices, then applied linguists may be moved to resist and become activists (Cowal & Leung, 2020). Given the disciplinary shift we mentioned earlier (from language pedagogy to language problems), the embracing of social action, with its inherent challenges, risks and vulnerabilities, is the natural consequence of much of our research and teaching, and so has come to characterise what we do.

Prospects

The foregoing offers a general overview of some of the main conclusions we draw from the chapters in this volume. But what next? What should be future areas of focus, to ensure that, in doing applied linguistics, we recognise, address and learn from the vulnerabilities, challenges and risks involved? Clearly the diversity of contexts within which applied linguists work, and the many components of their scholarly and pedagogical activity (organisational, psychological, theoretical, ideological, logistical) mean that best practices will be many, and will need to be fashioned locally. Yet from the work reported in this volume we can perhaps distil some general issues which we believe merit particular emphasis in the future.

One concerns processes of ethical review. Like other core values of academic activity and beyond (such as impact, quality and excellence), ethics has become a matter of mere accountancy for many, semantically enervated in the Ethics Form (cf. the Impact Agenda, the Quality Committee, the Excellence Rating, etc.). Ethical thinking runs the risk of being viewed as a bureaucratic process to be completed before research has begun, rather than an ongoing moral dimension of our activity, a major part of which involves the identification and mitigation of risks to vulnerable participants. 'Risk Management' perhaps suffers from the same 'Upper Case syndrome', inviting a tickbox mentality and, indeed, sometimes resulting in manufactured 'Risk', rather than real 'risk'. Filling in some ethics and risk assessment forms can, in fact, create the impression that research is inevitably a risky business. However, well-crafted forms can perhaps provide useful prompts. Unhelpfully, many forms are too generic, or are adapted from those used in the medical and psychological sciences, associated with detailed codes of ethical practice imposed by professional bodies. This can lead scholars in fields like applied linguistics to approach them as a challenge to be overcome, or as an irksome burden.

Missing still from many of these forms is contemplation of the risks to researchers themselves, which we have seen can be a particular concern for our discipline. Ways need to be found to make ethical review processes more responsive to the needs of individual disciplines, while not compromising overarching ethical principles. Beyond forms, ethical issues should play a fundamental role in our postgraduate teaching and training. The *Recommendations on Good Practice in Applied Linguistics* prepared by the British Association for Applied Linguistics (BAAL, 2021) is a helpful document in this regard.

Another issue highlighted in the chapters here and worthy of constant evaluation is the collaborative nature of applied linguistics. The range of collaborators is considerable: professional partners like interpreters and teachers; sponsors or commissioners of research; students, both in taught and research programmes; community members; political activists and policymakers; colleagues from both within or beyond our discipline, and within or beyond our traditional national and regional groupings. Some of the partnerships here come with increased risk to one or more of the collaborators and/or the project they are involved in. This is often due to unequal power relationships, and sometimes because of unexamined positionality. In some cases, a single individual can play more than one role: as Hall *et al.* (2017: 19) point out, 'collaboration in applied linguistics can be intrapersonal, embracing theory-building, theory interpretation, mediation and application, and professional practice, all in the same individual'. It is clear that in order to minimise risks, we need to be much more explicit about the roles we claim, more sensitive to those we may be performing unaware, and more alert to those ascribed to us by others. Such clarity will also perhaps reveal opportunities and solutions as well as challenges and risks.

When applied linguists collaborate with others, they inevitably do so with objectives that go beyond the academic. The intrinsic engagement of the discipline with vulnerable communities and individuals allows us to leverage our language-related research and teaching activities for social change. Unsurprisingly, therefore, the final issue we wish to highlight is the need for applied linguists to reflect on the ways we ourselves use language to communicate with those beyond academia (cf. Lewis, 2018, and responses following it; Schwartz *et al.*, 2016; Eisenstadt, 2020). One of our major vulnerabilities is the way we are positioned by populist media and political parties, as 'so-called experts' dealing in abstractions, rather than creators of powerful analytic and interpretive frameworks which can underpin considered actions for social justice. If we can capitalise on our experience in non-academic roles and with non-academic partners to connect more effectively with activists and policymakers, then perhaps we will be better able to meet the challenges of contemporary society, both language-based and language-mediated.

References

BAAL (2021) *Recommendations on Good Practice in Applied Linguistics* (4th edn). See www.baal.org.uk.

Cowal, J. and Leung, G. (2020) Activist applied linguistics. In S. Conrad, A. Hartig and L. Santelmann (eds) *The Cambridge Introduction to Applied Linguistics* (pp. 308–324). Cambridge: Cambridge University Press.

Eisenstadt, N. (2020) Evidence-based policy and other myths. What researchers need to know to influence government. London School of Economics blogpost, 22 September. See https://blogs.lse.ac.uk/impactofsocialsciences/2020/09/22/evidence-based-policy-and-other-myths-what-researchers-need-to-know-to-influence-government/.

Hall, C.J., Smith, P.H. and Wicaksono, R. (2017) *Mapping Applied Linguistics. A Guide for Students and Practitioners* (2nd edn). London: Routledge.

Lewis, M.C. (2018) A critique of the principle of error correction as a theory of social change. *Language in Society* 47 (3), 325–346.

Schwarz, N., Newman, E. and Leach, W. (2016) Making the truth stick and the myths fade: Lessons from cognitive psychology. *Behavioral Science and Policy* 2 (1), 85–95.

Index

Abdelhay, A. 22
academia 49–50, 65–66, 75–76, 148–149
Act to Ensure a Barrier-Free Canada 111, 113–115, 117, 118–119, 120
activism work
　in academia 75–76
　activist citizenship 199–200, 202
　activist-scholarship 49–62
　applied linguistics 5, 233
　Canada 118
　epistemic disobedience 32, 34–35, 45
　interdependency between biological and linguistic diversity 42–43
　Latin America 34, 44–45
　rights to language provision 198
　scholar-activists 50
　sign languages 51–53, 54–58, 118
　Southern epistemologies/Indigenous ontological orientations 19, 21
　vulnerabilities useful for 4
Africa 18, 20–26
Afro-Brazilian Portuguese 22
Ahmed, S. 63
AILA (International Association of Applied Linguistics) 75, 184
Albert, A. 123
Aldridge-Morris, K. 72
Allam, H. 139
Allwright, D. 147, 148
ALTE and Council of Europe 183, 184
Alt-Right 131–146
Amadasi, S. 151
American Sign Language 112, 113, 115, 116, 117, 118, 120–121
Amerindian sign languages 115–116
Amerindian spoken languages 32–33
Amidon, S.R. 25
Anderson, B. 31, 32, 34–35, 169
Andrews, J. 167, 168
Angouri, J. 140

animal/human interaction 26
anti-feminism 65, 134, 142
Aoyama, T. 154
Apple, M.W. 50
Arhuaco community 36, 41–45
arts 20–26, 74
Ashraf, H. 216
'assemblages' 16
assimilation 32, 92
Association of Internet Researchers 136
Atlee, T. 59
audibility 201–202, 207
audism 48
Auerbach, E. 202
authenticity 21
Avery, P.G. 198

Baca, D. 16
Bakhtin, M. 200, 205, 206
Balsam, K. 64
'Bantu' languages 22
Baynham, M. 72–74, 163, 201, 202, 204
Beatty, J. 119
Beck, U. 3, 4, 81, 82–83, 94
befriending 63–78
Belgium 116
Bell, M.K. 33
Berg, L.D. 50
Berger, J.M. 132
Bhabha, H. 25
Bhopal, K. 140–141
Bickford, A. 115, 117
bilingualism
　Canada 111, 116
　Finland 81–96
　Latin America 32, 39–40
　Wales 100
biodiversity 42–43
Blackledge, A. 209
Blackstock, C. 120

Block, D. 201, 207
blogs 136
Blommaert, J. 218, 225, 226
Boholm, M. 3
Bolander, B. 136–137
Booth-Butterfield, M. 150
Booth-Butterfield, S. 150
border thinking 16–17, 23, 24
Bourdieu, P. 216, 217, 218, 219, 221, 224, 226
Bradby, H. 167, 169
Braun, S. 57
Brazil 18, 20–26
Brazilian Portuguese 22
Brexit 5, 97–110, 199
BRICS countries 103
British Association for Applied Linguistics (BAAL) 1, 3, 75, 136, 234
British Council 98
Brown, P. 201, 206, 210, 211
Brumfit, C. 15
Buchanan, E.A. 136, 137, 143
Bunzl, M. 81
Burgess, A. 3, 5
Burley, S. 133
Butler, J. 4, 5

Caldas-Coulthard, C. 200
Calvelhe Panizo, L. 74
Cameron, D. 209, 210, 211
Cameroon 84
Campbell, D.E. 202
Canada 84, 111–127
Canadian Association of the Deaf–Association des Sourds du Canada (CAD-ASC) 112, 114–115, 116, 118, 119
Canadian Heritage 119, 121, 122
Canagarajah, S. 216
Candomblé 25–26
Cantillon, S. 49
capitalism 19, 23, 31–47 *see also* neoliberalism
Caplan, R. 133, 134, 140
Caretta, M.A. 167
carnivalesque 200, 205
Carruthers, J. 100
Castro, J. de 23
Center for World Indigenous Studies 45
Centre for Deaf Studies at Trinity College, Dublin 53

Chacón, G.E. 33, 34
challenges, definition of 2, 4–5, 232
chants 26
Charmaz, K. 218
Chatterton, P. 50
Christianity 22, 31, 34, 39–40, 42
citizenship 187, 197–213 *see also* democracy
civilizing projects 34
class, social 87, 100–101, 103, 215–216, 218–227
classroom instruction, language of 40
classroom-based research 147–161, 183–196, 197–213
climate change 3, 5
'close up' field research 138
co-learners 232
Coleman, J.A. 104
collaborative applied linguistics 234
collaborative dialogue 200, 204
Colombia 32, 33, 35, 36, 37, 41–45
colonialism
    and applied linguistics 17, 19
    and English 19
    as framework 16
    Indigenous communities in Latin America 32–33
    and indigenous sign languages in Canada 117
    language ideologies 84
    Latin America 33–34
    Pakistan 215–216, 217
    and sign languages 120, 121
coloniality of power 19, 40–41
computer-mediated communication (CMC) 136
Conama, J.B. 51, 53, 54, 56
concept-based instruction 210
Congress of Westphalia 90
Connell, R. 16
conscientizacao 200, 204
Consoli, S. 147, 149, 154, 157, 159
constructivist grounded theory 218
controversial issues 131–146, 197–213
Convention on the Rights of People with Disabilities (CRPD) 54, 55, 56, 112, 117
Conway, M. 132
Cooke, M. 201, 202, 204, 209
copyright 136

co-researchers, interpreters as
    169–170, 177
corpus linguistics 215
corpus-based critical discourse analysis
    71, 132, 142–143
cosmovisiones (worldviews) 34
Cote, J. 44, 45
counselling 139
counterfactual histories 81–96
counter-hegemony 50, 200
Cousin, G. 160
Couture, S. 50
Covid-19 pandemic 1, 3, 5
Cowal, J. 5, 233
Cox, L. 50
crab harvests 25–26
critical applied linguistics (CAL) 15
critical discourse analysis 132, 141
critical incidents 147–161
critical pedagogy 200, 202, 209
critical Southern perspectives 19
critical thinking 198, 200, 204, 210, 215, 220, 221, 223
cultural capital 217, 218
cultural dislocation 121
cultural essentialism 82, 104–105, 107, 151
cultural revitalization 34
cultural sensitivities in research 151, 156, 162, 168
Curran, R. 52
curriculum development 183–196
Cusicanqui, S.R. 18, 19, 20

Daly, A. 54
Daly, C. 58
Daly, M. 53
Daly, T. 57
Dantas, V.M.C.S. 26
Darmody, M. 57
Davies, A. 15
Dayter, D. 137, 139, 143
De Meulder, M. 53, 56, 58, 124
De Silva, E. 84
deaf activism 48–62, 118
Deaf Studies 50
'decolonial turn' 16
decolonialization 16, 19
decolonizing methodologies 15–30, 31–32, 36
Delacroix, J. 33
Deleuze, G. 24

democracy 75, 197–213
democratizing applied linguistics 16
Denney, D. 3
depoliticization of language 40
desensitization 135, 138–140
Deumert, A. 23, 24
Di Carlo, P. 16
Diaz, J. 32, 45
dictionaries 142
Digital literacy practices (DigiPrac) 163
diglossia 40, 187, 194
disability rights 89, 115, 117, 119
DiSalvo, D. 132
discourse management 168–169, 173–176
dissemination of research (extreme ideologies) 137–138
distance learning 193
diversity, biological 42–43
diversity, language of 63, 68–74
diversity, linguistic 41, 102–103, 201
Donaldson, G. 100
Doughty, H. 99
drama 74, 221–222
dual language immersion programmes 39
Duff, P.A. 40
Dutton, E. 134
dwelling place, language as 23

Eckert, P. 67
eco-linguistics 5
ecosystems 24
education
    bilingualism 39, 40
    and colonialism 34
    commodification of 199
    critical pedagogy 200
    decolonization of 43–44
    English in Pakistan 214–230
    Finland 88, 89, 91, 92–93
    Indigenous languages in Latin America 31, 35, 40
    language learning in the UK post-Brexit 97–110
    language of classroom instruction 40, 68
    in Latin America 34
    and neoliberalism 50
    researching sexuality and language use 63–78
    sign languages 52, 53, 57, 58, 115–116, 117, 120–121

Edwards, R. 166, 167, 169
Ekholm, L.K. 91
Elder, C. 15
elites 48, 87, 89, 216–223
emergent curriculum 202
Emery, S.D. 50
emic and etic constructs 141–143
emotional resilience 139–140
empathy, researcher 157
endangered languages 115, 120, 122–123
English
  in Cameroon 84
  in Canada 119
  and colonialism 19
  in Deaf communities 49
  English for Academic Purposes 148–149
  English for speakers of other languages (ESOL) 73–74, 197, 200, 201–202
  in Europe post-Brexit 106–107
  as a global language 97, 98–99, 102, 104, 106, 214, 227
  for international business 102
  linguistic imperialism 48
  in Pakistan 214–230
English Baccalaureate (Ebacc) 101
Engman, M. 86, 87, 89
'Enlightenment' 31, 34
epistemic disobedience 32, 34–35, 45
epistemological racism 17, 26–27
Equality Act 2010 (UK) 73
Equality and Diversity UK Post-16 Education Toolkit 72
Erasmus 102
Erich, Mikko 87
ethics
  analysing extremist discourse 132, 135–140, 143–144
  ethical review processes 233–234
  ethically important moments 149
  LGBTQ+ researchers 75
  researcher positionality 153–154, 159–160
  using an interpreter for multilingual research 166, 176, 177
ethnicity 19, 87
ethnographic research 36, 141, 162
Eurobarometer 98, 104
Eurocentricity 15, 21–22, 27, 31, 32, 36

European Charter for Regional or Minority Languages 89, 92
European Union 56, 101–102, 106–107
Europhobia 104–105
excluded people 22, 23, 201 *see also* marginality
exclusion from knowledge 55–56
existential risk 70
explicit material, researching 138–139
Exploratory Practice 147, 148–149, 154, 155, 159, 197
extremist discourse 131–146

face 166, 172–174, 176, 201, 205–206, 210, 211
fake news 144
Faludi, S. 65
Fang, F. 214, 227
Farr, M. 39
far-right politics 131–146, 184
Fassé, I. 84, 215
feminism 65, 131, 132, 133, 134, 142
fiction elements of risk 82–83
Fiehn, J. 198
field 217
Finland 81–96
Finnish 81–96
First Nations, Assembly of 119
FODIGUA (*Fondo de Desarrollo Indígena Guatemalteco*) 38–39
folksonomies 142
footing 165, 166, 170
Foreman-Peck, J. 102
Forest-Niesing, Senator 118
4chan 133, 134
Frank, P. 42
Freed, A.O. 167
Freire, P. 199, 200, 202, 204, 206, 209
French 84, 102, 106, 107, 119
Friedner, M. 117
future orientation of risk 82–83

Gal, S. 209
Galeano, E. 33
Galloway, N. 148
Gamergate 134
García, O. 163
Garcia, R. 16
Gardezi, H.N. 215–216, 224
Garzón, S. 38
Gawlewicz, A. 156–157

Gazzola, M. 106
Gee, J.P. 219
gender 19, 65, 68, 71, 190
Georgakopoulou, A. 204
Gephi 135
German 102, 184–195
Giddens, A. 82
Gillam, L. 149
Ging, D. 133, 142
Giroux, H. 199, 200, 209
Global Futures 100
Global South 15–30
globalization 32, 66, 97, 199, 214, 218, 226, 227
Goffman, E. 165–166, 170, 172, 173, 176, 201
Gomes, A. 27
Gonzalez, Eulalia 37
'good enough' data 152–153
Gorenflo, L.J. 34
Gorrara, C. 99, 100
Gotell, L. 134
Gove, Michael 4–5
graffiti 24
Graham, S. 105
grammar 209–211
Grandin, K. 37, 38
Granholm, C. 135, 139
Grosfoguel, R. 27
Guatemala 31, 33, 35, 36, 37–41
Guattari, F. 24
Guillemin, M. 149

Haas, M. 22
habitus 217, 220, 221, 225, 226
Hagenow-Caprez, M. 185
Haidar, S. 214, 215, 216, 218, 220, 221, 223, 225, 226
Hale, C.R. 50
Hall, C.J. 2, 234
Hall, R. 66
Halonen, M. 82
Hamilton, C. 215
Hanks, J. 147, 148, 152–153, 154, 197
Haque, E. 116
Hardie, A. 135, 138
Harré, R. 140
Harris, R. 22
Harvey, D. 199
Hatton, N. 187
Hauck, G. 16, 18

Hawley, G. 133
Heller, M. 32, 45, 84, 217
HEPI Report 123 (2019) 97, 98
Hepworth, M. 197, 198, 199, 201, 202, 203, 204, 206, 207, 211
Hess, D. 198
heteronormativity 63, 67, 71–72, 74
Heurich, J.D. 16
Hickman, C. 5
Hirsch, M. 4, 5
historical authoritarianism 22
Hobsbawm, E.J. 87
Hogan-Brun, G. 102, 104
Holliday, A. 4, 151, 155
Holmes, B. 103
Holmes, D.L. 152
homogenization 32, 34 *see also* standardization
homophobia 67–68, 74
Huerta, A. 49
Hult, F.M. 83
human rights 44–45, 119
human/animal interaction 26
humour 150–151, 205, 210, 211
Humphries, T. 48
Hutton, C. 16

Ihalainen, P. 81, 86, 87, 88, 89
Ika 36, 37, 41–45
imagined communities 31, 32, 34–35
incels 133, 134
indeterminate process, language is 22
Indigenous applied linguists 122
Indigenous knowledges 42–43
Indigenous languages
    Canada 111
    and colonialism 32
    Finland 88–89
    Indigenous sign languages 111–127
    Latin America 31–47
Indigenous Languages Act (Canada) 115, 117, 119, 121, 122, 124
Indigenous ontologies 15–30, 32, 34
Indigenous Sign Language Council 119
individualism 5
Ineese-Nash, N. 117
Ingersoll, K.A. 17
Ingvarsdotter, K. 168
integration 16, 183–196, 214–230
intellectual property 136
interdependency 42–43

interdisciplinarity 184, 191, 234
International Association of Applied Linguistics (AILA) 75, 184
interpreters
  in multilingual research interviews 37, 162–179
  sign languages 52, 54–55, 57, 112, 113, 120, 122, 123
Inuit Sign Language 115
Ireland, Marsha 119, 123
Irish Deaf Society 51, 56
Irish Gaelic 57–58, 100
Irish sign language 48–62
Irish Sign Language Act 2017 53–60
irony 198, 200, 211
Isin, E.F. 200, 202
isolated areas 42
Italian 102

Jewish communities 91
Johnson, D.C. 83

Karelian 88–89, 91, 92, 93–94
Kasperson, J.X. 3, 4
Kasperson, R.E. 3, 4
Kim, H. 116
Kjaran, J.I. 74
Klinke, A. 69
Koller, V. 135
Konstantinidou, L. 183, 184
Kramsch, C. 4, 187
Kroskrity, P. 16
Kubanyiova, M. 147, 149, 154
Kubota, R. 20
Kusow, A.M. 160
Kusters, A. 50

Lähteenmäki, M. 90, 91, 92
Laihonen, P. 82
land, language grounded in 17, 18, 20–26, 34
land reserves 42
language, concepts of 18–19, 21, 22, 26
Language Act 1922 (Finland) 86–87
language aesthetics 25
language didactics 188, 190, 191, 193, 194
language environments 219
language erasure 34, 116
language loss 83
language maintenance 32, 43

language planning 83, 93, 215
language prescription 211
language revitalization 20, 34, 38–39, 120, 122–123
languaging 200, 207, 210
Langue des signes québécoise (LSQ) 112, 113, 115, 116, 117, 118, 120–121
Lantolf, J. 200
Lanvers, U. 97, 98, 99, 100, 101, 104, 105
'large culture' paradigm 4, 151
Latin 34
Latin America 31–47, 66–67 see also Brazil
League of Nations 90, 94
Leap, W. 70
Lear, J. 35
Lebow, R.N. 84, 85, 89
Lee, G. 55
Leeson, L. 56
Lefebvre, H. 24
Lehtola, V.-P. 90, 92
Leitch, D.G. 121
Leite, I.B. 21, 23
Lemass, E. 56
Lenz, P. 185
Lett, J. 141
Leung, G. 5, 233
Levinson, S. 201, 206, 210, 211
LGBTQ+ 68–74, 141
LGBTQ+ researchers 64, 69–74, 75
Li Wei 163
Liamputtong, P. 156
life capital 147, 154
lingua francas 97
linguaphobia 97, 98, 99, 104–105
linguistic capital 4, 218, 220
linguistic imperialism 31, 48, 107
linguistic justice 4, 35
linguistic markets 216
linguistic repertoires 163
linguistic resources 217, 218, 225, 226
linguistic rights 83, 120–123, 124
linguistic/conceptual risk 70
literacy 33, 34, 162–179
local knowledge production 19
Locher, M.A. 136–137
longitudinal research 154, 155, 159
Lopes, Nei 22
López Hurtado, L.E. 38–39
Lynch, C. 53

MacDougall, J.C. 115
McKay-Cody, M. 115, 117
Maclean, K. 167, 176
Mainnín, M.B.Ó 100
Makoni, S. 4, 15, 17, 19, 20, 22, 27, 31
mangroves 18, 20–26
Manguebit/MangueBeat (rhythm of the mangrove) 20–26
Mann, S. 153, 157, 158
Manning, V. 53
manosphere 131–146
Māori 122
Maragogipe, Brazil 25
marginality 23, 66, 83
Markham, A.N. 136, 137, 143
Martin-Jones, M. 217
Martins, A.de M. 24
Marwick, A.E. 133, 134, 140
Marx, K. 204
Mateos, I. 183, 185
Mathews, E.S. 58
Mayan languages 33, 37–38, 39
McElhinny, B. 20, 32, 45
McEnery, T. 138
McGlashan, M. 71, 72, 74
McKee, R.L. 53, 121, 122, 123, 124
Mckinley, J. 147
media discourses 94
medium of instruction 40, 68
Meinander, H. 88
Meinhof, U. 22
memories, recording 32–33
Mendes, K. 65
mestizo identity 39–40, 41
meta-analyses 81, 97
Mignolo, W. 31, 32, 34, 35, 45
migration
 Guatemalans 38, 40, 41, 45
 integration 183–196
 queer migration 73
 Switzerland 184–186
 teaching controversial issues 197–213
 to the UK 199
mining 44–45
'minority stress' 64, 75
Modiano, M. 106
Monk, D. 67–68
monolingual ideologies 86, 97, 98, 100, 104, 105
moral panics 210
Morrish, L. 66
Mudde, C. 131

Muir, S. 91
multicultural classrooms 201
multicultural research 167–168
multiculturalism policies 116, 151
multimodality 24, 71
Murillo, L.A. 34, 43, 44
Murray, J.J. 53, 117, 124
Murray, W. 51
Mythen, G. 82

Nação Zumbi (Zumbi Nation) 23
Nagle, A. 133, 134
Nanã 25–26
Napier, J. 56, 57
Narrative Inquiry 147
Nascimento, Abdias do 21–22, 23, 25
nation states 31, 32, 41, 83, 86–89, 199
nationalism 32, 87, 131, 133, 199
negotiation of meaning 168
Neiwert, D. 131, 133, 134
neoliberalism 19, 49–50, 66, 75, 84, 198–199
Nero, S. 143
network analysis 134–135, 138
New Zealand 122
New Zealand Sign Language (NZSL) 122
Nguyen, D. 142
Ng'weno, B. 41
non-standard usages 211
Norlund Shaswar, A. 169
Northern Ireland 99, 100

O'Brien, D. 50
official language status
 Canada 111, 112, 116, 118–119
 and cultural capital 217
 Finland 81, 83, 85, 86–89
 Ireland 53–54
O'Flynn, M. 50
Oglesby, E. 37, 38
Olive, J.L. 141
Oliveira, N.M. 25, 26
Oneida Sign Language 123
online dictionaries 142
online extremism 131–146
online professional development 222
oral tradition 23, 36
othering 19, 199
outsider, researcher as 140–143, 156–158, 190, 232
Oxumaré 25

Pablé, A. 16, 21
Page, R. 136
Pakistan 214–230
Pakuła, Ł 64, 65, 67, 68, 69, 70, 71
Panayiotopoulos, A. 50
Paris Peace Conference (1919) 90
parody 205–26
participation framework, Goffman's 165–166, 170–177
participatory democracy 59, 187, 197–213
Pashtu 216, 219, 220, 225
passive interface 168
Patrick, D. 116
Paul, J.J. 120
Paulsrud, B. 163
Pearson, E. 141, 143
Pennycook, A. 4, 15, 16, 17, 19, 20, 27
Pérez-Milans, M. 83
Perrin, D. 187
Peseta, T. 66
Peutrell, R. 199, 200
phenomenological case studies 218
Philips, J. 202
Phillips, W. 133
Phillipson, R. 48, 106, 107
Pierson, C. 82
Pihlaja, S. 138
Pilkington, H. 141, 143
Plains Indian Sign Language 115, 123
playfulness 198, 205
Poland 68–69
politeness 198
Portuguese 22, 34
positionality of the researcher 147–161, 232
positivism 167, 176
post-colonialism 16, 19, 25
potentially exploitable pedapedagogic activities (PEPAs) 148–149, 155, 157
Povinelli, E.A. 38
Power, M. 3, 4
power relations
  collaborative applied linguistics 234
  coloniality of power 19, 40–41
  critical pedagogy 200
  Indigenous ontologies 19
  Latin America 34
  literacy as social practice 163
  multilingual research 167–168
  Quilombism 22

researcher-participant relations 147–161
and sign languages 123
sociolinguistics of globalization 218
Southern epistemologies 19
Pöyhönen, S. 90, 91
practitioner research 148, 152, 153, 154, 197
Press, J. 112
Prinsloo, M. 163
professional boundaries 147–161
professional linguistics organizations 75
proficiency in LOTE (languages other than English) 98
publicness of data 135, 136–137
publishing industry 74–75

Q'anjob'al 31, 36, 37, 38, 39–40
Qualtrough, Carla 118–119
queer applied linguistics 70
queer linguistics 63–64, 70
Quijano, A. 18, 19
Quilombism 18, 20–26

race
  Indigenous ontologies 19
  intersection with other discrimination 73
  racialized epistemologies 22, 39
  racism 17, 20, 26–27, 41, 135, 140, 144
  Southern epistemologies 19
radical hope 32, 33, 35, 46
Rahman, T. 214, 215, 216, 217, 221, 223, 226
Rajagopolan, K. 17
Raley, M. 55
Ramanathan, V. 220–221
Rampton, B. 107
Rancière, J. 25
rape and sexual assault discourse 134–144
rapport 149–150, 151, 155, 205
Rassool, N. 214
rationality 82
Recife, Brazil 23–24
Recommendations on Good Practice in Applied Linguistics (BAAL, 2021) 234
reflexive turn 167, 176, 234
reflexivity 159–160, 170, 187, 234
refugees 38, 73, 184

religion (as controversial topic) 203–206
Renn, O. 69
researcher bias 137–138, 143
researcher relationships with participants 147–161
resilience, researcher 135, 138–140
resistance *see* activism work
resource extraction 34, 44–45
rhetorical discourse 133
Rhodes, C. 102
Riazi, A.M. 149
right to the city 24
rights-based approaches 44–45, 115, 119, 120–123, 198
right-wing populism 183–184
risk, definition of 2, 3
Rivera-Cusicanqui, S. 33
Roberts, C. 204
Rodger, Elliott 134
Rodwell, G. 81, 84
Romaine, S. 40
Romani 88–89
Romano, A. 134
Roof, Dylann 144
Roosh V 137
Roots, J. 114
Rosa, J. 39
Rose, H. 54
Rüdiger, S. 137, 139, 143
Ruiz Vieytez, E.J. 90
Russian 86, 90, 91, 92, 93

Saarinen, T. 81, 87, 88, 89
sacredness 34, 42, 117
Said, E. 199
Salo, O. 87
Salzmann, Z. 141
Samata, S. 4
Sámi 88–89, 90–91, 92, 93
Santos, D. 105
Sarhimaa, A. 92
Sauntson, H. 66, 67, 68
scavenger methodologies 70
Schleiss, M. 185
scholar-activists 50
Schuit, J. 115
Science, Chico 23
Scotland 99, 102, 107
Seargeant, P. 107
second language acquisition 21, 219
self-determination 34

self-reflexivity 69
sensitive topics 64
Severo, C. 22, 31
sexuality 63–78
Shah, S. 166, 169, 176
Sibii, R. 152
Sierra Nevada, Colombia 41–42
sign languages
    Canada 111–127
    Finland 88–89
    Irish sign language 48–62
silencing 73
Silva, K. 65
Silverstein, M. 86
Simpson, A. 216
Simpson, J. 201, 202, 209
Skills for Life materials (UK) 202, 206–207
Skutnabb-Kangas, T. 116
slang terms 141–142
slavery 21, 33
'small culture' 151, 156
small stories 204
Smeltzer, S. 49
Smiler, K. 121, 123, 124
Smith, D. 187
Snoddon, K. 113, 115, 116, 117, 118, 119, 120, 121, 123
social capital 201, 217, 221–222, 226
social class 87, 100–101, 103, 215–216, 218–227
social construction and interpretation 167
social construction of risk 3, 82
social justice 4, 35, 54–59, 65–67, 75–76, 200, 208, 234
social media 51–52, 112, 136, 139
social networks 40
social practice, literacy as 163
socialization 23, 32
Sociocultural Theory 200, 207, 210
sociolinguistics 83, 193, 218
Solidarity Resistance Network (SRN) 24
songs 26
Southern epistemologies 15–30
Spanish 31–32, 34, 37, 39–40, 102
spatialization 23
Spencer, Richard 133
Spilioti, T. 135, 137, 138
spirituality 16, 42–43
Spöring, M. 99
Srivastava, P. 157, 159

stance 165
standardization 23, 32, 34
stereotypes 22, 23, 176, 206, 208
Stibbe, A. 5
stories-we-live-by 5
Stradling, R. 198, 211
structuralism 22
student-participant relationships 147–161
subaltern knowledges 23, 33, 34
Sunderland, J. 71, 72, 74–75
superdiversity 184–185, 201
Suwankhong, D. 156
Svedmark, E. 135, 139
Swain, M. 200, 204, 207, 210, 219
Swedish 81–96
Swedish for immigrants (SFI) 163
Switzerland 184–195
symbolic power 217, 225, 232
symbolic violence 225
systematization 23

taboos 64, 65, 66
Tagg, C. 137
Takam, A. 84, 215
Tamim, T. 214, 215, 216
taxonomies of risk 68–74
Taylor, C. 141
teacher education 41, 121, 209–211, 222–223
teacher-researcher relationships 147–161
technology
   distance learning 193
   online dictionaries 142
   online extremism 131–146
   online professional development 222
   and sign languages 57, 113–114
television and radio 114
Temple, B. 166, 167, 168, 169
TESOL (Teaching English to Speakers of Other Languages) 200, 201
textbooks 40, 68, 70, 71, 72, 220, 221
third spaces 25
Thompson, J.B. 199
Thornbury, S. 71
Tinsley, T. 100, 101, 102, 104
Tollefson, J. 83, 84
Toomey, R. 64
Torres, Antolino 37, 42
Townsley, G. 26
transdisciplinary approaches 184, 187, 195, 234

transformative intellectuals 209
translation 56, 113, 142, 165, 167–169, 170–173, 226
Trillos, M. 42, 43
Trinity College Dublin 49–50
Trudeau, J. 118
Tuhiwai-Smith, L. 31, 36, 42, 43
turn-taking 169, 198

UK 97–110, 132
UN (United Nations)
   Convention on the Rights of People with Disabilities (CRPD) 54, 55, 56, 112, 117
   Declaration on the Rights of Indigenous People 119
UNICEF 34
Underwood, K. 117
unintended undesirable outcomes 2–3, 231–2
universalism 15, 18, 21–22
'unlikeable subjects,' researching 137
Urban Dictionary 142
urban social movements 24
Urdu 216, 219, 220, 225, 226
US
   and English 102, 104–105
   extremist discourse 133
   migration to 38, 40
Ushioda, E. 158

van Dijk, T.A. 135
Van Herreweghe, M. 116
Van Langenhove, L. 140
Vanhanen-Aniszewski, M. 91, 92
Vertovec, S. 184
von Wendt, Georg 87
vulnerabilities, definition of 2, 3–4
vulnerable participants 135, 136–137
Vygotsky, L. 200

Wadensjö, C. 165, 166, 167, 168–169, 170, 176
Wales 99, 100, 102
Walsh, C. 31, 34, 41
Walter, R. 24
Wang, Y. 102
Weber, J. 121
Wedin, Å 170
Weeks, J. 70

Weisser, M. 136
Welsh 100
Wendling, M. 133
Wenzlhuemer, R. 85
Western bias 27, 35, 36, 221
'what ifs' 81–96
WhatsApp 151–152
White male heteronormative bias 19, 137
wicked problems 5
Wiley, T. 98
Wilkinson, E. 113, 115, 116, 118, 119, 121, 123
Willis, J.W. 141
Winter, A. 140
wisdom 34
Wodak, R. 69
women 25–26

workplace discrimination (as controversial topic) 206–209
World Association of Sign Language Interpreters 57
World Federation of the Deaf 56, 57
written language
  Deaf communities 56, 114–115
  German in Switzerland 185
  Indigenous languages 32–33, 36, 40

xenophobia 99, 104, 141, 183–184, 199

Yates, L. 152, 153
Yin, R.K. 141, 142, 143

Zalabata, L. 44–45
Zhang, Q. 151
Zieleniec, A. 24

For Product Safety Concerns and Information please contact our EU Authorised Representative:

Easy Access System Europe

Mustamäe tee 50

10621 Tallinn

Estonia

gpsr.requests@easproject.com

www.ingramcontent.com/pod-product-compliance
Lightning Source LLC
Chambersburg PA
CBHW070559300426
44113CB00010B/1318